Richardson and Fielding

Richardson and Fielding

The Dynamics of a Critical Rivalry

Allen Michie

Lewisburg
Bucknell University Press
London: Associated University Presses

Associated University Presses
440 Forsgate Drive
Cranbury, NJ 08512

Associated University Presses
16 Barter Street
London WC1A 2AH, England

Associated University Presses
P.O. Box 338, Port Credit
Mississauga, Ontario
Canada L5G 4L8

The paper used in this publication meets the requirements of the American National Standard for Permanence of Paper for Printed Library Materials Z39.48–1984.

Library of Congress Cataloging-in-Publication Data

Michie, Allen, 1963–
    Richardson and Fielding : the dynamics of a critical rivalry / Allen Michie.
      p.   cm.
    Includes bibliographical references and index.
    ISBN 0-8387-5419-8 (alk. paper)
    1. Richardson, Samuel, 1689–1761—Criticism and interpretation—History. 2. Fielding, Henry, 1707–1754—Criticism and interpretation—History. 3. English fiction—18th century—History and criticism—Theory, etc. 4. Criticism—Great Britain—History.
I. Title.
PR3667.M53   1999
823'.509—dc21
                                  99-25685
                                    CIP

For
Christine Michie

Contents

Acknowledgments

It is wonderfully ironic that a book about a rivalry should be the product of so many enjoyable exchanges with friends, family, and colleagues. John Burke, David Hensley, Robert C. Holub, John Jones, Laura Runge-Gordon, and Walter Sorrells have all offered ideas, clarifications, and good cheer from the earliest stages of the project. Maria Barbieri, Jerome Beaty, Dennis Burden, Martin Dannahay, John Dussinger, Suzanne Gibson, Joyce Goggin, David Mazella, and the collective wisdom of the C18-L listserv have all offered useful and provocative references. It was especially heartening to find enthusiastic general readers for Fielding thriving in the Literary Salon of Greenfield, Indiana, and I appreciate their encouragement. My research assistant, Tim Miles, handled all manner of research requests with accuracy, equanimity, and affability. Finally, the neighborly and extraordinarily efficient staff of Emory's Woodruff library quite literally made this research possible.

Special thanks go to the people of Bucknell University Press, especially Simon Varey for his beneficial reading and generous endorsement, Tawny Schlieski for her delicate textual surgery, and Gregory Clingham for his continued support and good taste. I was especially fortunate to have Martine Brownley and Walter Reed read the entire manuscript, and I am grateful for their insights. John Sitter, the Grandison and Dr. Harrison of this work from the beginning, has been a valued resource. His clarity of thought and editorial acumen lie silently behind everything that is good about this book.

To thank Joe and Julie Michie, Genevieve and Harriett Hawkins, Marguerite McDonald, and especially Christine Michie for their contributions to this book is also to thank them for everything I have written before it and will write after it. I owe each of them a debt of intellectual opportunity that I can only seek to repay by giving it to others in turn.

My greatest debt is to Stacey Cone. The energy of her mind does not stop to distinguish between intellect and emotion: curiosity is, for her, an expression of love. She has been a full partner in this project and became a full partner in life along the way.

Richardson and Fielding

1
Reception Theory

*There are three kinds of reader: one, which enjoys without judg-
ment, a third, which judges without enjoyment, and the one in
the middle which judges as it enjoys and enjoys as it judges.
This latter kind really reproduces the work of art anew.*
— Goethe, letter to J.F. Rochlitz, June 13, 1819

MORE SO THAN ANY OTHER TWO NOVELISTS, SAMUEL RICHARDSON AND
Henry Fielding are placed in a personal and literary rivalry which
began in 1741 with the publication of *Shamela* and which shows
few signs of abating even today. The methods and reasons for the
rivalry change with the times, but the names Richardson and Fielding seem destined for eternal contrast. Even when the rival is not
mentioned directly, it is usually clear from a critic's priorities that
one author is being privileged, usually at the direct expense of the
rival: the ghost of one author haunts the criticism of the other. As
Ronald Paulson and Thomas Lockwood write of Fielding's reception, "Finally, many . . . criticisms shade off into the criticism of
Richardson's novels, in which Fielding is almost always the un-
stated 'other' which helps to define Richardson (as Richardson is
the 'other' in many discussions of Fielding)."[1]

There is something to be said for not disrupting a critical tradition that brings Richardson and Fielding some attention they otherwise may never have had. The tidy simplicity of the opposition is
often a useful framework for teaching their works, making memorable (and in many cases perfectly accurate) illustrations of the
eighteenth-century literary climate. Unlike the other famous literary coupling of Jonson and Shakespeare, which is largely the cre-
ation of literary critics after John Dryden, Richardson and Fielding
did share a genuine personal animosity and repeatedly responded
to one another's works in print. There is no sense in denying the
realities and even the benefits of the Richardson/Fielding dichot-

omy, or for that matter the interesting and neglected theoretical nature of rivalries in general.

What I do intend, however, is to demonstrate the history of how this rivalry came to be established as one of the most unshakable "truisms" in all of English literary criticism. The stakes of this particular debate are high for our understanding of what the English novel is and how it came to be that way. By surveying the recurring dichotomies projected onto Richardson and Fielding by eighteenth-, nineteenth-, and twentieth-century readers, I argue that this is much more than a trivial literary parlor game. Because *Pamela, Clarissa, Sir Charles Grandison, Joseph Andrews, Tom Jones,* and *Amelia* are among the earliest and most influential of English novels, readers searching for family trees of literary influence often trace branches of the novel back to one author or the other. Literary history therefore tends to place entire sub-genres and narrative styles into "opposing" camps, and this can often be traced directly back to the Richardson/Fielding opposition.

Moreover, as a reception study, I hope to show how we cannot on the one hand dismiss rivalry-based criticism as biased and unfair and on the other hand claim personal taste as the honest basis for all aesthetic criticism. Studies of subjective critical responses are sometimes seen as pointless and (at worst) petty enterprises: as Northrop Frye writes in his influential *Anatomy of Criticism,*

> The literary chit-chat which makes the reputations of poets boom and crash in an imaginary literary stock exchange . . . cannot be part of any systematic study, for a systematic study can only progress: whatever dithers or vacillates or reacts is merely leisure-class gossip.[2]

It may be true that whatever dithers is leisure-class gossip. (From a cynical and materialist point of view, however, all of literary criticism can be seen as an extended exercise in leisure-class gossip.) What troubles me more, however, is Frye's primary objection that literary chit-chat cannot have a place a systematic study.

Frye could have found an illustrative example of his complaint in Frederic Blanchard's *Fielding the Novelist: A Study in Historical Criticism* (1926), an important book from which I want to distance my own. The fact that this monumental work has almost as much to do with Richardson as it does with Fielding demonstrates how closely the two authors' critical histories are intertwined. It may be true that pure objectivity is an illusory grail, but Blanchard undermines his own credibility on Fielding by making no attempt to disguise his partisan antipathy to Richardson. Recounting a letter where Richardson gloats over the failure of *Amelia*, Blanchard writes, "In the following letter one can almost *see* Richardson drawing a long face and rubbing his hands."[3] He frequently refers to Richardson throughout as "the little printer," labeling him as Fielding's "evil genius."[4] Blanchard perhaps fails to see that he is himself doing the very thing for which he ridicules Richardson: making petty and personal digs that are irrelevant to the genuine literary issues at hand. In other words, Blanchard ends up adding to the body of "vacillating literary chit-chat" in the act of recounting it. Blanchard's book is an excellent "study," but it is not particularly "systematic." It has static historical data, but it lacks a theory to make it (what Frye would call) "progressive."

The Richardson versus Fielding trial needs a court recorder, not another member of the jury. Any critical apparatus used to trace the evolution of the opposition should avoid, as much as language makes possible, taking sides for one author or the other. Otherwise it is only contributing to the situation it purports to analyze. The problem of "taking sides" is doubly problematic when we add the dimension of chronology. As René Wellek asks,

> Shall we judge frankly from the point of our own time, simply adding a link to the chain of the historical process, or shall we judge from the point of view of the time in which the work of art was created? Or shall we even judge from the point of view of a third time or of all times combined?[5]

Hans Robert Jauss proposes a solution, offering a theory of critical reception that is potentially more objective while providing a systematic approach to the analysis of historical criticism (or, if you prefer, "leisure-class gossip"). I will begin this chapter with an overview of Jauss's reception theory and a summary of its main tenets, followed by a detailed examination of one such tenet—the modes of aesthetic appreciation—which I plan to adapt for its particular relevance to the study of the Richardson/Fielding opposition.

Reception Theory: Chain Reactions

Jauss's words explain why his theory is particularly useful for an overview of the clannish Richardson/Fielding debate:

> [I]t is a virtue of the aesthetics of reception that it opposes the ambition of solipsistic interpretation, and is interested less in reciprocal falsifica-

tion than in the unifiability of different interpretations in which the
meanings of works of art—yielded to us and always only partially con-
cretizable—especially manifests itself.[6]

Jauss's theory proposes to not only take into consideration the past,
present, and future, but also to tie them together into one coherent
historical perspective on the given literary text. Past receptions are
seen as setting the context for present receptions, and present receptions are links in an evolutionary chain that feeds and is fed by
extraliterary history. The historicity of literature is seen three ways:
diachronically for the interrelationships of texts, synchronically for
the world view that is shared by texts of the same moment, and
generally for the ways that history at large contributes to the development of literature.[7]

Furthermore, reception theory does not allow literary history to
make the common mistake of losing the aesthetic dimension; to the
contrary, literary history is to be *based* upon aesthetics. Part of what
makes reception theory a viable tool for a study of how Richardson
and Fielding have influenced and irritated one another's readers
lies in its methodology of using subjective literary evaluations as the
data for constructing a more or less objective literary history. Jauss
views the overall critical reputation of an author as the result of a
cumulative process of mediation between the work, the reader, and
the social background:

> The aesthetic implication lies in the fact that the first reception of a
> work by the reader includes a test of its aesthetic value in comparison
> with works already read. The obvious historical implication of this is
> that the understanding of the first reader will be sustained and en-
> riched in a chain of receptions from generation to generation. . . . The
> step from the history of reception of the individual work to the history
> of literature has to lead to seeing and representing the historical se-
> quence of works as they determine and clarify the coherence of litera-
> ture, to the extent that it is meaningful for us, as the prehistory of its
> present experience.[8]

It is important that a reception study of Richardson and Fielding
emphasize the ways in which past readings have become a "prehis-
tory of present experience." Reception theory's alternative to the
polarized views of Richardson and Fielding lies in the simple jump
from synchrony to diachrony. Jauss provides (but does not emphasize) a catchall premise that establishes one of the many thematic
connections between German reception theory and American
reader-response theory: the engine of literary history is located in

the mind of the individual reader, "realizing" works in a random, unsynchronous order. When a text is seen as a "literary fact," capable of being realized over and over again by a continually changing body of readers, the connections between texts are formed by the audience rather than by a chain of historical events. "It is this intersubjective communication that separates the historicity of literature from the factual objectivity of pragmatic history," writes Jauss.[9] In other words, why not read Richardson in contrast to Smollett, or Fielding in contrast to Mackenzie, Austen, and John Grisham?

To get to the point where the Richardson/Fielding opposition can be transcended, however, one must ask certain questions about the ways it is created and sustained. Wlad Godzich raises precisely the issues at stake:

> What happens when we read? Do we bring ourselves to the work or do we get something from it? What sort of prejudgments do we bring to our readings? Do we expect, e.g., certain things in certain genres? Are we intimidated by certain genres, certain authors, certain reputations? What is the image of the author that we bring to a reading? Do we, as the reading audience, exercise some influence upon the author as s/he writes for us? Do we have immediate access to literature or not, and if not what mediations can we repertory? To what extent can we be manipulated so that we respond in an expected manner? How can it be determined that we will respond aesthetically to something that may not have been intended that way?

Godzich's words were written in definition and explanation of Jauss's reception theory. "All these questions, and more, especially those having to do with value, emerge in the forefront of attention as soon as a reader- or a recipient-centered approach to literature is attempted."[10]

Origins and Alternatives

In 1967 at the University of Constance, Jauss delivered his famous inaugural lecture, "What Is and for What Purpose Does One Study Literary History?", amid considerable political and cultural turmoil. The title was meant to echo Friedreich Schiller's inaugural speech in 1789 at Jena, "What Is and for What Purpose Does One Study Universal History?". The connection between the lectures is twofold: each proposes new ties between the artifacts of the past and the realities of the present, and each proposes a revolutionary

new era in academic scholarship. It may seem presumptuous now
for Jauss to relate "revolution" in Germany during the 1960s with
revolution in France during the 1780s, but this was nevertheless
an extremely volatile period within the German academy.[11] A re-
vived study of literary history was part of the search for a new political "relevance" for literary studies, the familiar demand made in
French, British and American universities during the same period.[12]

What made reception theory "revolutionary" among literary theories was its offer of an alternative to (or perhaps a fusion of) the
two dominant theories of the day: formalism and Marxism. Jauss
designed reception theory to capture what was best about both
methods without reproducing their flaws. Jauss argues that Rus-
sian Formalists such as Yuri Tynjanov hold that genres evolved out
of other genres with literary history being the story of innovation,
change, and exhaustion of old forms; while Marxists such as Raymond Williams hold that literature evolves when economic and social changes alter the ideology of authors and readers. Formalists
such as Yuri Tynjanov have an "almost purely intrinsic" view of literary history, and Marxists such as Raymond Williams have an "almost purely extrinsic" view.[13] Jauss's theory has elements of each:
literature is believed to evolve alongside changes in society, but
much of this evolution also has to do with literature engaging in a
dialogue with itself. Jauss was reaching for a more accurate, practical and applicable method of literary history, one that is sufficiently
free of dogma to observe and analyze the effects of dogma in others.
The goal is to forge an interdependent relationship between the
history of literature (formalism) and the history of the world at
large (Marxism), without reducing one to the other or forcing literature to lose its artistic character by pressing it into nothing more
than commentary.[14]

American academics have given more much more attention to
Wolfgang Iser than to any other single reception theorist.[15] Robert
Holub claims the reasons for this are not hard to understand in
light of American academic concerns. Iser's theory is not "at odds
with the best traditions of textual criticism and close reading. . . .
Speculating on how the reader reacts, filling in the 'gaps' as it were,
involves little more than interpreting the text," writes Holub.[16]
Iser's primary concern in *The Act of Reading* and *The Implied
Reader* is to locate the ways that individual readers create meanings out of the "indeterminacies" built into literary texts. Both
Jauss and Iser deal with "the problem of what meaning is and of
how a literary text conveys meaning," writes Jürgen Schlaeger,

with "Jauss concentrating more on the historical and hermeneutic aspects of the problem and Iser more on the actual processes of meaning constitution involved in reading a literary text."[17]

I have chosen to break with American tradition and emphasize Jauss's theory rather than Iser's, because my concerns with Richardson and Fielding are more with "historical and hermeneutic" issues than with "meaning constitution involved with reading a literary text." I take for granted that readers are able to construct a range of meanings from Richardson and Fielding's novels. I am not planning to investigate the epistemology or psychology behind how readers arrived at their meanings. Instead, I feel it would be more helpful (and possible) at this point to chronicle what those meanings were, why they emerged in their specific historical moments, how they changed over time, and how they influenced subsequent readers. One of the primary differences between Iser and Jauss can be summarized in the distinction between "meaning" and "significance." Holub writes that "Iser's work is involved with meaning, and the production of meaning . . . [whereas] significance (for Iser, the reader's response to meaning), a territory which entails sociology and history, lies outside of Iser's theoretical terrain."[18] Naturally one cannot have "significance" without "meaning" (or, I would argue, vice versa), but there are already many excellent "meaning" studies of Richardson and Fielding's novels.[19] What I believe needs attention at this point in critical history is a new look at their mutual canonical "significance."

Readers, Real and Imagined

From the point of view I have outlined above, it should be clear that Jauss's theory assumes and contains a great deal of Iser's. What may not be so clear to American readers is how reception theory differs from reader-response theory, and why this matters to a study of Richardson and Fielding in particular.[20] The differences between the two theories summarize, to a great extent, the differences between Jauss and Iser. Not only do Iser and Jauss differ on the ways that readers are to be analyzed, they also differ on the nature and identity of the readers themselves.

Iser writes that his "reader as a concept" has "his roots firmly planted in the structure of the text; he is a construct and in no way to be identified with any real reader."[21] Iser's ideal reader avoids the messy reality of shifting cultural sands because "he" remains resolutely theoretical. Actual readers are complex individuals and they make even more complex groups. A detailed study of the individual and collective readers who have recorded their reactions to Richardson and Fielding requires a more sophisticated and flexible tool, one that Jauss offers in his book *Toward an Aesthetic of Reception*.

Jauss does agree that authors assume an "ideal reader" for their works, thereby incorporating the core of Iser's theory into his own, but this hypothetical reader exists in an equivocal relationship with the actual readers. According to Jauss, "[T]here are works that at the moment of their appearance are not yet directed at any specific audience, but that break through the familiar horizon of literary expectations so completely that an audience can only gradually develop for them."[22] For example, it is simplistic to say that Richardson conceived of a single "implied reader" for *Pamela*. On one level he was writing for young middle-class servant girls in need of model letters, but on another level he was writing for specific readers in his devoted coterie of personal friends (none of whom, incidentally, were middle-class servant girls). Regardless of the original audience, Richardson's novels are now at their second peak of popularity with a body of feminist readers who would be deeply alien to (and would probably not be wholly approved of by) Richardson. Once an audience does develop, the continued popularity of the literary work depends to an extent upon the literary tastes which the work itself has directly or indirectly influenced. This is not always good news for the author: "When, then, the new horizon of expectations has achieved more general currency, the power of the altered aesthetic norm can be demonstrated in that the audience experiences formerly successful works as outmoded, and withdraws its appreciation."[23] As I will demonstrate in chapter three, the phenomenon of an all too pervasive influence is at work behind the radical reversal of Richardson and Fielding's popularity at the beginning of the nineteenth century.

Jauss and Iser may differ on their theoretical constructions of readerships, but there are other, more complementary ways in which they are working on the same larger project. Jauss's theory can be seen as beginning where Iser's ends. Jauss is perhaps thinking of Iser when he makes this distinction between two kinds of reception, synchronic and diachronic:

> [Reception theory] must on the one hand shed light on the actual process through which the effect and significance of the text concretizes itself for the present reader, and on the other reconstruct the historical process in which readers have received and interpreted the text at different times and in varying ways.[24]

Just as Jauss points out the way his theory works with Iser's to complete the whole reception picture, Schlaeger points out how Iser bolsters Jauss's weakness: Jauss's theory accounts for how the chains of meaning create literary history, but fails to analyze the dialogic ways in which these individual meanings are constructed. "And this is exactly the point where Wolfgang Iser's theory of aesthetic response takes off," writes Schlaeger.[25]

"Realization" of Texts: The Continuity of Literary History

Reception theory and reader-response theory have one additional idea in common, an important one which I believe has not received sufficient attention in the few existing comparative studies. Both theories claim that a text essentially does not exist until the reader "realizes" it. Their conceptions of exactly what this "realization" is and how it works are not the same, however. Reader-response theory tends to use "realization" as part of the process of semantics and the phenomenology of reading, whereas reception theory uses "realization" as the linchpin for all of literary history. As a result, Iser's (and Stanley Fish's) "realization" is rooted in the deep structures of language, authority and culture; whereas Jauss's "realization" is, perhaps more naively, related to broad questions of sociology and background reading. The "history of literature is a process of aesthetic reception and production that takes place in the realization of literary texts on the part of the receptive reader, the reflective critic, and the author in his continuing productivity," Jauss states simply.[26]

Jauss broke with conventional paradigms of literary history by affirming that the "facts" of literary history are not enough: they do not capture the nonchronological continuity of an individual's reading experience, nor the "event" nature which makes a work useful and allows it to be "transmitted" from the past to the present.[27] It may not seem too radical an innovation to declare that meaning can only exist in an unending sequence of present moments, but in the context of an evolutionary model of literary history, the contrast to static structuralist modes is clear. Jauss writes a strong defense of the aims of the reception-based approach:

[T]he best chance for success for a new literary theory would come . . . by utilizing the insight into historicity which is peculiar to art. Not the panacea of perfected taxonomies, closed systems of signs, and formalistic descriptive models but a historical investigation that did justice to the dynamic process of production and reception, of author, work, and public . . . [the answer is] to renew the study of literature and lead it out of the blind alleys of a literary history that was running aground in positivism, the sort of interpretation that had stopped serving anything other than itself. . . .[28]

The alternative to literature serving nothing but itself is a literature that serves what Jauss calls "history at large." Jauss formulates this interdependent relationship between literature and "reality" not only to make his theory more accurate, but also to recapture the humanistic function of literature that traditional "authors-and-movements" histories commonly ignore and political histories commonly oversimplify.[29] Jauss instead believes that the most important way in which literature relates to general history, and the way in which I hope to use Richardson and Fielding's literature in this book, is in its "socially *formative*" function.[30] The literary work is not just received against the backdrop of social norms and expectations, it is perceived against other works of art and the experiences of day-to-day life.[31] Because literature is not somehow separate from other phenomenological experiences, it contributes to the flow of undifferentiated experience as well as reflects it. Jauss writes that there exists a "properly *socially formative* function that belongs to literature as it competes with other arts and social forces in the emancipation of mankind from its natural, religious, and social bonds."[32]

The work itself therefore plays an active role in shaping the cultural norms that in turn shape its own reception (remembering, of course, that works need not be "received" in the chronological order in which they were written). Applying this to the history of Richardson and Fielding criticism, the two authors have contributed to the evolution of the critical criteria that are, ironically, sometimes used to discount their own novels. For example, Nancy Armstrong's theory of the novel in *Desire and Domestic Fiction: A Political History of the Novel* emphasizes the power that female characters are given within the domestic sphere, leading her to privilege novels such as Richardson's *Pamela*. Citing the premise that "Fielding found it ludicrous to think that a man of such station would so overvalue the virginity of a woman who was not particularly well born," Armstrong therefore assumes that "Richardson's representation of the individual inspired Fielding to write two novels in rebuttal."[33] Armstrong reduces the quantity and quality of literary life to be found in Fielding's works to a single vindictive motive. Who is to say that Fielding's *Amelia*, however, did not have its share of influence over society's expectations of women's moral authority in the domestic sphere? Directly or indirectly, Fielding helped to shape the literary criteria and expectations of novelistic writing that are used to discredit him.

Reception and Author-to-Author Influence

As in the above example with Armstrong's reading of *Pamela*, the seeds for the reception of a wide body of works can be found buried within one influential text. The authors of fictional texts themselves respond creatively to their predecessors, adding another dimension to the complex interactive process between authors, texts and readers. "In the step from a history of the reception of works to an eventful history of literature . . . the next work can solve formal and moral problems left behind by the last work, and present new problems in turn," writes Jauss.[34]

Jauss's method in his book *Question and Answer: Forms of Dialogic Understanding* is to approach literary works as "answers" to "questions" posed by earlier literary works. The premise is not too dissimilar from Harold Bloom's "anxiety of influence," only less pessimistic and less overtly Freudian: Jauss uses the word "reconstitute" rather than Bloom's "misread" for what authors do to their predecessors' texts. ("Reconstitute" has connotations of creativity that suggest authors rising to the challenge of their predecessors rather than sinking beneath their weight.) Jauss illustrates his theory with Bloom's famous example: *Paradise Lost*. Jauss sees Milton's work as a reception of, and poetic commentary on, the third chapter of Genesis, establishing "a new horizon of meaning for the words."[35]

Richardson and Fielding are particularly tempting for this kind of author-to-author reception study. Using the same model, one could produce an analysis of *Joseph Andrews* as a reception of *Pamela*, *Amelia* of *Clarissa*, or *Grandison* of *Tom Jones*. Critical works such have these have been done often and well, so I have no plans to "reconstitute" them here.[36] These are reception studies only under a broad definition of the term (a definition which somewhat loses sight of the theory's original revolutionary aims), tracing literary history within its own self-contained boundaries with little or no reference to a collective body of readers or to "history in general." As a corrective, therefore, I will consider how creative writers respond to the Richardson/Fielding rivalry, but only in the context of a wider reception history and the social/historical conditions which permeate it.

The Recovery of Alterity:
The Interactions of History and Aesthetics

"Aesthetic perception is no universal code with timeless validity, but rather—like all aesthetic experience—is intertwined with historical experience," writes Jauss.[37] Jauss conceives of aesthetics, the engine that runs the entire literary enterprise, to be no more isolated and self-sufficient than the readers themselves. It is inaccurate to say that reception theory is simply the study of how works exist in relation to their readers; the heart of the theory lies instead in the three-way relationship of works, their readers, and history.

The premise is more original than it sounds. Aesthetics is seen as a function of history, not a commentary on it, something that literature causes rather than the other way around. Jauss is therefore able to reconcile his belief in the importance of the aesthetic's historical dimension with his belief in the importance of a non-chronological aesthetic response. In other words, an understanding of the *original* historical context of a work adds a dimension to our *present* aesthetic appreciation (which is itself framed by its own historical context). For example, Richardson and Fielding's historical canonicity has become the chief reason why they are still read, and the fact that they are still read is of course the reason for their continued canonicity. Our awareness of *Pamela* and *Tom Jones*'s eighteenth-century popularity is certainly a source of their ongoing twentieth-century appeal.

Jauss differs sharply from the New Critics who tend to reject historical understanding as superfluous to aesthetic perception. Jauss does not even consider historical understanding to be an option, attractive only to academic or unusually curious readers. Whether we may like it or not, or *know* it or not, historical understanding is what makes aesthetic appreciation possible in the first place. A literary work exists in a subtle conflict with its historical moment, and our ability to gauge the distance between the work and the horizon of its historical backdrop is the key to its canonical (if not artistic) significance. Jauss writes that the "artistic character of a work" is in proportion to "the distance between expectation and experience, tradition and innovation."[38] Texts that pose no challenging questions to their times—works that lack "alterity"—are likely to be seen as marginal, "popular," or (ironically) of "historical interest only."

There are two kinds of history: general and personal. Jauss means to include both. Works are written as "answers" to "questions" posed by history, be those questions abstract or intimate. A modern reader approaching an eighteenth-century novel, for instance, is free to read that text for the answers which the historical author originally intended (e.g., Fielding's views of Methodism), for answers to historical questions of which the author never could have conceived (e.g., how *Clarissa* can relate to women being given rophynol and "date raped" at a fraternity house), or for answers to questions significant only to the individual reader (e.g., what Lady Western can teach you about how to handle your mother-in-law). The list is by no means all-inclusive, and should not be dismissed as trivial or facetious. Jauss believes that these are the reasons why we read literature in the first place, and that this is as close as we are likely to come in a post-Marxist age to a humanistic function for the humanities, which is to "wrest works of art away from the past" and continually pose new questions to which older works can provide modern answers.[39] These "answers" to the various "questions" of history do not necessarily have to fall in a tidy chronological order, however. Samuel Richardson can answer Danielle Steele as much as Danielle Steele can answer Samuel Richardson.

Such a view holds serious implications for the canonization of authors in general and for Richardson and Fielding in particular. If canonization depends upon aesthetic response and aesthetic response depends upon recovering a sense of a work's alterity, then the history of Richardson's and Fielding's slippery canonical status is the story of when readers have chosen to reconstruct that alterity, why, the degree of alterity they find, and the point from which they choose to measure it.[40] The "newness" is often lost on later readers, however. Jauss claims that the elements of what was once a new perspective are still within the text, but once they become familiar, they require "special effort to read them 'against the grain' of the accustomed experience to catch sight of their artistic character once again."[41]

Whenever Richardson or Fielding are overtly contrasted, it is almost always because the critic is trying to "catch sight of their artistic character." Reading the novels "against the grain" frequently means reading one author's works against the other, using them as sandpaper for one another in an attempt to recover a sense of freshness or new relevancy. I would argue that since Richardson and Fielding have been seen as filters for one another's work from the very beginning, their original audiences had an unusual kind of "alienating new perspective" that makes it problematic for us to find a clear point of reference from which to mark our "aesthetic distance." It seems to have always been, and to always be, almost impossible to read one author free from the horizon of the other.

The Horizon of Expectation

The concept of the "horizon of expectation" is obviously central to Jauss's approach. Jauss defines the horizon as a "historical marker and, at the same time, the necessary condition for the possibility of experiential knowledge—constitut[ing] all structures of meaning related to human action and primary modes of comprehending the world."[42] Richter summarizes the horizon as something beyond the mere history of taste. The horizon of expectation is much more inclusive: it is a "history of all the various preconceptions—about art, reading, and the cultural milieu in general—which audiences bring to literary texts."[43] Furthermore, Godzich points out the way that the concept of the horizon distances Jauss from structuralism:

> The pitfall that the Russian Formalists could not avoid, namely the separation of literature and life, is thus overcome, for it is in their daily lives that readers build up their horizons of expectations and it is in the same lives that any work-induced changes will have to take place.[44]

"Changes" is the key word in Godzich's sentence. The relationship between reception and horizon is circular: the horizon of expectations informs our responses to literary works which in turn alters our horizon, leaving us with subtly different expectations for the next literary work. How a work meets, falls short of, or exceeds "expectations" contributes to our estimates of its literary significance. For example, a new work which fits neatly within the preexisting horizon of expectation may be seen as little more than a commercial commodity, whereas a work which challenges expectations may, depending upon the extent of the challenge, be accepted as artistic or rejected as unintelligible. Rejected works may be rehabilitated, however, as in the cases of D.H. Lawrence or James Joyce. Richter points out that rejected or misunderstood works "may succeed in entering the canon later when the literary horizon has, in effect, caught up with them."[45] Literary works change horizons, and horizons in turn change receptions.[46]

It is exactly this notion of "change" that Terry Eagleton objects to in his book *Literary Theory*: not that change does not occur in transactions between texts and readers, but that "change" presumes certain contradictory assumptions and happens in ways that reception critics seldom admit. "If one considers the 'text in itself' as a . . . set of 'schemata' waiting to be concretized in various ways by various readers, how can one discuss these schemata at all without having already concretized them?" writes Eagleton. "In speaking of the 'text itself', measuring it as a norm against particular interpretations of it, is one ever dealing with anything more than one's own concretization?"[47] More specifically, Eagleton locates a facet of "change" that is a weakness in Jauss's new version of literary history: "It is not that literary works themselves remain constant, while interpretations of them change: texts and literary traditions are themselves actively altered according to the various historical horizons within which they are received."[48] To add relevant examples to Eagleton's point, when modern critics read *Clarissa* they are responding to a text that Richardson substantially revised from the time of its initial appearance and peak popularity (not to mention abridged editions). Also, when modern readers refer to *Pamela* they are virtually always referring to only the first part of what an eighteenth-century reader might have known as *Pamela*. As for literary traditions changing, the clearest example is the fact that Richardson's novels are now seen as pioneering works in the history of the feminist novel; a category wholly alien to Richardson himself, who was more inclined to see himself working out of the conservative conduct book tradition.

Jauss is aware of the difficulties that the "horizon of expectations" entails. It is not fair to reception theory, Jauss's version at least, to accuse it of being naive or blind about the subjectivity inherent to the hermeneutic process. To the contrary, how we interpret the past through the eyes of the present is precisely what reception theory sets out to study and reveal. Jauss aims to celebrate the distance between two cultures, not repress or narrow it. Since earlier assumptions are by necessity already contained within our own, historical understanding is possible only when we are able to differentiate between what is created and what is inherited. "The work of historical understanding requires a conscious, fully implemented mediation between the two horizons," writes Jauss.[49] In other words, Jauss acknowledges that subjectivity is inevitable in works of literary history, but the critic should nevertheless lean toward objectivity by making that subjectivity a "conscious, fully implemented mediation."

Identifying the precise parameters of a horizon of expectations requires that its analysis be "objectified" as much as possible. Pure objectivity may indeed be an illusory goal, but some opinions are nevertheless more objective than others. Jauss proposes a way that the inevitable subjectivity can be objectified. The general principle is, not surprisingly, one of mediation: conflicting horizons between readers can be transcended easier than they can be resolved. Like a true diplomat, Jauss suggests that there is always a level of shared experience behind any difference, and that questions of the subjectivity, taste, types, and levels of readers can be asked meaningfully "only when one has first clarified which transsubjective horizon of understanding conditions the influence of the text."[50] Extrapolating principles from Jauss's account of the ways a novel constructs a horizon for its new readers, there are three things that we can look for in a text to arrive at the level of the "transsubjective horizon:" the familiar norms of the genre, the connections to familiar works within the literary-historical surroundings, and the opposition between "the poetic and the practical uses of language."[51]

These three levels of reading may provide a map to the "transsubjective horizon," but they nevertheless remain primarily within the realm of the reader's private experience (or "concretization") of the text. Jauss is on firmer ground asserting his differences from Iser and the reader-response critics, basing his reception studies on the more conventionally "objective" groundwork of historical data. For example, Jauss provides sample areas of research that could produce a reception history of Rousseau's *La Nouvelle Héloïse*: anecdotes of how busy people made time to read it, crowds at the bookstalls, inflated prices of new editions because of the demand, spurious continuations by obsessive readers, anecdotes of dramatically sentimental reactions, blow-by-blow accounts of the reading process found in people's letters, sales figures, rapid reprint schedules, and accounts of people "converted" morally by the book.[52] These are roughly the types of receptions I will be tracing for Richardson and Fielding.

Just because Jauss is able to provide an example of the research required to identify an objectifiable reception history does not necessarily mean that he is prepared to do the research himself. Jauss's own criticism of individual works is almost always directed toward locating the receptions of the *gipfelsebene*, the body of authors who read one another's works for source material. Jauss thereby leaves out the vast majority of "ordinary" leisure readers who have committed their reactions to paper. Iris Zavala points out an important player who is often left out of this and all other reception models, putting his finger on what is perhaps the single greatest problem in Jauss's claims for reception theory as a new model for literary history: "We have so far not mentioned the *silenced readers*, those who could not make public their reception of other texts. We must await . . . those textual strategies that allow the initiated to slip into the borderland of what cannot be said."[53] In other words, there is something less than purely democratic about a literary history that limits itself to the study of only those readers who write. "The Murphy's Law of reception-theory is that the most naïve readers are the least likely to leave evidence of their response to texts," claims Richter.[54]

It is important to remember at this point that reception theory is based not upon *individual* instances of reception, but upon the *chains* of reception which constitute the collective fate of a literary work. "Silenced" readers may not leave written records of their opinions, but if their views of a work have had any influence on other readers who influenced other readers who at some point wrote literary criticism, then they have had their small role in the modification of a literary horizon. Works that inspire no commentary or cause no change in behavior are doomed to have no reception history beyond the moment of their initial appearance. (Jauss is proposing a new theory of literary *history*, not a new theory of literature.) Ideally, therefore, no reader of a significant book is ever truly "silenced," and the power of influence is traced directly to the work itself.

Question and Answer

Jauss does detail one method for locating how historically distant audiences probably saw their contemporary literature. The last of his major books, *Question and Answer: Forms of Dialogic Understanding*, explains a straightforward procedure: simply investigate what questions to which the work is an answer. Although he does not cite Jauss directly, a good recent example of the technique is Hunter's *Before Novels: The Cultural Contexts of Eighteenth-Century English Fiction*. Hunter's literary history starts with literary texts and works backwards, investigating what cultural forces (or horizons of expectations) were at work in prompting the emergence of the English novel.

Jauss's version of question and answer is more dialogic and interactive than that of his source, Hans-Georg Gadamer's *Truth and Method*. Gadamer claims that the reader does not address the text directly, but instead addresses the same questions along *with* the text, bringing his or her own "horizon of interrogation" to the text. There is an inevitable tension between the text of the past and the reader of the present. This tension can be overcome by the question and answer dialogue between author, text, and reader which "concretizes meaning in ever different ways, and therefore more richly."[55] I hope to emphasize yet another dimension of dialogue implicit in Jauss's dialogic model: that of reader-to-reader. New readers of Richardson and Fielding respond not only to the questions within and outside of the texts, but also to questions posed by other readers. Modern critics of Richardson and Fielding are, for example, just as likely to be responding to questions posed by Ian Watt as they are to be responding to questions posed by Richardson and Fielding or the times in which they lived.

Types of Readers and Modes of Reading

The "dialogic" nature of Jauss's theory may need to be clarified at this point and dissociated from Mikhail Bakhtin's more familiar use of the word. Jauss's theory posits that there are three types of readers who act in the question-and-answer dialogue with the text. For each of these three types of interactive readers, there are three modes (or "attitudes") of aesthetic appreciation.

The first type of reader is the type mentioned above as the most frequent subject of Jauss's own practical criticism: the *gipfelsebene*, or readers who are also themselves creative writers. The second type is the *mittlere ebene*, or those professional readers and critics who have influence without being creative writers themselves. The third type of reader is the *präreflexive ebene*, the body of general readers that serves as the market of production for the *gipfelsebene* and the unconverted audience for the *mittlere ebene*. While all three levels naturally coexist within any one moment, my own reading of the reception history of Richardson and Fielding suggests that they are never exact equals, creating a diachronic element to Jauss's synchronic model. Different types of readers ascend over others across time, one type having more influence than another at any one moment.

The three types of readers operate within three modes of aesthetic enjoyment: poiesis, aesthesis and catharsis. Jauss borrows his terminology from Aristotle's *Poetics* and is faithful to their original Aristotelian meanings. The first mode is "poiesis," the attitude of experiencing art as an active process. Jauss describes it as "the producing consciousness, in the production of world as its own work." Quoting Hegel, Jauss writes that the reader " 'strips the external world of its inflexible foreignness,' makes it into his own product, and by this activity acquires knowledge that differs from the conceptual knowledge of science and the instrumental practice of self-reproducing craft".[56] The reception theorist who has the most to say about the subtleties of this mode is Iser, not Jauss. Although he does not use the word "poiesis," Iser focuses almost exclusively on this attitude, detailing how the reader actively fills in indeterminacies and creates (rather than "finds") a coherence within the text. Jauss's theory allows room for the other two aesthetic modes, however, and (perhaps more importantly) for the junctures, overlap, and conflict between them.

The second mode is in contrast to poiesis. "Aesthesis" is a passive and contemplative appreciation from the reader, the mode of reading we use for admiration and pleasure. Jauss writes:

Aesthesis as the fundamental receptive aesthetic experience thus corresponds to various definitions of art as 'pure visibility' (Konrad Fiedler) which understand the pleasurable reception of the aesthetic object as an enhanced, deconceptualized seeing . . . a 'disinterested contemplation of the object in its plenitude' (Moritz Geiger).[57]

The third mode is "catharsis," the part of a reading experience that brings about a pragmatic change in our beliefs or behavior. Jauss defines this familiar "instruct-and-delight" mode of reading by combining Aristotle's and Gorgias' meanings:

Catharsis as the fundamental communicative aesthetic experience thus corresponds to the practical employment of the arts for the social functions of conveying, inaugurating, and justifying norms of action. Catharsis also corresponds to the ideal object of all autonomous art which is to free the viewer from the practical interests and entanglements of his everyday reality and to give him aesthetic freedom of judgment by affording him self-enjoyment of what is other.[58]

It may initially seem that the three types of readers (poet, critic, and general) neatly parallel the three kinds of reading (active, passive, and didactic). Creative writers may indeed read "actively" insofar as their own works are part of a fuller realization of what they have previously read, and the general public may indeed read passively for entertainment or didactically to experience alien situations and "the other." It is the second kind of reader, the critic, who seems most unaccounted for in Jauss's model.

Theoria

"[T]he requirement that one evaluate for a mass publication with rapid-fire deadlines a heavy pile of fiction is not likely to encourage a stance of reverie and escape," writes Richter. "The reviewer is not escaping the workaday world in reading: reading *is* the reviewer's workaday world."[59] Professional critics read actively insofar as it is their vocation, but this is not the "Iserian" sense of the word "poiesis" that Jauss defines. They read passively insofar as they give themselves over to the text for as full of an experience as possible, but this is secondary to what makes them a unique class of readers. They read didactically, but it is they who hope to do the teaching. I am adding, therefore, a fourth category of aesthetic experience to Jauss's model: "theoria," Aristotle's word for "sight" or "study and investigation."

Jauss is unclear as to the true nature of *critical* reading. He states in *Toward an Aesthetic of Reception* that the critic and literary historian are "first simply readers before their reflexive relationship to literature can become productive again," dismissing the critical mode of reading as ancillary to the "reader in his genuine role."[60] This is a puzzling assertion because it uses a sequential distinction as a basis for the analysis of reading, as if people are physically or psychologically unable to experience a text in two or more ways simultaneously. The elevation of one kind of reception as being more "genuine" than another also seems contradictory to Jauss's empirical aims. Jauss cites Walther Bulst saying "no text was ever written to be read and interpreted philologically by philologists," but I see no reason why such a reading should not be valid.[61] (There are certainly many contemporary works of literature that seem to court critical readings by literary theorists, and for generations books have been written with an eye toward "pleasing the critics.") Later in the same section of *Toward an Aesthetic of Reception*, Jauss writes that "it is only through the process of its mediation that the work enters into the changing horizon-of-experience," bringing about the "perpetual inversion . . . from simple reception to critical understanding" that is the essence of a reception-based literary history.[62] Who "mediates" literature and works toward "critical understanding" more directly than professional critics and academics? I therefore intend no contradiction or insult to Jauss by asserting that the critical mode of reading be given equal standing, even at times priority, as a valid mode of appreciation and reception.

The theoria mode—which I am defining as reading for insight, understanding, or professional purposes—also accounts for two other omissions in Jauss's theory, one minor and one major. The minor omission is the failure to discuss readers (professional or otherwise) who read non-literary texts, that body of publications that make up the vast majority of the body of the printed word. Jauss does not mention texts such as instruction manuals, news magazines, medical journals, biographies, military histories, etc. The omission is relatively minor because Jauss claims only to advance a theory of literary history based upon a certain approach of aesthetics, not a theory of mass communication in general. Even so, there is no reason why some readers should not be able to find a personally meaningful aesthetic value in any of these genres which may affect their world view more concretely than any poem or novel. There is certainly an art to writing a clear, creative, and well-designed cookbook, for example, which is read primarily for information but entertains and inspires nevertheless. This is one reason why the theoria mode, while dealing with the potentially dry concerns of insight and understanding, nevertheless remains alongside Jauss's categories of *aesthetic* appreciation.

Politics, Conflict, and Domination

The second and more important omission in Jauss's categories of aesthetics is one that several readers have singled out as the greatest single weakness in reception theory overall: the absence of a political dimension. "Without a model of society or history, non-Marxist advocates of reception have trouble steering a course between a complete relativity and an uncritical legitimation of tradition," writes Holub.[63] Jauss's general argument in *Aesthetic Experience and Literary Hermeneutics* is that the aesthetic function of pleasure makes the text resist ideological determination. As we have seen, however, Jauss also believes that "it is only through the process of its mediation that the work enters into the changing horizon-of-experience." In today's critical climate it is difficult to accept that any kind of mediation is free from a political dimension pushing the work toward some kind of ideological determination. The theoria mode of aesthetic appreciation allows room for the political dimension, as reading for *knowledge* is never a wholly neutral process.

When critics approach a text, they know roughly what kind of insight they expect or want to prioritize. A critic reading a text with a self-conscious feminist identification, for example, will find in that text some kind of insight into feminist issues. (Catharsis allows the work to bring a new ideology to the reader; theoria allows the reader to bring a new ideology to the work.) Ideology is not simply an academic issue, however, as the political attraction or repugnancy of a text is inextricably bound up in a critic's aesthetic appreciations. There is no clearer proof of this than the fascinating history of the moral criticism of Fielding and Richardson. "It contains such a surprising variety of nature, wit, morality, and good sense, as is scarcely to be met with in any one composition, and there is such a spirit of benevolence runs through the whole, as I think renders it peculiarly charming," writes Elizabeth Carter of *Joseph Andrews* in 1743. "It must surely be a marvelous wrongheadedness and perplexity of understanding that can make any one consider this complete satire as a very immoral thing."[64]

The polarized, political rhetoric that marks the opposition of Richardson and Fielding from their day to this suggests another necessary modification to Jauss's paradigm. Jauss writes that his three modes of aesthetic pleasure "are not to be conceived hierarchically, as a structure of layers but as a nexus of independent functions."[65] A study of readers themselves, at least the highly motivated ones of Richardson and Fielding, suggests otherwise. If reception-based literary history is to be truly based upon the collective judgments of the readers rather than the individual judgments of the trained historian, then we must allow that readers are seldom as fair-minded and judicious about acknowledging that others' aesthetic appreciations are just as valid as their own. Richardson and Fielding's audience is among the most hierarchically-thinking body of readers in the history of the novel. Aesthesis, poiesis, catharsis, and theoria may be a network of independent functions, but they conflict more often than they cooperate.

Tracing the reception history of a dichotomized pair of authors and their opinionated readers requires a methodology that can identify which readers stand on which side of the boundary, when the majority is on what side and why, and who is sitting in the middle. Richter writes that Jauss's aesthetic modes are "dialectical alternatives" and the "shifting of the audience's motivation for reading from one of these alternatives to another is one of the chief causes of literary change."[66] As the critical history of Richardson and Fielding is so polarized, one author being read constantly against the grain of the other, it is useful to loosely categorize readers' aesthetic modes as being as dialectical as the Richardson/Fielding opposition itself. In other words, when one mode of reading leads to an aesthetic appreciation of one author, another mode of reading usually works to simultaneously denigrate the other author.

As an example of this dialectical approach, consider the following passage from the anonymous *Critical Remarks on Sir Charles Grandison, Clarissa, and Pamela* (1754):

> Grandison's benevolence has something showy and ostentatious in it; nothing in short of that graceful and beautiful nature which appears in Fielding's Allworthy. . . . To conclude [addressing Richardson], I think your writings have corrupted our language and our taste; that the composition of them all, except Clarissa, is bad; and that they all, particularly that [*Clarissa*], have a manifest tendency to corrupt morals.[67]

The reader is obviously a type-two reader, a professional critic, as general readers rarely go to the trouble of publishing entire works of literary criticism. Fielding is privileged because his character shows "graceful and beautiful nature," whereas Richardson's characters "have a manifest tendency to corrupt morals." Appreciation of "grace" and "beauty" in Allworthy's nature is a passive mode of appreciation, while concern for the integrity of the English language and the purity of British morality is a socially active and pragmatic mode of appreciation. In Jauss's terms, therefore, the Fielding/Richardson opposition for this *mittlere ebene* falls most readily into the aesthesis/catharsis opposition.

Taking my cue from Richter's observation, I will trace the turning points in the predominantly British and American reception history of Richardson and Fielding by documenting which type of reader transitions to and from which mode of reading.[68] (Clearly it is better to think of these "modes" as *orientations* rather than categorical imperatives. There are few perfect examples of each mode, and I will make an effort to value clarity over the imposition of artificial structures.) Different types of readers and reading were clearly dominant at different periods. My results tend to validate Levin Schücking's argument in *The Sociology of Literary Taste* that opinion does not really evolve; rather, one body of readers becomes dominant over another body and received literary "taste" changes accordingly. It is therefore a mistake to look too hard for a unified horizon of expectation (or "spirit of the age"), as there are really only differing bodies of readers: "What happens is not as a rule that a taste is modified, but that other persons become the advocates of a new taste. . . . Only constancy of the social structure guarantees a certain constancy of taste."[69] Because shifts between dominating bodies of readers naturally affect the literary horizons of expectation that are used for and against Richardson and Fielding, I will devote a chapter to each major critical era in the debate. Shifts in who controls the discourse of reception fall coincidentally and conveniently into the rough parameters of the eighteenth, nineteenth, and twentieth centuries. Generally speaking, the most articulate readership of Richardson and Fielding in the twentieth century is the professional literary critic. In the nineteenth century, it is the creative writer.

In the eighteenth century, as the next chapter illustrates, the "general readers" for whom Richardson and Fielding's novels were carefully tailored dominate the critical landscape. The nature of that landscape, however, rapidly became more volatile than either Richardson or Fielding could have anticipated.

2

The Eighteenth Century: *Shamela* to Richardson's *Correspondence*, 1741–1804

Your fine Tom Jones and Grandisons
They make your youthful fancies reel!
They heat your brains, and fire your veins,
And then you're prey for Rob Mossgiel.
—Robert Burns, "Farming Memorandum"

IN 1728 AN OBSCURE, UNSUCCESSFUL AND STUBBORNLY AMBITIOUS POET named Henry Fielding submitted his first play to one of the most prestigious theatres in England, the Theatre Royal at Drury Lane. He may have called upon his well-connected aunt, Lady Mary Wortley Montagu, to put in a good word for him with the intimidating "Triumvirate" which managed the Theatre Royal: Robert Wilks, Barton Booth, and the biggest star of the London stage, the poet laureate/dramatist/comedian/entrepreneur/actor Colley Cibber. One anonymous observer at the time writes that to get a hearing from the management at the Theatre Royal, including Cibber himself, one had to

> pay his Complements severally to the Menagers, who, with much Unwillingness, were prevail'd upon to appoint some leisure Day for the Reading of it . . . Yet this was a Favour not easily to be obtain'd; for we are to know, when an Author had got thus far, he had made a considerable Progress, not one in Twenty being ever able to gain this Point.[1]

The Triumvirate eventually accepted Fielding's *Love in Several Masques*, which was a modest success and ran four nights, despite having to follow Cibber's own enormously popular *The Provok'd Husband*. Fielding and Cibber became acquaintances, then close friends. Fielding praised Cibber's talent in several prefaces, and Cibber acted in several of Fielding's plays. In 1729, however— probably because Cibber was disappointed at the attendance of

Fielding's *Love in Several Masques* and refused to stage Fielding's next completed work, *The Temple Beau*—Cibber and Fielding became bitter enemies.[2]

The literary culture of Grub Street encouraged authors to hold grudges. Fielding satirized Cibber several times in *The Champion* throughout 1740,[3] as well as in the revised *Author's Farce* (1734) and "The Apology for the Life of Theophilus Cibber" (1740). In 1741, however, Fielding launched his most merciless attack. Annoyed at seeing Cibber achieve enthusiastic acclaim again and again with amateurish and inelegant writing, Fielding burlesqued what he may have thought was Cibber's most insipid work to date, the phenomenally popular novel *Pamela*.[4]

Fielding had fired the first shot in an ongoing battle which was to effect his entire literary career and subsequent reputation, as well as the career and reputation of the author of *Pamela*. Fielding's quarrel with Cibber was to be a trivial warm-up for a much larger and consequential literary contest, however, because this time Fielding had picked a fight with the wrong man.

How it Started

No one knows if Fielding and Richardson ever met face-to-face.[5] Fielding certainly knew the true author of *Pamela* by the time he came to write *Joseph Andrews*, and in the minds of their eager readership, Fielding's parody of the Andrews family was to harden the cement that would bond the names "Richardson" and "Fielding" together. Richardson's doctor, George Cheyne, is the first of many to annoy Richardson with an expression of enthusiastic curiosity for Fielding and the first to mention the rival author by name in Richardson's voluminous correspondence: "I beg as soon as you get Fieldings Joseph Andrews, I fear in Ridicule of your Pamela and of Virtue in the Notion of Don Quixotes Manner, you would send it me by the very first Coach."[6] Richardson was no doubt offended by what he read in *Joseph Andrews* but wrote nothing about it in his letters at the time.

Occasionally Richardson and Fielding were civil enough to correspond. Fielding is one of those who urged Richardson to give *Clarissa* a happy ending, and Richardson seems flattered by his concern. Richardson also claims to have helped Fielding obtain better accommodations during Fielding's declining months in Lisbon.[7] Fielding wrote positive things about Richardson's works in several essays: in the *Jacobite's Journal* (2 January and 5 March 1747–

48), Fielding praises *Clarissa* for its penetration and ability to raise the passions, and in the *Covent Garden Journal* No. 10 (4 February 1752) he endorses Richardson by way of censoring Rabelais and Aristophanes, an eerie preview of the technique which so many critics would soon use against Fielding himself.

Letters and essays were not the primary media in which each writer wished to be immortalized, however. It is in the texts of their novels that Richardson and Fielding weigh in with what they intended to be their most damaging personal criticism. (I am leaving aside *Shamela* and *Joseph Andrews*, where Fielding's attitude toward Richardson's work is too transparent for commentary here.) Richardson offers little internal evidence in *Clarissa* that he is responding directly to *Joseph Andrews*.[8] On the contrary, a move in that direction would call attention to the fictionality of the text and undermine his pretense of being an "editor" of recently discovered letters (at least while the pretense was taken seriously during the early volumes). Aurélien Digeon suggests Fielding was spurred on in writing *Tom Jones* by the knowledge that Richardson was working on *Clarissa*, but there is little internal evidence.[9] (As we can see in *Shamela* and *Joseph Andrews*, when Fielding wants to make a stab at Richardson, he will do it in plain sight.) In the introduction to Book X of *Tom Jones*, however, Fielding makes the most extensive of his several arguments for the aesthetic and moral benefit of "mixed characters." Fielding may be aiming at *Clarissa* when he encourages the reader to reject the alternative mode of characterization:

> [W]e must admonish thee, my worthy friend, (for, perhaps, thy heart may be better than thy head) not to condemn a character as a bad one, because it is not perfectly a good one. If thou dost delight in these models of perfection, there are books enow written to gratify thy taste. . . . [N]or do I, indeed, conceive the good purposes served by inserting characters of such angelic perfection, or such diabolical depravity, in any work of invention: since from contemplating either, the mind of man is more likely to be overwhelmed with sorrow and shame, than to draw any good uses from such patterns.[10]

Searching for direct internal evidence in the novels is probably not the best way to locate Richardson and Fielding's literary influence on one another, however. Following Jauss, it is better to see their works in a more general context and ask how one work is an "answer" to another work's "question." Richardson's response to the "problems" he saw in *Tom Jones*, for example, is not only seen directly in the *Correspondence*, but also indirectly in the entire conception of *Sir Charles Grandison*. "Richardson himself saw at once that (however much Fielding may have praised *Clarissa*) Tom was an anti-Richardsonian hero, and moreover a decidedly popular one, overshadowing *Clarissa* in sheer sales," write Ronald Paulson and Thomas Lockwood. "Richardson very soon began to plot a novel that would produce both a male equivalent of Clarissa and an anti-Tom Jones."[11] Richardson designed Sir Charles Grandison to be an anti-type of his own Mr. B. and Lovelace, also. Nevertheless, in the concluding note to *Grandison*, Richardson claims as a primary motivation for the book the effort to counter the effect of a certain novel in which "Human Nature has often . . . been shewn in a light too degrading." *Grandison*'s stated intention is to demonstrate that "characters may be good, without being unnatural":

> It has been said in behalf of many modern fictitious pieces, in which authors have given success (and *happiness*, as it is called) to their heroes of vicious, if not of profligate, characters, that they have exhibited Human Nature as it *is*. Its corruption may, indeed, be exhibited in the faulty character; but need pictures of this be held out in books?[12]

Fielding responded in kind in *The Journal of a Voyage to Lisbon*. "The highest instruction we can derive from the tedious tale of a dull fellow scarce ever pays us for our attention," he writes in the preface, probably thinking of *Sir Charles Grandison*.[13] Fielding's criticism is more direct than Richardson's, naming names, addressing the reader personally, and going straight to the question of artistic motive: "One hint, however, I must give the kind reader; which is, that if he should be able to find no sort of amusement in the book, he will be pleased to remember the public utility which will arise from it. [E]ntertainment, as Mr Richardson observes, [is] but a secondary consideration in a romance. . . ."[14]

Fielding is not only the first to start the rivalry, but also the first to try and end it. In a famous letter of 15 October 1748, Fielding offers Richardson a truce and denies he is envious:

> [T]he World will not suppose me inclined to flatter one whom they will suppose me to hate if the[y] will be pleased to recollect that we are Rivals for that Coy Mrs. Fame. . . . I love [fame] as coldly, as most of us do Heaven, so that I will sacrifice nothing to the Pursuit of her, much less would I bind my self, as all her Passionate Admirers do, to harbour in my Bosom that Monster Envy which of all Beings either real or imaginary I most heartily and sincerely abhor. You will begin to think I believe, that I want not much external Commendation. I will conclude

then with assuring you. That I heartily wish you Success. That I sincerely think you in the highest manner deserve it.[15]

It is remarkable and fortunate that this is one of the few letters from Fielding that have survived. The fact that Fielding's correspondence is largely lost may have influenced our expectations for his reactions to Richardson—there could have been other letters, now lost, which were every bit as vindictive toward Richardson as Richardson's were toward Fielding. It is a strange paradox that Fielding is so complementary in his letters and so critical in his novels.

Richardson, however, remains absolutely consistent in his disparagement of both Fielding and his works. He uses the imagery of competition, warfare, and overthrow:

> He is, in every paper he publishes under the title of the Common Garden, contributing to his overthrow. He has been overmatched in his own way by people whom he had despised, and whom he thought he had vogue enough, from the success his spurious brat Tom Jones so unaccountably met with, to write down; but who have turned his own artillery against him, and beat him out of the field.[16]

Richardson's caustic letters about Fielding, including all of his commentary on *Shamela* and *Joseph Andrews*, date from *after* the appearance of *Tom Jones*. Richardson's motive is therefore either jealousy of *Tom Jones*'s popularity, or he did not consider Fielding significant enough to merit commentary until that time. Either way, it is clear from Richardson's correspondence between 1749 and 1754, the period between the publications of *Tom Jones* and *Sir Charles Grandison*, that he is working his way toward a response to the novel he sincerely thinks is contributing to the decay of everything he values in society. As Richardson perceived Fielding's popularity to rise, so did he perceive Fielding's morality to fall.

For someone who hides the relationship between his personal authorship and his narration, Richardson was unusually quick to make assumptions about Fielding's. Richardson bases conclusions about Fielding's personality on what he finds in *Tom Jones*, combined with what little he finds out from Sarah Fielding and society gossip, and then recycles all of this back into a re-reading of the novels. There is no evidence that Fielding was living a particularly corrupt private life, and his public life as a lawyer and magistrate was distinguished. Richardson's antipathy for everything Fielding supposedly stood for did not, however, prevent Richardson from maintaining a long and public association with a man who was too hedonistic and morally reprehensible for Fielding himself: Colley Cibber. Perhaps Richardson thought the enemy of his enemy should be a friend.

Author/Reader Relationships

There is always a part of the reception history of any given work that is unique—the period while the author is actually writing. Authors with an ambition for immortality must write for anonymous generations of readers, and those future generations will in turn be influenced by the text and influence other readers' readings. During the author's lifetime, however, readers are able to influence the production of new texts, and they are not necessarily anonymous. "Reader-response" becomes not just a theory, but also social action.

Richardson and Fielding both gave oral readings of their manuscripts to select groups of friends. There is no evidence to suggest Fielding gave readings very often, but there is ample evidence that Richardson read often enough, and solicited opinion enough, to invite some splendid ridicule. William Hazlitt, conversing with Charles Lamb about whom they would most like to have seen at work, proposes Richardson:

> 'Richardson?'—'By all means, but only to look at him through the glass-door of his back-shop, hard at work upon one of his novels (the most extraordinary contrast that ever was presented between an author and his works), but not . . . to go upstairs with him, lest he should offer to read the first manuscript of Sir Charles Grandison, which was originally written in eight-and-twenty volumes octavo, or get out the letters of his female correspondents, to prove that Joseph Andrews was low.[17]

Few things are as important to Richardson as the opinions which others held of his works. He is anxious to know not only their aesthetic evaluations, but also how their thoughts and behavior change (like those of Mr. B.) by experiencing the texts. Richardson depended heavily upon his "little circle of adoring females," as Paulson and Lockwood call them, that includes Elizabeth Carter, Sarah Chapone, May Delany, Anne Donnellan, Frances Grainger, Susanna Highmore, Urania Hill, Astraea Hill, Minerva Hill, Hester Mulso, Mary Prescott, Isabella Sutton, Catherine Talbot, Sarah Fielding, Jane Collier and Sarah Westcomb.[18] This group overlaps with, but is not identical to, the "Blue Stocking ladies" which often met at the homes of Elizabeth Vesey and Elizabeth Montagu. Their loyalty to Richardson and his novels is unquestioned, but if loyalty is measured by a corresponding rejection of Fielding and *his* novels, it is often overestimated.

Women in Richardson's circle often express admiration for Fielding's novels, but because of their personal relationship with his rival author, the expression of admiration often takes a certain "under the breath" tone. The individual reactions of these readers will be discussed below, but it is worth pointing out here that they were, as a group, caught in a difficult position between the texts and the authors.[19]

Lady Dorothy Bradshaigh, for example, is Richardson's "beloved incognita" throughout their lengthy correspondence. Reading between the lines of a letter from 16 December 1749, it is clear that she probably thinks better of *Tom Jones* than she is willing to admit directly to Richardson. Although she disapproves of the novel's morals and trifling characters, she nevertheless reports "there are many good things" in it. Her condemnation of Fielding is muted at best:

> The girls are certainly fond of Tom Jones . . . tho' I give you my word, I never let a faulty word or action pass me without a visible disapproba-tion. . . . Had you gone thro' it, your censure or praises would have had agreeable weight with me, as some things I approve, but disapprove many more. I should have been glad to have known how far my opinion corresponded with yours. . . . I do assure you, Sir, Mr. Fielding's private character makes him to me appear disagreeable; so I am no ways preju-diced in his favour, I only impartially speak my opinion.[20]

Bradshaigh is not alone in "clearing" her opinion of Fielding with Richardson, apologizing for any inadvertent praise, asking for cor-rection, and reassuring him that any admiration of Fielding's works is not confused with admiration for the man himself. Urania, As-traea and Minerva Hill naively broke protocol by enthusiastically recommending *Tom Jones*, and Richardson disciplined them with a strongly worded reply. Their father, Aaron Hill, sent this account to Richardson:

> They are with me now: and bid me tell you, You have spoil'd 'em Both, for Critiks.—Shall I add, a Secret which they did not bid me tell you?— They, Both, fairly *cry'd*, that You shou'd think it possible they cou'd ap-prove of Any thing, in Any work, that had an *Evil Tendency*, in any Part of Purpose of it. . . . And, as soon as you have Time to read [*Tom Jones*]

for yourself, tis there, pert Sluts, they will be bold enough to rest the Matter.—Mean while, they love and honour you and your opinions.[21]

An analysis of receptions from those among Richardson's personal acquaintances, therefore, must take into consideration the important implications of this powerful author/reader relationship. Richardson is influential, and hardly impartial, in shaping the critical criteria which critics apply both to Fielding's novels and to his own. We should also consider the possibility that Urania, Astraea and Minerva Hill may have spoken aloud the guarded opinions of other devout "Richardsonians."

Fielding, as far as we know, did not have the benefit (or curse) of a similar coterie. On the contrary, Fielding's body of enemies is as large or larger than Richardson's body of admirers. Richardson avoided the political, theatrical and journalistic arenas, espousing a conservative and noncontroversial moral philosophy.[22] Richardson's novels occasionally sparked a burlesque or critical broadside, but the man himself generally escaped criticism in his own time. Fielding, on the other hand, gave almost everyone who was inclined to dislike him a good reason for doing so. He was by a cross-section of people who could have objected to either his aristocratic family or his marriage to a "cook maid," his high-minded court reforms or his drinking with "low" associates, his merciless satires (and their role in bringing about the theatre-closing and career-ending Licensing Act) or his battles with the libelous hacks from Grub Street, and his opposition to Walpole or his support of Walpole.

Praise of Fielding's novels often carefully disassociates itself from praise of Fielding the man. *Criticism* of Fielding's novels, however, usually works in the opposite direction. Contemporary readers eagerly followed Richardson's lead and took what they knew or had heard about Fielding's allegedly corrupt private life and found traces of debauchery in his works. As James Boswell says of Samuel Johnson's criticism, "Johnson's severity against Fielding did not arise from any viciousness in his style, but from his loose life, and the profligacy of almost all his male characters."[23]

Types of Readers

There is a certain "group mentality" represented in the history of the Richardson/Fielding opposition which we may find difficult to understand today. We usually reserve such group identification for followers of sports teams whose loyalty is often as ferocious as it is essentially arbitrary. "It is plain that we are born Tom Jonesists or Anti-Thomists, as we are born to be Platonists or Aristotelians," writes a facetious author in the *Saturday Review* as late as 1893.[24] This group identification is often what makes the Richardson/ Fielding opposition possible, however, and marks a significant point of separation from other literary rivalries. The William Shakespeare/Ben Jonson opposition, for example, has always been largely an exercise for literary critics, initiated by John Dryden a century later. The Richardson/Fielding opposition, however, began as a phenomenon of popular culture, was passed on from generation to generation of casual readers, and only relatively recently became the sport of professional academics (for whom loyalty is often a very real, if not always acknowledged, issue).

The group identification of readers contributes to the harsh tone of much eighteenth-century criticism in and out of Grub Street. The decline of literary patronage allowed public opinion alone to make or break literary careers, so statements of loyalty often became exaggerated in direct proportion to statements of hatred for the rival. "Under patronage and within the code of classicism the writer was expected to be self-effacing, adding his anonymous brick to the high cultural edifice of tradition," writes Roy Porter. "The rise of a wider, more varied and anonymous readership changed all that. . . . Yet freedom from noble patronage might take one out of the frying-pan into the fire."[25]

The dynamics of a group mentality among readers have not been discussed in depth by reader-response or reception critics. Groups are defined mostly by other groups—it takes a group mentality to recognize another, and since groups must patrol their borders defensively, artificial rivalries are easily initiated. (Why is it traitorous, for example, to be a loyal fan of two or more football teams?) In terms of the Richardson/Fielding dichotomy, the group mentality informs the perceived distances between between the "implied" and "real" readers (to borrow terms from Iser). An important part of Richardson and Fielding's reception history hinges upon the difference between the audience the author conceived of and the audience which actually did the reading. Simply put, Richardsonians have distorted ideas of who the Fieldingites are, and vice versa, and they use these ideas as a basis for their criticism.

The success of Richardson's didactic purpose hinges upon his novels reaching their intended readers. Ostensively, *Pamela* targets young lower-class women, *Clarissa* targets young middle-class women and their parents, and *Grandison* targets young upper-class men. The actual readership, however, consists of highly literate, middle-aged adults from the middle and upper classes. Joseph Bartolomeo points out an interesting difference in one person's impression of Richardson's readership: in a letter from 9 March 1751, Samuel Johnson urges Richardson to include a topical index to *Clarissa* since it would be consulted by "the busy, the aged, and the studious." But Bartolomeo notes that just one year earlier Johnson had written in the *Rambler* 4 (31 March 1750) that modern novels should meet a high moral standard since they are "written chiefly to the young, the ignorant, and the idle, to whom they serve as lectures of conduct, and introductions into life." The two trios of perceived readerships are exact opposites. "Despite Johnson's often-expressed admiration for Richardson's masterpiece, this parallel implies that Richardson is not reaching the readers whom both authors most desire to instruct," writes Bartolomeo.[26] Either Johnson keenly observed a change in those he personally saw with copies of the novel in hand, or his estimations of the readership are a matter of personal speculation subject to change according to the purposes of the critic.

Fielding's implied reader is more difficult to pin down, but he makes very clear the kind of reader he does *not* want.[27] "Reader, it is impossible we should know what sort of person thou wilt be: for, perhaps, thou may'st be as learned in human nature as Shakespear himself was, and, perhaps, thou may'st be no wiser than some of his editors," he writes in *Tom Jones*, referring to the critical reader as "my good reptile."[28] Again, generalizations about the readership depend largely upon the aims of the person making the observation. Earlier in our century Wilbur Cross found a different result based upon a different set of assumptions:

> [A] sober narrative with a moral purpose, real or affected, is understood by everybody; whereas humour and irony perplex the average mind. Richardson's novel ran its course down through all classes to the servant's hall, while Fielding's novel ran upward through a less numerous class to the gentry and nobility.[29]

More recently, and completely differently, Michael McKeon makes a sophisticated argument for the emergence of a group of displaced middle-class readers caught between conflicting currents of economic and intellectual history who are drawn to Fielding's "parable of the younger son."[30]

During the eighteenth century, people with a strong group identification tend to look into the mirror rather than the bookstalls when estimating Fielding's readership. Creative writers often make the assumption that Fielding's readers are other creative writers: Charles Jenner, for example, writes in *The Placid Man* (1770) that the purpose behind Fielding's learned introductory chapters is to secure himself from unthinking imitators.[31] This phenomenon is not markedly noticeable for Richardson's readership until the twentieth century,[32] when modern literary critics almost always assume—usually with good reason—that Richardson's only readership is fellow literary critics.

With this background and its qualifiers in mind, we can now turn to a more detailed consideration of each type of reader (as defined by Jauss) and the role each plays in the eighteenth-century Richardson/Fielding opposition.

Type-One Readers: Creative Writers

It is virtually a cliché by now to say the influence Richardson and Fielding have had on the novel is incalculable. I am certainly making no attempt to calculate it here. What has received little attention, however, is how novelists have responded creatively to Richardson and Fielding *as a pair*.

As we have seen, the *gipfelsebene* (in Jauss's terms) tends to conceive Richardson's and Fielding's audience to be one of fellow novelists. Not surprisingly, therefore, one of the primary criteria they use for a comparative evaluation of Richardson and Fielding is their craftsmanship and narrative technique. In a denunciation of romances in *The World* #19, 10 May 1753, the future poet laureate William Whitehead complains that few novelists have mastered the art of "writing upon low subjects without writing in a low manner," so readers should not even "attempt to open any novel, or romance . . . unless it should happen to be stamped Richardson or Fielding."[33]

A more specific but less accepting example is in *Letters Between Henry and Frances* (1757) by Elizabeth and Richard Griffith. This sentimental novel in the Richardsonian mode, admired by Johnson, nevertheless has a character named Henry who concludes that *Tom Jones* is a "true copy of human life; the characters thoroughly kept up to; the story well told; the incidents humorous; the sentiments noble; and the reflections just and moral." Lest the Richardson influence be diluted, however, the authors have Henry find fault with Fielding's wit, which manifests itself in "poor allusions, bald conceits, or wretched puns."[34]

Perhaps the most detailed analysis of Richardson and Fielding's comparative techniques is in Jenner's *The Placid Man: or, Memoirs of Sir Charles Beville*. For Jenner, all contemporary novelists fall into one of two schools of influence: Richardson or Fielding's. The superior camp is that of "the ingenious Mr. Henry Fielding, whose memory ought to be as dear to every novel-writer, as his authority ought to be respectable." Jenner writes essays in praise of Fielding's technique of interpolating essays. Of epistolary novelists, on the other hand, Jenner writes:

> I am aware that the generality of them will plead that they are inlisted under another master and therefore are not under any necessity of conforming to his rules; that by throwing their materials into the form of letters, they confess themselves disciples of Mr. Richardson, and so, in imitation of their master, have a right to begin in the middle of their history, without ceremony open half a dozen characters upon you at once, and leave you to find out who they are as you can.

Of the two methods and authors, "Mr. Fielding seems to deserve a little more respect."[35]

Nicolas T. Barthe takes a more philosophical view in *La Jolie Femme: ou La Femme du Jour* (1770), reading the prose poetically like few other readers of the eighteenth-century novel. The result is an account that grows less partisan as it grows more philosophical: "No Author, I believe, ever metamorphosed himself into his characters so perfectly as Richardson. . . . [Fielding's] style has the same effect as that ancient music, whose art made the soul pass gently, or, as it were, insensibly, from joy to sorrow. . . ."[36]

These few examples demonstrate what Ian Watt, Paul Hunter, McKeon and many others have written of the early novel: it "rises" as a hybrid of many pre-existing literary forms. One form that Hunter and McKeon do not mention as a "pre-text" for the novel, however, is the essay in literary criticism.[37] It is impossible to distinguish the above passages, all from works of fiction, from the rhetoric of criticism we find in any number of eighteenth-century journals. These authors make their comments by way of narrative intrusions; other authors create characters who express their creators' opinions as part of the narrative.

Novels of manners, for example, can draw out the fashions of the times, unwittingly giving future generations an insight into the smaller cross-currents of popularity that make up the shifting tides of the Richardson/Fielding reception. Albinia Gwynn has two society ladies discuss the issue in *The Rencontre: Or, Transition of a*

Moment (1785), both of whom see "fashion" as an enemy to the stable morality of Richardson. The first speaker repeats the unoriginal dictum that Fielding portrays the world as it is while Richardson portrays it as it ought to be, and she contrasts the conventional moral implications of each method. The second speaker steps in:

> Good God! Lady Charlton, interrupted Charlotte, who would have thought such an old-fashioned author had been your favourite! Why, one runs the hazard of having one's taste called in question by ever mentioning his Clarissa, or Sir Charles Grandison. That person must be void of both taste and sentiment, who can read either with dislike, my dear. . . . This is a very whimsical age! . . . So capricious a thing is fashion, and public taste![38]

Richardson and Fielding are both praised by characters in Miss Smythies' *The Stage Coach* (1753). Smythies suggests there was some debate about which books to recommend to an uninitiated reader unfamiliar with the new and controversial genre. If we can read a subtext of fact into the fiction, then *Clarissa* and *Amelia* were often the first novels many people encountered. Richardson and Fielding, as a pair, were therefore a powerful shaping influence in the horizon of expectations which these contemporaries brought to all future encounters with the novel:

> Mr. Manly said he had never read any thing of that kind, but the works of Cervantes, till lately he had been persuaded to pursue Clarissa, and some of the Covent-Garden justice's performances; and though he formerly had thought such fictions below his notice, he was now not ashamed to aver, there were some which . . . were capable of yielding profit with amazement, particularly those he had mention'd.[39]

Whereas many critics and general readers state their preferences for Richardson or Fielding within the framework of a sharply-defined dichotomy, many authors state (or imply) their preferences within a framework of paradox and ambiguity. As in *Letters Between Henry and Francis*, praise of one novelist is written in the style of the other author. (In other words, characters may write letters to one another praising Fielding, or intrusive narrators may digress on a panegyric on Richardson.) The result is an interesting situation where one author's novels have entered the horizon of expectations partially governing the criticism of the rival's.[40] The Reverend Richard Graves, for example, is obviously following Fielding's style in *The Spiritual Quixote* (1773) with digressions, narrative intrusions, interpolated stories, essays (including an essay on "Quixotism"), and a character modeled on Parson Adams. Nevertheless, the preface states "Clarissa or Sir Charles Grandison, will furnish more hints for correcting the follies and regulating the morals of young persons . . . than volumes of severe precepts seriously delivered and dogmatically inforced."[41]

Perhaps one reason why the criticism of Richardson and Fielding tends to be mixed in works of fiction is that there is a different kind of "group mentality" operating among the type-one readers. Personal preferences aside, novelists may have felt that Richardson and Fielding are both due a degree of respect for their contributions to the genre. There are several epistolary novels written in the high sentimental style which make complimentary references to Fielding, as if to acknowledge the other side of the argument and find a critical middle ground between the two rivals. These sometimes fleeting references to Fielding may reflect his popularity with the general readership, if not necessarily his enthusiastic popularity with those writers who choose to follow Richardson's form: Maria Cooper's *The Exemplary Mother; or Letters Between Mrs. Villars and her Family* (1769) is an epistolary domestic romance which has a young character who "made choice of Fielding's works" which he reads "with eagerness" while his sister is charmed by the "pathetick Richardson."[42]

Other passages which seek a common ground between the rivals are more comprehensive and spill over into the plotting. The anonymous author of *The History of Charlotte Summers, the Fortunate Parish Girl* (1750) declares himself a "son" of Fielding, but creates a narrative which has self-conscious elements of *Pamela*, *Clarissa*, and *Tom Jones* (the heroine declines to marry a deceiving man, only to discover later she is of noble birth and can marry her true love, a gentleman of higher rank). The narrator also shows an early, perceptive awareness of the Richardson/Fielding opposition in a passage of balanced reader-response evaluation:

> The one tickled me till I had like to die laughing, and the other moved me so I had like to have died crying. . . . [Fielding] wrote nothing but what tickled his own Fancy, and never put Pen to Paper but when he was perfectly pleased with himself and all about him; by this Means nothing flowed from him but what was facetious and witty. On the other Hand, the Historian of *Clarissa* . . . never wrote till he had wrought up his Imagination into a real Belief of the Reality of the Misfortune of his Heroine. His Sighs, his Tears, and Groans guided his Pen, and every Accent appears but the Picture of his own sad Heart, that beats with tender Simpathy for the imaginary Distress of his favourite Fair.[43]

Other authors refer to the crossbreeding ironically and humorously, confirming via the authenticity of the satire that some circles must have taken the dichotomy very seriously. Henry Brooke's novel *Fool of Quality* (1766–70), for example, is a novel of sentiment complete with interpolated essays, giving the name "Fielding" to a family of characters, along with a pair of brothers named Richard (the irresponsible debaucher) and Henry (the hard-working tradesman). Robert Burns, who admired Fielding's realism and found Richardson's characters "beings of another sphere," is one of the few poets to comment on the Richardson/Fielding dichotomy.[44] His poem "Farming Memorandum" (1784) has these lines about the devilish spirit Rob Mossgiel:

> Your fine *Tom Jones* and *Grandisons*
> They make your youthful fancies reel!
> They heat your brains, and fire your veins,
> And then you're prey for Rob Mossgiel.[45]

Another good-humored example is Richard Cumberland's novel *Henry* (1795), written in Fielding's style, which has the genial narrator make the Richardson/Fielding comparison via a change in the usual critical approach to Fielding's consumptive personality: Fielding "furnished his baiting-places with such ingenious hospitality, as not only to supply his guests with the necessary remissions from fatigue, but also to recruit them with viands of a very nutritive as well as palatable quality." Richardson, on the other hand, plays the Pardoner to Fielding's Host:

> Others there have been, and one there was of the same day, who was a well-meaning civil soul, and had a soft simpering kind of address, that took mightily with the ladies, whom he contrived to usher through a long, long journey, with their handkerchiefs at their eyes, weeping and wailing by the way, till he conducted them, at the close of it, either at a ravishment or a funeral, or perhaps to a madhouse, where he left them to get off as they could. He was a charming man, and had a deal of custom, but the other's was the house that I frequented.[46]

By 1769, when *Tristram Shandy* is in its full popular rage, Richardson and Fielding's works are still the most imitated. The *Gentleman's Magazine* for 1769 mentions the anonymous *History and Adventures of Arthur O'Bradley* (1769) as one example in the Fieldingesque mode and Pierre Treyssac de Vergy's *Mistakes of the Heart* (1774) as one in the Richardsonian. The end of the century saw shifts in Richardson and Fielding's popularity according to the different types of readers: general readers are gaining admiration for Fielding, critics are paying somewhat less attention to either, and novelists gravitate closer to Richardson. "During the closing years of the century the novel was chiefly in the hands of women, who . . . were becoming somewhat reticent about the author of *Tom Jones*," writes Blanchard. "The revolutionary writers—Godwin, Holcroft, and others—presumably found Fielding too orthodox for their liking; while the Gothic romancers . . . flew in the face of his injunction against ghosts, and, on the sentimental side, aligned themselves with Richardson."[47]

Type-Two Readers: Critics

The *mittlere ebene* (or the set of critics who are mediators between the creative writers and the general readership) is a diverse group throughout the eighteenth century that includes ministers, reviewers, journalists, moralists, hack writers, philosophers, and aristocratic *literati*. Drawing distinctions between type-two and type-three readers is at times difficult, and often the only significant difference is that critics voice their opinion in publications and general readers voice their opinion in letters or journals. Of the fifty-three people I have found from 1749–1804 who make direct comparisons of Richardson and Fielding, thirty-one of them are critics. It is ultimately impossible to tell with the Richardson/Fielding opposition if the critics are following an issue that is important to the general readership or if the general readership has been preconditioned by the critics—probably both. Either way, it is not unexpected to have more written commentary (at least that which has survived 250 years) from published writers than from general readers, and we can safely assume a vast amount of opinion from general readers has been lost. While the voice of the general readership is at its strongest during the eighteenth century, the dominant voice on the opposition is still that of the *mittlere ebene*.

Type-Two Readers: Sources of Opinion

If the critic is the mediator between the text and its reception, then the critic's text is mediated in turn by the media which publishes it. *What* opinions we have on the Richardson/Fielding opposition are conditioned by *where* those opinions appeared. Our conception of the ups and downs of the rivalry might well be unrecognizable to an informed observer from the eighteenth century, as our impressions are of course based upon the available texts. These texts tell us Richardson is more popular than Fielding up until the mid 1760s, but essentially all we have is Richardson's correspondence. "The surviving records of early reception are unusually copious and rich, offering intriguing evidence not only of particular responses arrived at by particular readers but also of the larger terms of reference within which their reading were typically framed," writes Tom Keymer of *Clarissa*.[48]

No such statement would be possible in behalf of *Shamela*, *Joseph Andrews*, *Jonathan Wild* or the early reception of *Tom Jones*. Most of Fielding's letters have been lost, probably in the fire which destroyed his brother's home in June 1780.[49] The loss is particularly damaging to research into the early reception of *Joseph Andrews*. Fielding decided not to risk the repercusions of his notoriety as a dramatist and left his name off the first three editions of *Joseph Andrews*, thereby stifling a great deal of attention which possibly would have been his otherwise. Even Richardson offers no commentary on *Joseph Andrews* until after the publication of *Tom Jones*. There is no comment on *Joseph Andrews* in its first year in *The Gentleman's Magazine*, *The London Magazine*, or *The Works of the Learned*, all of which reviewed *Pamela*. We know *Joseph Andrews* did have a substantial readership, however, as there were three London editions printed in thirteen months, along with two editions of a French translation. All three editions amounted to 6,500 copies, roughly half that of *Pamela* in its first year.[50] The early reception of *Pamela*, by contrast, is scrupulously well-documented. In addition to the novel becoming the new center of fashionable conversation, the epistle-oriented Richardson preserved virtually his entire correspondence, and the letters were published before calamity could intervene.

There has been some question about the proportions of letters, journals, essays, books, and other material which provide our sources for eighteenth-century opinion on Richardson and Fielding. "The scarcity of public comments after publication [of *Joseph Andrews*] is perhaps explained by the scarcity of journals that reviewed such an anomalous and doubtfully reputable form," write Paulson and Lockwood. There were several active journals in London at the time, however, and most of them *did* review *Pamela*.[51] Paulson and Lockwood go on to state that most of the Richardson criticism comes in the form of "reactions" rather than reviews, letters from readers to one another or to Richardson.[52] That may be true for the sum total of responses to Richardson's works, but it is

far from the truth if we isolate statements which also mention
Fielding. Of the fifty-three responses surveyed here, only thirteen
are from letters and nine from periodicals, compared with *twenty-
one* which come from books. (Additionally, seven come from novels, two from journals, two from poems and one from a sermon.)

Paulson and Lockwood are not alone among critics who isolate
letters and periodicals—"reactions" and "reviews"—as the primary
sources for reception history in the period. My findings suggest,
however, that Richardson's reputation throughout the eighteenth
century has been significantly distorted, not only because of the im-
balance of primary sources, but also because modern critics tend
to neglect the very well-established genre of book-length studies in
literary history and criticism. Ioan Williams, for example, has it
completely backwards. He states that one reason Richardson has
the edge in criticism of the time is that he is reviewed and Fielding
is not:

> The essays from the essay-journals, traditionally conservative and con-
> cerned to preserve an ideal of middle-class behavior in a changing
> world, are radically different from the work of the reviewers, who were
> expected to be more willing to accept each variation on the new form
> on its own merits.[53]

On the contrary, Richardson did *not* have the edge as the century
progressed. Richardson fares better in the reviews than in the essays, even if "essay" is taken to include passages from larger books.
Fielding, however, tends to suffer in the reviews and thrives in the
"traditionally conservative" essays.

The conspicuous silence of the reviewers says the most about the
reception of *Tom Jones*. In the first month *Tom Jones* appeared
(February 1749), Thomas Astley's *The London Magazine* devoted
its first four pages to a laudatory, detailed review. *The Gentleman's
Magazine*, however, with Johnson probably influencing Edward
Cave's editorial decisions, said nothing, choosing instead to run the
plan and epilogue from Johnson's *Irene*. The first significant mention of *Tom Jones* in *The Gentleman's Magazine* is reprinted in a
long article from *Old England* criticizing Fielding personally as a
press informer. In the same issue, no doubt deliberately timed, the
editors devoted even more space to a laudatory review of *Clarissa*,
which overflowed into four pages of the next issue. This second
issue, August 1749, did include a brief poem by a "Cawthorn" addressed to Fielding, "On Reading His Inimitable History of *Tom
Jones*." "How this stowaway compliment managed to creep into the

Poet's Corner, nobody knows; possibly Mr. Urban was misled as to the identity of the author," writes Blanchard.[54] Richardson admirers protested the poem, and the occasional poet James Cawthorne wrote the magazine to disclaim responsibility. By the end of the year, *The Gentleman's Magazine* and *The London Magazine* had become bitter rivals—Whig versus Tory, Samuel Johnson versus Thomas Astley, and Richardson versus Fielding.

Type-Two Readers: Prestige for the Genre and Canonization for the Authors

"When it comes to credit for literary history, readers seldom figure, but when it comes to blame, taste and desire (rather than pens and publishers) often become culprits," writes Hunter, indirectly defending a reception study over traditional literary history. "The story of the novel . . . often is mistold because of too precise a division of labor based on literary predispositions and class prejudice. The suspicion of ordinary readers and the distrust of the ordinariness of the novel were almost the same thing."[55] In other words, it is impossible to separate the developing prestige of the novel as a genre from the perceived prestige of its readership. Critics of the period united Richardson and Fielding as a pair, and by doing so helped to change expectations of the novel from suspicion to respectful canonization. Richardson or Fielding may rise or fall throughout literary history, but as they do so, the novel does nothing but rise.

As late as 1783, Hugh Blair's book *Lectures on Rhetoric* was accepted as authoritative on laws of literary taste. From his privileged position as Professor of Rhetoric at Edinburgh, he states in his lecture on "Fictitious History" that after Philip Sidney, the romance "dwindled down" to the "insignificant" novel. Novels are only important insofar as they "discover the errors into which we are betrayed by the passions." His aesthetic standard is clear, as it was to be for Ian Watt: "Interesting situations in real life are the groundwork of novel writing." As with Watt, interestingly enough, the only three British writers discussed at length are Defoe, Richardson and Fielding. Even within the third-class genre of the novel, Richardson and Fielding are placed side by side as notable exceptions to the rule of "trivial performances which daily appear under the title of lives, adventures, and histories, by anonymous authors":

> Fielding's novels are highly distinguished for humour and boldness of character. Richardson, the author of Clarissa, is the most moral of all

our novel writers; but he possesses the unfortunate talent of spinning out pieces of amusement into an immeasureable length.[56]

Blair's opinion is fairly typical for an academic of the time. The novel tended to be seen as a relatively low genre which nevertheless attracted great individual geniuses. The critical horizon of expectation is therefore working against both Richardson and Fielding. When their novels met with such success, however, the horizon had to adjust to account for it. "In quite different ways those two novelists addressed directly the strong cultural resistance to any new form of fiction, and even if the resistance did not immediately fall away, their impact was substantial on both a general readership and the moral and literary establishment," writes Hunter. "In effect, Richardson and Fielding considered together became a kind of double-barreled answer to the literary and moral objections raised by the Augustans against innovation and novelty a generation earlier."[57] Simply put, Richardson and Fielding asked new kinds of literary questions which needed new kinds of critical answers.

As the number of novels grew, so did the range of literary criticism. Ioan Williams goes so far as to claim that there are two periods of prose fiction during the eighteenth century, before and after the publication of *Pamela* and *Joseph Andrews* in the 1740s. Criticism after 1740 began to consider the novel as a genre equal to poetry and drama once these novels proved that the genre could be intellectually demanding, artistically significant, and entertaining. Whether there is a direct causal link or not, literary journals multiplied and began to publish more commentary with the simultaneous escalation of the Richardson/Fielding debate.

Literary criticism rapidly began to outgrow the journals and began to take book-length form. Clara Reeve's *The Progress of Romance*, written just two years after Blair's *Lectures on Rhetoric*, reflects a significantly more stable position for the novel as a *bona fide* literary genre. *The Progress of Romance*, the first extended history of the novel (or at least the first to deal with the specific traits of specific novels), is written by a Richardsonian. Reeve was a close friend of Richardson's daughter who helped edit the final proofs for the book. Fielding is deemed superior in "wit and learning" (categories Richardson does not compete in), but works of wit are declared to be of only "secondary merit." Reeve acknowledges more men than women prefer Fielding. Inaugurating the now-familiar phrase often used both for and against Fielding, Reeve finds Fielding a bad influence on young boys because he "painted human nature as *it is*, rather than as *it ought to be*."[58] Reeve's analysis may not be terribly original or insightful by modern standards, but the fact that a history of the novel is undertaken in the first place is testimony to the growing prestige of the genre by 1785. From the beginning, Richardson and Fielding as a contrasted pair are used as cornerstones for the entire history of the genre.

Before Reeve's book, it was more common for discussions of the novel to be in terms of the "Ancient Romance" and the epic. "The novel labored under the suspicion of being a mere waste of time, a frivolous and even pernicious amusement. Many critics are definitely embarrassed in dealing with it," writes René Wellek. Wellek uses Richardson and Fielding in particular to trace a decline of interest in conventional epic theory that parallels the growing interest in the novel, an insight that helps explain the question behind Fielding's answer of an experimental "comic epic poem in prose": "Fielding's excellent plotting and Richardson's sentimental morality helped to raise the novel in critical evaluation. . . . Classical epic theory more and more became a purely academic subject."[59]

John Moore's *The Commencement and Progress of Romance* (1797) is typical of such classically-based criticism, despite being written at a time that calls Wellek's claim into question. Moore traces the development of prose fiction from the Romans to Smollett, elevating the novel by associating it directly with the classics. Richardson and Fielding are not compared directly, but their entries are placed side by side. Both are seen to follow Cervantes in the "realistic" rather than "idealistic" tradition. Richardson is admired primarily for adapting his writing style to different characters, a particular strength of his epistolary form. Lovelace has great spirit, so much so that he may be counter-productive by evoking too much admiration. Fielding is defended against his critics and is admired for his plots and the skillful way *Tom Jones* moves from its darkest crisis to a natural and still surprising conclusion. Moore provides us with a dramatic reader-response reception of *Tom Jones*, saying it is a work where

> the imagination of the reader has been gratified by the exhibition of a variety of interesting scenes and characters, and his heart warmly engaged in the fortunes of the hero, his mind is agitated and alarmed by a series of incidents which seem to cross and obstruct the schemes and blast the hopes of him for whom he is now deeply interested. . . .[60]

By the time Moore was writing his history of the romance at the end of the century, readers would have fully expected entries on

Richardson and Fielding and would have expected one to follow the other. One generation's cliché is another generation's debate, however. The transformation from popularity to canonization is remarkably brief for Richardson and Fielding, especially for an eighteenth century so protective of its literary traditions. If Richardson and Fielding could look back on their own 250 year reception history, each would probably be horrified by how much they have helped one another into a seemingly permanent place in the literary canon.

After the publication of *Pamela* and *Joseph Andrews*, Richardson and Fielding were the two best-known novelists of their day. Readers quickly linked them together, many without knowing the name of *Pamela*'s author, anticipating the next work of each to be a career masterpiece. According to Hunter, it is remarkable not only that Richardson and Fielding are paired together, but also that eighteenth-century readers recognized them as even being in the same genre:

> [C]ontemporaries of Fielding and Richardson tended to think of the two as having jointly made the claim for 'what was new about "the new species of writing" '. . . . [T]he surrounding critical context offers a kind of overview of what the newness consisted in. Followers of Richardson tended to emphasize certain features and those of Fielding rather different ones, but . . . there was no noticeable tendency to regard their accomplishments as two separate species or forms.[61]

Hunter overstates the case—relatively few critics comment directly upon their favorite author's "newness," canonizing him instead by emphasizing the strength of the pre-existing elements they already know how to find. As Richardson and Fielding enter the canon, the novel does not so much shock with its formal innovations as it simply becomes familiar.

Critics gradually began to use Richardson and Fielding as touchstones for excellence in other novels. "By the time of Fielding's death he and Richardson, however ranked in relation to each other, were established in an unofficial pantheon," write Paulson and Lockwood. "Although they continued to be compared and contrasted, they had become twin norms by which later novelists were judged and placed."[62] On one hand Richardson's and Fielding's position as "twin norms" consolidated their places in the literary canon. On the other hand this position tended to exaggerate their differences, because critics used them as poles between which the entire diversity of the eighteenth-century must necessarily fall. *The*

Monthly Review and *The Critical Review*, for example, were two new magazines in 1754 created to respond to the explosion of popularity for prose fiction, and they both frequently use Richardson and Fielding as touchstones. In a 1758 *Monthly* review of *The History of Amanda*, the critic writes that the heroine "must not think herself qualified to keep company with Madam Clarissa, or Miss Western: ladies of the first distinction in the records of romance."[63]

There are many other examples of Richardson and Fielding's linked canonization. The anonymous author of *The Adventures of a Valet* writes as early as 1752 that all but two modern authors write descriptions as if they suffer from hallucinations: "It will not look like Adulation to except the Authors of *Tom Jones* and *Clarissa* from this general Censure; nor would it have been needful indeed to have named their Works, if we had but said there were two such."[64] A young Edward Gibbon states in 1767 that Richardson and Fielding are "the two great geniuses who in their different manners have pushed their genre to perhaps the highest degree. . . ."[65] Even Johnson, no friend to Fielding generally, admits his standing as a critical touchstone alongside Richardson when he says of Francis Burney, "Richardson would have been really afraid of her . . . Harry Fielding, too, would have been afraid of her."[66] The *Monthly* reviewer for *Cecilia* agrees, stating in December, 1782, that Burney shows "much of the dignity and pathos of Richardson; and much of the acuteness and ingenuity of Fielding."[67] Finally, when Reeve came to write her history of the novel in 1785, it was clear to her and her readers that Richardson and Fielding were "the most eminent writers of our country."[68]

Of course not all statements of Richardson's or Fielding's canonicity place them on such level ground. At times the canonical status of one author is dependent upon the critical rejection of the other. Anna Williams, the blind woman who lived with Johnson, writes, "In distant times, when *Jones* and *Booth* are lost, / *Brittania* her *Clarissa's* name shall Boast."[69] J.W. Von Archenholz agrees in 1782 that *Tom Jones* is temporary while *Clarissa* is for the ages.[70] The *Gentleman's Magazine* proves in 1749 that canonization does not always come from evaluative criticism—almost every issue for the year contains some type of charged reference to Richardson and Fielding in the form of allusions to characters and events, gossip, lists of the most influential novels of the year, and even a frontispiece drawing of a pile of books with *Tom Jones* underneath *Clarissa*.

A curious side-effect of the process of canonization is, as we have already seen with certain type-one readers, a certain hesitancy on the part of some critics to risk criticizing Richardson or Fielding too harshly. George Canning, a Richardsonian, guards his own respectability in his "On Novel Writing" (1787): "Were I to prophane these by impertinent criticism, I might with justice be accused of avowed enmity to wit; of open apostacy from true feeling, and true taste."[71] In *The Pursuits of Literature* (1794) Thomas Mathias avoids the crossfire by damning with faint praise. In a work De-Quincey says was "the most popular book of its day," Mathias writes, "Every person should be well acquainted *with the whole* of Cervantes, of Le Sage's unequalled and unrivalled Gil Blas, and of Tom Jones, (that great comick Epick poem) by Fielding. These perhaps are all, which it is *necessary* to read." He then turns to Richardson, and this is his complete entry: "Let us turn to Clarissa, the work of a man of virtue and genius, which is too celebrated for any additional praise."[72]

Type-Two Readers: Canonization by Comparison

Additional praise for both authors came nevertheless. In addition to canonizing Richardson and Fielding by linking their names together as touchstones for excellence, critics often canonized them by way of comparing them with other established authors. Surprisingly, critics seldom compare Richardson and Fielding with pairs of authors associated by a pre-existing rivalry.[73] For example, there are no eighteenth-century allusions to Fielding playing Jonson to Richardson's Shakespeare. Instead, Richardson and Fielding are usually both compared to a single author as a mark of their status rather than as part of a larger contrast of their particular literary techniques. Richardson and Fielding are already linked to the point where critics consider them as a single literary unit.

Shakespeare is the most frequently cited. Typical is the chapter titled "Catalogue of the most celebrated Writers of the present Age, with Remarks on their Works" in *Letters Concerning the Present State of England: Particularly Respecting the Politics, Arts, Manners, and Literature of the Times* (1772). The anonymous author compares both Richardson and Fielding to Shakespeare but hardly does so equally. The critic clearly wants to reflect the opinion of his times but seems to feel that an overly-enthusiastic acknowledgment of Richardson's status would somehow weaken his praise for Fielding:

> Perhaps of all men none ever saw deeper into the human mind than Shakespear and Fielding . . . that immortal poet is not greater in the

superior walks of tragedy and comedy, than this inimitable writer is in comic romance. His characters are not only true to nature, they are nature itself. . . . His humour is incomparable; his plots excellent, and his incidents superior to those of any writer the world ever produced. . . . Never lived a man that saw in a quicker manner the foibles, vices, and wrong side of a character with such keenness.

The entry on Richardson is much shorter and not as effusively positive:

The delineation of character in his romances, exceeds that of any writer antient or modern: but the portraying the passions peculiar to certain personages in a long novel in prose, is easier than making a strong impression from the same effort in the space of a play. Shakespear's great excellence is his character drawing—Richardson is equally original.[74]

Other classical references favor the middle-class printer, not the scholar who writes the comic epic poem in prose. French critics in particular seemed to be in a kind of contest for the most euphoric praise of Richardson. Denis Diderot's eulogy (1761) places Richardson on the same shelf with Homer, Euripides, Sophocles, and, famously, the Bible itself.[75] As McKillop writes, "The *Éloge* marks the limit which other less hardy souls should approach in fascination, or seek to avoid."[76] Sébastien Mercier takes the challenge, however, when he claims in 1773 that Richardson is the modern Homer and that *Clarissa* surpasses the *Aeneid*.[77]

It is far more typical for critics to compare Richardson and Fielding with their (usually) canonical contemporaries. After Fielding, critics most often compare Richardson (usually unfavorably) to Rousseau. Throughout the 1770s in Germany, for example, Rousseau is seen as Richardson's primary rival even more than Fielding (the line was drawn between "Philistine rationalism" and the "new enthusiasm," claims McKillop).[78] Samuel Pratt prefers Fielding to Richardson, but believes Le Sage is better than Richardson, Fielding, Smollett and Rousseau put together.[79] Among the strangest of other comparisons to Richardson is the question Diderot eagerly asked anyone who had recently returned from England: "Avez-vous vu le poëte Richardson? Avez-vous vu le philosophe Hume?"[80]

After Richardson, critics most often compare Fielding (usually favorably) to Tobias Smollett. The comparison occurs much more often than the comparison between Richardson and Rousseau and can be seen as a second, shorter-lived rivalry for Fielding. Theirs is a battle in print, waged mostly by the authors themselves rather than by their partisan readers.[81] Smollett attacks Fielding, probably out of jealousy, in *Peregrine Pickle* (1751), "Habbakkuk Hilding" (1752), and Bonnell Thornton's newspaper *The Drury-Lane Journal*. Fielding responded occasionally in his own *Covent Garden Journal*, ending the feud on 28 January 1752 by sadly ending his own career as a novelist:

> I do not think my Child [*Amelia*] is entirely free from Faults. I know nothing human that is so; but surely she doth not deserve the Rancour with which she hath been treated by the Public. . . . [I] shall submit to a Compromise, which hath been always allowed in this Court in all Prosecutions for Dulness. I do, therefore, solemnly declare to you, Mr. Censor, that I will trouble the World no more with any Children of mine by the same Muse.[82]

("One can almost *see* Richardson drawing a long face and rubbing his hands," writes Blanchard.)[83]

Fielding is sporadically compared with Smollett after the "Paper War" of 1751–52, but Smollett was not as popular at the end of the century as Richardson still was. By the 1790s readers were looking back over the sum-total careers of all three: "Fielding was gaining; Richardson, losing; while Smollett was held in less esteem than either," writes Blanchard.[84] Or as Andrew Lang measures another kind of reception, "About 1780, the vendors of children's books issued abridgments of 'Tom Jones' and 'Pamela,' 'Clarissa' and 'Joseph Andrews,' adapted to the needs of infant minds. . . . but the booksellers do not seem to have produced 'Every Boy's Roderick Random,' or 'Perigrine Pickle for the Young.' "[85] An extended dispute on the issue in 1817 between George Crabbe and Thomas Campbell, with no clear winner, seemed to put the cap on it. More interesting for my purposes, however, is how critics who wanted to advance Smollett did so by comparing him with a united and canonical Richardson and Fielding: "*Roderick Random, Perigrine Pickle*, and *Humphrey Clinker* . . . undoubtedly . . . rival the productions of the moral, the pathetic, but tiresome Richardson, and the ingenious but diffuse Fielding, with all his knowledge of the human heart" writes Robert Anderson in 1794.[86]

Type-Two Readers: Oppositional Comparisons

Critics may not have paralleled Richardson and Fielding to other pairs of authors, but critics almost always used some kind of clearly defined opposition as their aesthetic criteria for comparison. Richardson and Fielding are usually read "against the grain" of one another in an attempt to recover the alterity which makes them historically and culturally relevant. Jauss writes that the "artistic character of a work" is in proportion to the "distance between expectation and experience, tradition and innovation."[87] One of the best ways to gauge a culture's horizon of experience, tradition, and innovation is to examine the network of oppositions that recur in its thinking.

The first and most formal of the oppositions, epistolary versus narrative, may at first seem too obvious to mention. For several eighteenth-century critics, however, the two modes carried very different and oppositional connotations. The dichotomy is virtually identical to that of tragedy versus comedy, as Cumberland writes in *The Observer*, 1785:

> [T]o subjects of this sort, perhaps, the epistolary mode of writing may be best adapted, at least it seems to give a more natural scope to pathetic descriptions; but there can be no doubt that fables replete with humorous situations, characteristic dialogue, and busy plot, are better suited to the mode which Fielding has pursued in his inimitable novel of 'The Foundling,' universally allowed the most perfect work of its sort in ours, or probably any other language.[88]

Barthe similarly finds the opposition between Richardson and Fielding to be one of tragedy versus comedy (among other things). As he writes in *The Gentleman's Magazine* 40 (October 1770) with uninvited annotation from the magazine's Richardsonian editors, Fielding is

> less sublime . . . than Richardson, but more chearful, more original [editor: 'This will scarce be allowed by the admirers of Richardson, nor does it seem true'], he engages us as much as the other makes us weep. . . . In short, Richardson is more grand . . . more simple, more instructive [editor: 'This too will not be allowed'], and his admirers being less idolatrous, he will have, perhaps, a still greater number of readers.

Related to Barthe's tragedy/comedy opposition is the internal/external opposition which readers find so often throughout the nineteenth and twentieth centuries:

> When I read *Clarissa*, I am of the family of the Harlowes. . . . By turns, I could embrace and fight with Lovelace. His pride, his gaiety, his drollery charm and amuse me: his genius confounds me, and makes me

smile; his wickedness astonishes and enrages me; but at the same time, I admire as much as I detest him; he is the Cromwell of women.

By contrast, Fielding, who "may justly be styled his rival," is praised for his variety of characterization and portrait of the external mannerisms of British life: he is "the Author who has best seized the manners of the people, though it is said that they generally form the nation."[89]

Barthe's observation about Fielding's "seizing the manners of the people" can be contrasted with another of Cumberland's statements about Richardson in *The Observer*: "As to the characters of Lovelace, of the heroine herself, and the heroine's parents, I take them all to be beings of another world."[90] This type of opposition, realism versus idealism (or the natural versus the artificial) is the dichotomy most frequently used by eighteenth-century critics.[91] The dichotomy was an important one for these readers, as high moral value was attached to both sides of the contradiction, and it was not yet clear exactly how the novel would be expected to respond. James Beattie writes in 1783, for example, that "Fielding might be vindicated in regard to all the censurable conduct of Tom Jones, provided he had been less particular in describing it."[92]

Dr. John Ogilvie makes a major statement on the Richardson/Fielding opposition in his *Philosophical and Critical Observations on the Nature, Characters, and Various Species of Composition* in 1774. Ogilvie associates idealistic characters with the intellect and realistic characters with the imagination:

> [*Clarissa*] is in no respect original. She appears adorned with an assemblage of virtues, and of intellectual endowments . . . in order to have the force of an *example*, these are raised considerably beyond the common level. . . . The *Adams* of Fielding on the contrary, strikes us wholly in the light of an original. . . . [H]is character is marked with *little strokes* which render it *truly comic*, and there is scarce a single instance in the whole work, in which the originality either ceaseth to appear when it ought to be conspicuous, or is carried beyond nature.

Ogilvie sees Fielding's realism providing a full "knowledge of mankind, which to some readers may in a great measure supply the loss of a limited acquaintance, and a defective education."[93] This is exactly the kind of praise Richardson expected for his own pragmatic novels which are rooted in the traditions of the conduct book.

Richardson's regular correspondents usually remain loyal, however, finding Richardson on the opposite side of Ogilvie's artificial/natural dichotomy. Thomas Edwards writes to the Reverend Lawry on 12 February 1752 that Fielding's technique suffers in comparison to Richardson's:

> [W]hat is really great seems to be above [Fielding's] powers. . . . a man will but weakly describe passions and affections which he himself cannot feel; there will be a certain stiffness, as we see in copying a picture, which will make it fall vastly short of that freedom and nature which shews itself in a good original.
>
> I think it scarce possible not to feel this difference between the Author I just now mentioned and my friend Mr. Richardson . . . the one we see every moment does *personam gerere*, he is an Actor, and not a Garrick neither, the other is the thing itself.[94]

Robert Bisset (the biographer of Burke), writing in *The Historical, Biographical, Literary, and Scientific Magazine: The History of Literature and Science, for the Year 1799*, believes the issue of idealism/realism is also one of probability, prefiguring twentieth-century arguments about the moral symbolism of Fielding's structure in *Tom Jones*. Both Richardson and Fielding are improbable, but Fielding handles it with better technique: "The lower kind of novel-writers, a very numerous herd, have betaken themselves to the imitation of Richardson much more than Fielding; but are totally deficient in that lively genius which renders extravagance and improbability agreeable."[95] Bisset also makes the insupportable claim, repeated throughout the nineteenth century, that Fielding based his characterizations on real-life observations:

> Squire Western, Partridge, and Tom Jones . . . were the result of accurate observation of actual existence: Sir Charles Grandison was a mere personification of all bodily and mental perfections. The materials for Fielding's novels were taken from a very extensive range of knowledge, which must have employed great attention to the human character. . . . Richardson's did not require so numerous materials, his chief characters might have been formed from a contemplation of the *Whole Duty of Man*.[96]

Other critics who use the idealism/realism dichotomy, all of them giving the balance of praise to Fielding's realism, include Reeve ("[Fielding] certainly painted human nature as *it is*, rather than as *it ought to be*"); an anonymous critic in *Olla Podrida* ("If we wish for delicate and refined sentiment, refer to Grandison and Clarissa; if we would see the world more perhaps as it is, than as it should be, we have Joseph Andrews and Tom Jones"); again in the very next issue ("The angelic qualities of a Grandison, or an Harlowe, are reflected but by the hearts of a few solitary individuals, whilst those of Jones find a never failing mirrour in the better half of mankind"); and Barthe (Fielding draws nature "as she really is").[97] Johann Gottfried von Herder is the only exception, prefiguring much nineteenth- and twentieth-century criticism by reading Richardson's idealism as social reform and Fielding's realism as an endorsement of the status quo.[98]

Type-Two Readers: Questions and Answers

If the dichotomies of epistolary versus narrative, tragedy versus comedy, and idealism versus realism are the answers of the critics, then what exactly are the questions from Richardson and Fielding? To consider the question precisely, it is best to think of these dichotomies as tools that place Richardson and Fielding into conceptual categories. Works in a new genre always challenge the horizon of expectation in some way, at least they do if they are going to spark any critical debate and become nominees for literary canonization. The relationship between reception and horizon is circular: one influences the other and creates a new point of departure for our next encounter with other texts. How new works meet or fall below our expectations has close connections with our evaluations of their aesthetic worth (ranging from "same old thing" to "innovative" to "unintelligible"). Richardson and Fielding's novels were experiments within their genre, and at the time they were written, their genre itself was an experiment. One of the central questions to which preconceived oppositional categories were the answer is, therefore, how did Richardson and Fielding conform to and rebel against the existing genres of their day.

The results of this generic pigeonholing, as with most everything else in the Richardson/Fielding reception history, are not neutral and impartial. Readers generally perceive Richardson's novels to be more amenable to the available literary categories. Fielding's formal experiments received much more negative commentary than Richardson's, but were it not for the established rivalry it is likely they would have received almost no commentary at all. "[I]n the new *genre* of prose fiction it was no doubt difficult for the formal world to accept as profound an author who depicted the homely scenes of common life and told truth laughingly," writes Blanchard of Fielding. "It was *Grandison*, not *Amelia*, that won the praise of the eminent; the *Journal* of Fielding's voyage was proffered with apology and received without applause."[99] Perhaps, but at least

Fielding's final works *were* received, where countless other domestic romances and travel narratives of the time are now forgotten.

The one text of Fielding's that is of a more familiar genre to the critics than the parallel text from Richardson is *Shamela*. "*Shamela* had offered no serious crux for the critics, who had not, in fact, made up their minds about the novel it was parodying," write Paulson and Lockwood.[100] *Joseph Andrews*, however, is an entirely different case. The preface to *Joseph Andrews* outlines a complex matrix of influences, tendencies, and inspirations which make up his bewildering and paradoxical "new species of writing." Fielding moves carefully through an established classical argument, comparing and contrasting his novel with the familiar genres it most resembles: dramatic comedy, romance, epic, and the picaresque.[101] The early reception of its experiment in genres makes the lack of documents on *Joseph Andrews* particularly unfortunate, but it is probably safe to read at least *some* significance into the silence. "It is true that one hears more of it after the publication of *Tom Jones*, when the two novels provided a theme for people who like to discuss comparative merits," writes Cross. "But there is nothing unusual in this, for it takes time for a novel to get into letters and memoirs outside an author's circle of friends."[102] Perhaps the more vocal side of the reading population did not quite understand the question to which the preface and the novel were the answer. Richardson assumed that the question was wholly *Pamela*, and the fact that Richardson himself began much of the (preserved) discussion on *Joseph Andrews* cements the rivalry into the very roots of *Joseph Andrews*' early reception.

James Beattie is the best of the early critics who records an effort to reconcile Richardson and Fielding's experiments, as a pair, with existing genres. In *Dissertations Moral and Critical* he considers different styles of what he calls the "new romance." In Aristotelian fashion he identifies two primary types of romance: the serious (Richardson and *Robinson Crusoe*) and the comic (Marivaux, *Gil Blas*, and Smollett). A sub-genre of the comic romance is the "Epick Comedy" which includes Fielding's novels: "*Epick*, because it is narrative; and *Comick*, because it is employed on the business of common life, and takes its persons from the middle and lower ranks of mankind." He finds *Clarissa* rambling and tedious in its minuteness of detail, but he appreciates the unified, "epic" qualities of *Tom Jones*:

Since the days of Homer, the world has not seen a more artful Epick fable. The characters and adventures are wonderfully diversified: yet

the circumstances are all so natural, and rise so easily from one another. . . . And when we get to the end, and look back on the whole
contrivance, we are amazed to find, that of so many incidents there
should be so few superfluous.[103]

Type-Two Readers: Samuel Johnson

Of all the critics to address the Richardson/Fielding opposition,
Samuel Johnson has emerged as the most memorable and influential. Johnson's modern canonization has made us see his slight and
informal comments on Richardson and Fielding, for better or for
worse, controlling the terms of the debate until at least Samuel
Coleridge. To isolate one contemporary example, the blurb on the
back of the Penguin edition of *Tom Jones* begins with these words:
"'I am shocked to hear you quote from so vicious a book,' said
Johnson of *Tom Jones*. . . . Few readers will nowadays subscribe to
such a view." (Jacket blurbs should not be dismissed—they are an
interesting and neglected part of the reader-response experience,
and they often play a subtle but major role in the preconceptions
and expectations that govern readers' initial receptions.) *Tom Jones*
sells more copies now in Penguin than in any other single edition.
If we can assume the blurb is most readers' first encounter with the
text of *Tom Jones* (after the unexceptional cover art), then readers
are still being conditioned, from the first moment, by the opinions
of Samuel Johnson. Even though the text does not mention Richardson's name, the comment is taken from a comparison of Richardson and Fielding. Johnson is, then and now, often a primary
channel through which the implications of the Richardson/Field-
ing opposition seep into popular opinion.

The full quotation was recorded by the person to whom it is addressed, Hannah More. More mentions she had read and enjoyed
Tom Jones, and Johnson responded with his famous words, followed by a "noble panegyric on his competitor Richardson; who, he
said, was as superior to him in talents as in virtue, and whom he
pronounced to be the greatest genius that had shed its lustre on
this path of literature."[104] More had not mentioned Richardson;
Johnson's thoughts of Fielding just naturally brought Richardson to
mind.

Johnson contributes to most of the century's standard dichotomies on Richardson and Fielding. "Sir, there is all the difference in
the world between characters of nature and characters of manners;
and *there* is the difference between the characters of Fielding and

those of Richardson," he says in 1768, recalling the distinctions of idealism versus realism and internal versus external. "Characters of manners are very entertaining; but they are to be understood, by a more superficial observer, than characters of nature, where a man must dive into the recesses of the human heart."[105] In 1772 Johnson replied similarly to a question from Boswell, again taking the opportunity to change the subject in order to elaborate on Richardson's merits.[106] Boswell asks if Johnson will admit that Fielding draws "natural" pictures of life:

> Why, Sir, it is of very low life. Richardson used to say, that had he not known who Fielding was, he should have believed he was an ostler. Sir, there is more knowledge of the heart in one letter of Richardson's, than in all "Tom Jones." I, indeed, never read "Joseph Andrews."[107]

The internal versus external opposition which Johnson uses so often leads him to invent one of the more persistent metaphors to dog Richardson and Fielding over the years. Johnson tells Boswell in 1768 "that there was as great a difference between [Richardson and Fielding] as between a man who knew how a watch was made, and a man who could tell the hour by looking on the dial-plate."[108] Johnson may have borrowed the metaphor from Richardson, who claims to be borrowing it from someone else.[109] In a letter to Sarah Fielding commending her *Familiar Letters*, Richardson writes:

> Well might a critical judge of writing say, as he did to me, that your late brother's knowledge of it was not (fine writer as he was) comparable to your's. His was but as the knowledge of the outside of a clock-work machine, while your's was that of all the finer springs and movements of the inside.[110]

It is interesting (and amusing) that opinion has differed over the years as to which author is the watch-maker and which is the watch-reader. Boswell seems to assume that Johnson places a positive connotation (as Richardson does) on the watch-maker for his insight and expertise. Boswell reverses the connotation, privileging the clarity of the dial over the hidden springs: "I cannot help being of opinion, that the neat watches of Fielding are as well constructed as the large clocks of Richardson, and that his dial-plates are brighter," he writes. "Fielding's characters, though they do not expand themselves so widely in dissertation, are as just pictures of human nature, and I will venture to say, have more striking features, and nicer touches of the pencil."[111] Fielding's biographer,

Wilbur Cross, reads Johnson's ambiguous metaphor the other way around, giving the credit to Fielding:

> It was, I suppose, Fielding who could explain the mechanism of a watch to a reader who had patience enough to listen; it was Richardson who constructed the clock on whose bright dial one might see at a glance where the hands stood. The one lost himself in unimportant details; the other gave broad and clear pictures of human nature.[112]

Watt allows Fielding to rise out of the dichotomy altogether: "Fielding is surely entitled to retort that there are many other machines in nature besides the individual consciousness . . . he was engaged in the exploration of a vaster and equally intricate mechanism, that of human society as a whole . . . ."[113]

Johnson was a devoted advocate of Richardson; nevertheless, he contradicts himself on several occassions which would suggest, unless one knew otherwise, that he preferred Fielding. "Fielding's opinions on literature are constantly and consistently reflected in Johnson," writes Robert Moore, expressing an opinion shared by many critics who see Richardson's rival as being more in tune with Johnson's expansive humanism, verbal flair, and philosophical conservatism. "Fielding's novels are in large measure splendid illustrations of many of Johnson's most deeply-felt principles, better illustrations by far than the novels of Richardson."[114] Johnson would seem to undermine his comments on the "unnatural" morality of *Tom Jones* in the *Works of the English Poets*, for example, under the entry on Addison:

> Whatever pleasure there may be in seeing crimes punished and virtue rewarded, yet, since wickedness often prospers in real life, the poet is certainly at liberty to give it prosperity on the stage. . . . The stage may sometimes gratify our wishes; but, if it be truly the *mirror of life*, it ought to show us sometimes what we are to expect.[115]

In the "Preface to Shakespeare," Johnson draws out the implications of this view of literary mimesis into a full aesthetic manifesto. As he writes in support of Shakespeare's rejection of the classical unities,

> Mankind was not then to be studied in the closet; he that would know the world was under the necessity of gleaning his own remarks, by mingling as he could in its baudiness and amusements. . . . [H]is descriptions have always some peculiarities, gathered by contemplating things as they really exist.[116]

Remarkably, there is at least one occasion where Johnson prefers Fielding's work to Richardson's in terms of moral characterization, if not necessarily editorial control. Johnson responds to Mrs. Thrale, who had praised Clarissa Harlowe as "perfection" in 1776: "On the contrary you may observe there is always something which she prefers to truth. Fielding's Amelia was the most pleasing of all the romances." The praise is short lived, however. Johnson continues, "[B]ut that vile broken nose never cured, ruined the sale of perhaps the only book, which being printed off betimes one morning, a new edition was called for before night."[117]

There are a number of theories as to why Johnson, usually quite an independent thinker, is so blindly supportive of Richardson and harshly critical of Fielding. One hypothesis is simply that Johnson and Richardson were good friends. There is textual evidence to support the circumstantial evidence: one of Richardson's few attempts at the periodic essay is in one of the few issues of the *Rambler* which Johnson did not write himself. Johnson introduced the essay on the "Modern Woman" as by "an author from whom the age has received greater favours, who has enlarged the knowledge of human nature, and taught the passions to move at the command of virtue."[118] Johnson's admiration for Richardson's works clearly translates into admiration for the man himself, as Johnson does Richardson the honor of preserving his fame in the *Dictionary* with more references than any other single author (except himself). Finally, and perhaps most importantly, Richardson once sent six guineas to bail Johnson out of a sponging house, for which Johnson sent Richardson a copy of Sir Thomas Browne's *Christian Morals*.[119]

Charles Vaughan proposes that Johnson's enmity against Fielding stems from Fielding's rejection of the laws of Aristotelian criticism.[120] As we have seen, however, Johnson's rejection of the Aristotelian dramatic unities is the cornerstone of his impassioned defense of Shakespeare. Johnson may oppose Fielding's Whig politics, but this is not wholly consistent with the wide compass of Johnson's acquaintance.

My own theory is that magnifying one's opinions about an author by contrasting him with a rival was certainly not an original or remarkable thing to do in the eighteenth century. Johnson's opinions of Fielding's novels might have been different had there been no Richardson. We will never know for sure, but then as now, to have something to say about one author is to have something to say about the other. Johnson's literary status has simply resulted in his opinions being put under closer academic scrutiny. Perhaps when trying to find consistency in Johnson's remarks, it is helpful to remember that Johnson never published a considered essay about Richardson or Fielding, and all we have is his off-the-cuff conversation reported second hand.[121] It may also be helpful to remember Johnson's own comment: "Nobody talks more laxly than I do."[122]

Type-Three Readers: the General Public

The *präreflexive ebene* is the largest body of readers at any time, but it is also likely to be the least vocal. Both writers and critics do exactly that—write and criticize—whereas general readers generally *read*. Therefore, we have relatively few surviving documents from general readers about the Richardson/Fielding opposition. Those documents we *do* have, however, demonstrate trends in reception that are often markedly different from the concerns of creative writers and professional critics.

A reception-based literary history is one based upon *chains* of reader-response, not necessarily an exhaustive list of *individual* responses. In this way, silenced readers make their presence known by influencing other readers who in turn influence other readers who in turn record their opinions based upon the cultural climate of the times. In this way, texts enter the horizon of expectation by pragmatically influencing the tastes and ideas of the general public; tastes which flow back into the criticism of future literary works. For example, every time a critic repeats the realism versus idealism cliché (e.g., "Fielding paints the world as it is, Richardson paints it as it ought to be"), it is informed by a popular consensus of not only *what* the real world is and *how* it ought to be changed, but also a consensus that Richardson and Fielding are going to be recognizable authorities on the matter. For further evidence of how eighteenth-century writers and critics spoke for silenced readers, simply notice how many of them write "we" rather than "I."

Richardson and Fielding were without question reaching unprecedented numbers of general readers. Estimates of sales figures in the eighteenth century are untrustworthy and do not provide an accurate gauge of the number of actual readers.[123] Contemporary estimates are unreliable as well, because publishers often exaggerated for advertising purposes. It is nevertheless safe to say that Richardson and Fielding's novels were unprecedented best-sellers and that the two men were in a position to change the general public's expectations of prose fiction more than anyone since Cervantes.

Type-Three Readers: Parallels to the Critics

The oppositions and dichotomies used by general readers are sometimes the same as those used by the professional critics, suggesting at least some overlap in their aesthetic criteria. Hester Thrale, for example, is a general reader in direct contact with a domineering critic: Samuel Johnson. " 'Tis general nature, not particular manners, that Richardson represents," writes Thrale in 1778, recalling Johnson's favorite internal/external nature dichotomy. "Honest Joseph, and Pamela's old father and mother, are translatable, not like Fielding's fat landladies, who all speak the Wiltshire dialect."[124] Thrale feels that although Fielding and Smollett "knew the Husk of Life perfectly well," yet "for the Kernel— you must go to either Richardson or Rousseau."[125] Similarly, Thomas Edwards, without having even read *Tom Jones*, is convinced that the novel would only be approved by those "who look more to the head than the heart."[126]

Other critical oppositions are used less often by general readers. The artificial versus natural dichotomy is in the letter from Edwards to the Reverend Lawry ("[Fielding] we see every moment does *personam gerere*, he is an Actor, and not a Garrick neither, the other is the thing itself"), quoted 12 February 1752. As for other parallels to the expectations of the critics, Anna Seward reveals her conception of how Richardson and Fielding fit into preestablished genres in a letter from 10 May 1787: she hates the "coarse unfeeling taste" of those who value Fielding over Richardson, believing that Fielding writes "romances" whereas Richardson writes "the highest efforts of genius in our language, next to Shakespeare's plays."[127]

Type-Three Readers: Morality, Manners, and Didacticism

The idealism/realism dichotomy holds a special significance for general readers who tend to see it slightly differently than most of the critics. Critics generally use the dichotomy to make strictly aesthetic evaluations, but for general readers (and, admittedly, for several creative writers and critics as well),[128] aesthetics and ethics are one and the same. So much so, in fact, that many readers throughout the eighteenth century believe morality is the reason novels exist in the first place. Protestant morality "is, no doubt, the indispensable duty of every writer to promote, as far as lies in his power," writes the author of *Critical Remarks on Sir Charles*

Grandison, Clarissa and Pamela.[129] When readers approach a text
with "no doubt" about the "indispensable" merits of such a rigid
critical approach, we can expect it to have serious effects on a reception of Richardson and Fielding, two authors for whom morality
and social duty are primary themes.

It is no surprise that eighteenth-century readers were obsessed
with morality—if there is a surprise, it is a wonder that they did not
write about it more often than they did. Literacy itself is seen as
one piece of a larger social obligation to virtue. Hunter writes that
piety and personal improvement are related throughout the century, with literacy rarely an end in itself. "[R]eaders believe they do
it for the sake of some higher good. No one argues that people
should learn to read just for the sheer joy of the skill or in order to
read works of entertainment or imagination," writes Hunter.
"[T]he sequence was from serious reasons—religious, economic, or
social—to personal pleasures that came as a bonus."[130] The novel,
with its roots in the romance and popular journalism of the day,
is often a suspicious genre of entertainment. Couple with this the
pragmatic motivations for writing and reading, and it is not at all
surprising that didacticism is such a powerful force in the reception
of the eighteenth-century novel.[131]

Authors who have demonstrated less than perfect Christian
moral behavior in their lives or in their novels were often singled
out and pilloried mercilessly. When Richardson and Fielding are
the subjects, it is usually Fielding who suffers. "[H]is political and
personal assailants were shrewd enough to take advantage of the
temper of the times and accuse him of the very 'lowness' he sought
to extirpate," writes Blanchard.[132] A mid-century critic lucky
enough to be named Joseph Addison has the following public admonition for Fielding in 1754:

> Wit, the most dangerous Weapon in the Hands of an ill-natur'd or ill
> Man . . . you possess, or have possessed in a Degree superior to all your
> Contemporaries. . . . [But] anything that has the Face of Morality
> [seems] to have fallen in your Way by Chance, rather than to have been
> an original Part of the Design . . . for the future, [direct your] Artillery
> against Vice.[133]

The general readers who come down hardest on Fielding for reasons of morality are the clergymen, no friends of the novel in general. Even as late as the end of the century they still align
themselves with Richardson and recommend his works with all the
holy authority of their office. God Himself, it would seem, is a Rich-

ardsonian. William Wilberforce, an Evangelical whose *Practical View of the Prevailing Religious System of Professed Christians* (1797) went through fifty editions in fifty years, made a special point in 1797 to exempt Richardson from his blanket condemnation of the fiction of the day, attacking instead the "vicious" doctrine of "goodness of heart."[134]

Morality is always a matter of perception, of course, although naturally it never seems that way to the absolutists of the time. The switching back and forth over the years about whether Richardson or Fielding is the most perverse reveals a great deal not only about literary history and changing aesthetic tastes, but also about changing interpretations of morality. Didacticism offers eighteenth-century readers not only traditional expectations of morality, Hunter claims, but also a psychological sense of order and an aesthetic sense of closure.[135] Wherever there is interpretation of any kind, it seems, aesthetics is never far behind.

The critical cliché most beloved by all types of Augustan readers is the Horatian dictum that art should "instruct as well as delight." Art and morality are each most effective when they are side-by-side.[136] Astreae and Minerva Hill, for example, write of *Tom Jones* in 1749 that

All the changefull windings of the Author's Fancy carry on a course of regular Design; and end in a extremely moving Close, where Lines that seem'd to wander and run different ways, meet, All, in an instructive Center. . . . Its *Events* reward Sincerity, and punish and expose Hypocrisy. . . .[137]

There has always been, and still is, a powerful relationship between moral standards and aesthetic taste, even if in the case of Richardson and Fielding they are not always as united as the Hills find them to be in *Tom Jones*. To sketch just one historical example with Richardson, by the end of the century he was still praised for his morality, but people seemed to be growing bored with him aesthetically. His position was secure in the canon, but he was not finding a steady general readership. In other words, moral criteria superceded aesthetic criteria during the transition to the nineteenth century (until Coleridge and others reunited them).

Readers were often sensitive to the distance between fine artistic touches and moral efficacy, but that distance was not always inversely proportional to their praise. In other words, readers sometimes gave an author substantial credit for either art or morality, but rarely both, suggesting that didacticism had not reached so far into the cultural consciousness that it became an all-consuming aesthetic criterion (as it would in the nineteenth century). Reeve simply puts it, "As I consider wit only as a secondary merit, I must beg leave to observe, that [Fielding's] writings are as much inferior to *Richardson*'s in morals and exemplary characters, as they are superior in wit and learning."[138] When an author was praised for his technique but criticized for his morality, however, the balance of critical priority usually fell to the morality. Canning writes of Tom Jones, worried about his moral effect on young readers,

> That it is a character drawn faithfully from Nature, by the hand of a master, most accurately delineated, and most exquisitely finished, is indeed indisputable. But is it not also a character, in whose shades the lines of right and wrong, of propriety and misconduct, are so intimately blended, and softened into each other, as to render it too difficult for the indiscriminating eye of childhood to distinguish between rectitude and error?

Canning uses this double-sided critical rhetoric in the opposite direction when discussing *Sir Charles Grandison*. Richardson's weakness, just as Fielding's, is cited as an excess of his strengths: "I cannot hesitate a moment to consider that 'faultless monster' *Sir Charles Grandison*, whose insipid uniformity of goodness it is so fasionable to decry, far the more preferable to be held up to a child, as an object of imitation."[139]

Elizabeth Carter, in a letter to Catherine Talbot dated 20 June 1749, comes to similar conclusions in her moral reading of Richardson and Fielding. The art of each author has a tendency to run counter to their morality, in opposite directions for each, and the result is an impartial and slightly confused critical evaluation:

> Fielding's book is the most natural representation of what passes in the world, and of the bizarreries which arise from the mixture of good and bad, which makes up the composition of most folks. Richardson has no doubt a very good hand at painting excellence, but there is a strange awkwardness and extravagance in his vicious characters. . . . he has drawn such a monster [Lovelace], as I hope never existed in mortal shape. . . .[140]

Carter is a remarkable figure in the eighteenth-century reception history of Richardson and Fielding, not because her opinions are necessarily unique, but because she is the kind of reader about whom other general readers seem almost pathologically concerned. She is a young woman, unmarried, living at home, and yet to make her formal debut into society. She is highly literate, enjoys reading novels, and is a lively, frank, and frequent correspondent with other young ladies. There is reason to believe there were hundreds more readers of Richardson and Fielding just like her. What she represents to most writers, critics, and general readers, however, is an impressionable young mind whose innocence must be preserved lest the entire moral fabric of Christian England become unravelled. "The fact that anxiety about 'evil' centers explicitly on young people implies not only the deep caring about the future that the moralists themselves allege," writes Hunter, "but also a deep distrust of the prevailing tendency of things to change, to threaten received values, and to destroy those who support received values."[141] The assumption underlying the concern is that young people have a tendency to actually imitate what they read. "But that a Child must admire the character, is certain; that he should wish to imitate what he admires, follows of course," writes Canning, "and that it is much more easy to imitate faults, than excellencies, is an observation too trite, I fear, not to be well founded."[142]

The quaint worries of eighteenth-century parents and moralists should not be smugly dismissed by modern readers. Social action, or "praxis" as Jauss calls it, is specifically invoked by both Richardson and Fielding, and they seem to invite it as a valid response to their literature. Richardson's novels come from the tradition of conduct books and model letters, and Fielding (writing during careers as a political journalist and judge) states in the dedication to *Tom Jones* that he attempts to "engage a stronger motive to human action in [Virtue's] favour, by convincing men, that their true interest directs them to a pursuit of her."[143] Eighteenth-century moralists assume that general readers must by necessity also be role-players, and so do Richardson and (perhaps to a lesser extent) Fielding.[144] As Jauss writes,

> The horizon of expectations of literature distinguishes itself before the horizon of expectations of historical lived praxis in that it not only preserves actual experiences, but also anticipates unrealized possibility, broadens the limited space of social behavior for new desires, claims, and goals, and thereby opens paths of future experience.[145]

When young men are the subject of concern, readers find Tom Jones a far more threatening character than Blifil (or, for that matter, even Lovelace). "Mixed" characters were as off-limits for minors as mixed drinks are today. "Young men of warm passions and not strict principles, are always desirous to shelter themselves under the sanction of mixed characters, wherein virtue is allowed to be predominant," writes Reeve. "In this light the character of *Tom Jones* is capable of doing much mischief."[146] Canning agrees it is the *combination* of Tom Jones's good qualities with his bad that make him an inappropriate model:

> The character of *Jones* can neither operate as an incitement to virtue, or a discouragement from vice. He is too faulty for the one, and too excellent for the other. . . . [T]he Character becomes the more dangerous, in proportion as it is the more amiable.[147]

The same thing is said of Lovelace from exactly the opposite perspective. Carter hints at having admiration for Lovelace's spirit when she speaks of his "strange extravagance."[148] Richardson must have listened to his readers, because one reason why he felt compelled to make such extensive revisions to *Clarissa* was to make Lovelace more unambiguously evil and less attractive to women.

General readers tend to see the minds of young women to be in much graver moral peril than those of young men. The reasons are not hard to understand, explains Cumberland in *The Observer*. Since the expansion of publishing and the establishment of lending libraries, "novels are now become the amusing study of every rank and description of people in England." We must therefore pay close attention to who has access to what novels, as young minds "are so apt to be tinctured by what they read," especially "daughters, who are brought up in a more confined and domestic manner than boys." Girls are more impressionable than boys because their upbringing gives them less individuality, and they are therefore "tempted to form themselves upon any characters, whether true or fictitious, which forcibly strike their imaginations."[149]

Keymer takes a somewhat more sophisticated view of the ways in which readers, especially women, allow Richardson's characters to "forcibly strike their imaginations." He argues in *Richardson's Clarissa and the Eighteenth-Century Reader* (1992) that Richardson's didacticism operates similarly to Fielding's insofar as each author's narrative technique invites active participation (Jauss would say "poeisis") in the moral dilemmas of the story. What many of Richardson's contemporaries see when they consider his didacticism is not a simple effort to preach moral platitudes, writes Keymer, but instead "a far more intelligent, extensive and dynamic endeavour."[150] Keymer's interpretation is perfectly valid, but I have not found it borne out by instances of comparative receptions. (A possible exception is the reaction of Diderot, cited on page 90.)

Many readers comment on the "to-the-moment" quality of Richardson's narrative, but no one comments on Fielding's first-person addresses to the reader (apart from dismissing them as "digressions" or "distractions"). What few immediate reader-response examples we have for Richardson's works take the form of a series of emotional outbursts rather than steady intellectual advances.

Instead, general readers seem to be much more concerned with the imitation of specific behaviors than abstract moral lessons, especially when the readers are assumed to be female. So much so that young women's imitations of characters are often seen as quite mindless and robotic, as in Cumberland's warning about the dangers of *Clarissa*:

> I suspect that it has given food to the idle passion for those eternal scribblings, which pass between one female friend and another, and tend to no good point of education. . . . Young people are all imitation, and when a girl assumes the pathos of Clarissa without experiencing the same afflictions, or being put to the same trials, the result will be a most insufferable affectation and pedantry.[151]

Clarissa is seen as a book to be admired, its characters as ones to imitate, and its author as one to be flattered, but there is little evidence that the book actually inspires any serious moral thought. This is one reason there are so many *reactions* to Richardson, but surprisingly little *criticism* from type-three readers. Readers often credit Fielding, on the other hand, with the dubious benefit of inspiring new thoughts: *Pamela, Clarissa*, and *Sir Charles Grandison* elicit affectation, but *Joseph Andrews, Tom Jones*, and *Amelia* wake the sleeping passions. Oliver Goldsmith writes an excellent statement in "The Citizen of the World" of the eighteenth-century moral horizon which did so much to help Richardson and hurt Fielding (to whom he is probably implicitly referring):

> [In] dangerous fictions . . . Assignations, and even villainy, are put in such strong lights, as may inspire even grown men with the strongest passion; how much more, therefore, ought the young of either sex to dread them, whose reason is so weak, and whose hearts are so susceptible of passion? . . . There are many passages that offend good morals, overthrow laudable customs, violate the laws, and destroy the duties most essential to society.[152]

Even more powerfully, the Reverend James Fordyce in a sermon in 1764 read his recommendation of "the beautiful productions" of

Richardson, and while not mentioning Fielding by name (Who else would be referred to following praise of Richardson?), warns that

> certain books, which we are assured (for we have not read them) are in their nature so shameful, in their tendency so pestiferous, and which contain such rank treason against the royalty of virtue, such horrible violation of all decorum, that she who can bear to peruse them must in her soul be a prostitute, let her reputation in life be what it will.[153]

This is a remarkable passage and one of the century's most extreme condemnations of "Fieldingesque" literature. Just the act of passively reading *Tom Jones*, or novels like it, makes young women prostitutes in their souls.

In conclusion, it is worthwhile to compare these alarmist predictions to the surviving receptions of Richardson and Fielding that actually come from young women. What they say is radically different from what many of the above readers would expect, or wish. These young women include Elizabeth Carter (introduced above); her correspondent Catherine Talbot; and the two daughters of Aaron Hill, Astraea and Minerva.

One of the first to record substantial praise for one of Fielding's novels is, ironically, a twenty-five-year-old woman. Despite identifying herself throughout her life as a Richardsonian, Elizabeth Carter recommends *Joseph Andrews* to her friend in 1743:

> It contains such a surprizing variety of nature, wit, morality, and good sense, as is scarcely to be met with in any one composition, and there is such a spirit of benevolence runs through the whole, as I think renders it peculiarly charming. The author has touched some particular instances of inhumanity which can only be hit in this kind of writing, and I do not remember to have seen observed any where else. . . .[154]

Carter demonstrates a hesitancy to criticize too harshly, avoiding translating praise for Fielding into a parallel rejection of Richardson. Talbot, too, was a devoted Richardsonian, so in her defense of Fielding she perhaps chooses to mention no names and quickly change the subject:

> It must surely be a marvellous wrongheadedness and perplexity of understanding that can make any one consider this complete satire as a very immoral thing, and of the most dangerous tendency, and yet I have not read any thing time immemorial, as I have been greatly engaged in the important affair of working a pair of ruffles and handkerchief.[155]

Carter is just as aggressive in support of *Tom Jones*. Four months after its publication, Carter defends it from attacks by Talbot in a letter (quoted above) which Blanchard calls "perhaps the most vigourous defense of *Tom Jones* made during this period by a critic of ability which has found its way into the annals of literature."[156] Her awareness of the powerful Richardson/Fielding opposition makes her defense even more courageous. Carter finds examples of good morality in *Tom Jones* and examples of bad artistry in Richardson— the opposite of what moralists in the century would have a young woman conclude. Yet, for all that, her moral outlook is both individualistic and wholly conservative.

Talbot, for her part, is much closer to the ideal Richardsonian that is the fantasy of many readers and the scorn of many others. Nevertheless, after carefully advertising her unambiguous allegiance, she has this observation on Fielding's novel in a letter to Carter dated 22 May 1749: "The more I read Tom Jones, the more I detest him, and admire Clarissa Harlowe—yet there are in it things that must touch and please every good heart, and probe to the quick many a bad one, and humour that it is impossible not to laugh at."[157]

The daughters of Aaron Hill, Astreae and Minerva, are the readers who had the misfortune of sending their kind thoughts of *Tom Jones* to Richardson himself. They had previously accompanied their father on a visit to Richardson in 1741 to compliment him on *Pamela*. Richardson remembered them years later and wrote to Hill asking for his daughters' reactions to *Tom Jones*, which Richardson himself had not read, assuming the jury was fixed. "[W]e went through the whole six volumes; and found much (masqu'd) merit, in 'em All: a double merit, both of Head, and *Heart*," they wrote on 27 July 1749, referring to themselves as "a Pair of forward Baggages" of "untittering disposition." They commend Fielding's intricate plotting, and conclude with an endorsement of his morality:

Its *Events* reward Sincerity, and punish and expose Hypocrisy; shew Pity and Benevolence in amiable Lights, and Avarice and Brutality in very despicable ones. In every Part it has Humanity for its Intention; in too many, it *seems* wantoner than It was meant to be: It has bold shocking Pictures; and (I fear) not unresembling ones, in high Life and in low.[158]

Richardson's bitter response, quoted on pages 43–44 above, "spoil'd 'em Both, for Critiks."

What is so surprising and unexpected about the reactions of the young women here is that they all recorded substantial praise for Fielding and relatively little for his rival, yet all of them ultimately went on record in support of Richardson. Perhaps they were intimidated by Richardson personally, as were the Hill sisters, or perhaps they were self-conscious of what was "proper" for young ladies to believe about the novels they had read. In any case, critics' concerns about didacticism in Richardson and Fielding, the stuff of standard literary histories, is significantly undermined by the reactions of actual readers, the stuff of reception-based literary histories.

Type-Three Readers:
Richardson, Fielding, and Popular Culture

Not until the late twentieth century with its multimillion dollar publishing promotions has there been anything in the history of literature to compare to the immediate reception of *Pamela*. "Reception seems too mild a word for the *Pamela* craze that swept through eighteenth-century Europe and inspired emulation in virtually every medium," writes James Turner. Turner points out that an avid *Pamela* fan could, on a typical day in the 1740s, buy any number of editions (large or small print, with or without engravings, with or without a sequel), read at least ten spin-offs (including *Shamela* and *Joseph Andrews*), visit the Pamela waxworks, see the twelve *Pamela* paintings in Joseph Highmore's studio, see Garrick in *Pamela, a Comedy*, and end the day in Vauxhall gardens in front of *Pamela* murals while cooling off with a *Pamela* fan.[159]

Walter Scott's novels were a sensation, but it is doubtful that they affected as wide a cross section of readers, shaping or changing their attitudes about prose fiction so profoundly. Fielding was surely not the first to notice that the fashion for *Pamela* was reaching the point of spontaneous absurdity. Mrs. Barbauld reports that fine ladies in public places held up their copies of *Pamela* to prove they were reading it.[160] Erasmus Reich, visiting England on a vacation from his native Germany, visited Richardson's home: he found the fruits in Richardson's garden to taste "of the golden age," kissed the inkwell in the arm of Richardson's writing chair, and brushed away tears as he departed.[161] In print, Joseph Warton compared the pathetic power of *Grandison* with that in *King Lear*, and Johnson, the one-man arbiter of the literary canon, declared Richardson to be "the greatest genius that had shed its lustre on this path of literature."[162] Perhaps the most famous and effusive praise of Richardson, however, comes from Diderot's eulogy in 1763: "O! Richardson, if you did not, during your life, earn all the praise that you deserved, how great will be your fame among our descendants when they see you at the distance that we see Homer. Who then will dare to erase a line from your sublime work?"[163]

There is an aspect of reception aesthetics that Jauss does not consider: a work can sometimes become too popular for its own good, and readers may begin to reject it for social, rather than "literary," reasons. Goethe at one point is "decidedly lukewarm" on Richardson because, writes McKillop, he had been "repelled in his Frankfurt and Leipzig days by the *Grandison*-fever of his associates."[164] Mathias follows a long consideration of Fielding in his *Pursuits of Literature* with the following brief but telling entry on Richardson: "Let us turn to Clarissa, the work of a man of virtue and genius, which is too celebrated for any additional praise."[165] Gwynn has a character exclaim, "Good God! . . . Who would have thought such an old-fashioned author had been your favourite! Why, one runs the hazard of having one's taste called in question by ever mentioning his Clarissa, or Sir Charles Grandison."[166] Finally, if Barthe is correct in 1770, Richardson's own out-of-control fame may ironically serve to prolong the fame of his rival: Fielding's "admirers being less idolatrous, he will have, perhaps, a still greater number of readers."[167]

The immediate popular reception of *Tom Jones* was significantly smaller than that of *Pamela*, but it seemed to be more volatile. Readers loved it or hated it, but no one apparently was indifferent. It is impossible to identify an "average" reception in the way we can for *Pamela*. The popularity of *Tom Jones* infuriated Fielding's enemies, and these were the same enemies who left us most of the famous written records of the novel's early reception. For every written negative reaction, however, there are sales figures in the thousands. An advertisement from Fielding's publisher in 1749 claims it was "impossible to get Sets bound fast enough to answer the Demand."[168] As early as 1751, even Fielding's enemies admit that *Tom Jones* is "in every Hand, from the beardless Youth, up to the hoary Hairs of Age."[169]

There are other signs that Fielding is finding his own way into the popular consciousness. Lady Bradshaigh, Richardson's "beloved incognita," lets it slip that in the first year of publication the "girls are certainly fond of Tom Jones . . . tho' I give you my word, I never let a faulty word or action pass me without a visible disapprobation."[170] One of the strangest occasions where Fielding causes a change in the critical horizon (via the preface to *Joseph Andrews*) is when Jane Porter writes in the preface to *Thaddeus of Warsaw* (1803) that the "pure morality" and "unity of design" in Richardson's novels qualify his works to be called "epic poems in prose."[171]

Yet there are signs that Fielding's popularity could have backfired against him just as Richardson's did, although, as Barthe writes, the effect is muted since Fielding's fans tended to be less "idolatrous." Lady Henrietta Luxborough writes in 1753, for example, "I remember I heard so much in *Tom Jones*'s praise that when I read him, I hated him."[172] Lady Bradshaigh, under the name of Mrs. Belfour, is bored by *Tom Jones* as early as 1749. Her reasons have nothing to do with the book itself, but she offers a powerful testimony of the extent to which Fielding had infiltated popular culture:

> As to Tom Jones, I am fatigued with the name, having lately fallen into the company of several young ladies, who had each a Tom Jones in some part of the world, for so they call their favourites; and ladies, you know, are always talking of their favorites. . . . A few days ago, in a circle of gentlemen and ladies, who had their Tom Jones's and their Sophias, a friend of mine told me he must shew me his Sophia, the sweetest creature in the world, and immediately produced a Dutch mastiff puppy.[173]

Non-Literary Influences on Reception

"The social function of literature manifests itself in its genuine possibility only where the literary experience of the reader enters into the horizon of expectations of his lived praxis," writes Jauss in his explanation of the central theses of reception theory.[174] As we have seen, however, "lived praxis" also circulates back into interpretations of literature. Lived praxis is not always as tidy a category as the term suggests, however. "Real life" factors that have little or nothing to do with literature *per se* often influence comparisons of Richardson and Fielding.

We have already seen several of these factors at work. Fielding is the more dangerous man to support because of his earlier political, theatrical and journalistic writings. Richardson personally intimidated many of his followers into positive criticism, causing many of the Blue Stockings to carefully preface anything that might seem like praise for Fielding and to hesitate before critiquing Richardson or his ideals too harshly.

Lady Mary Wortley Montagu and Sarah Fielding present an interesting twist on the subject of how nonliterary factors play a role in the Richardson/Fielding opposition. Both women have kind words for Richardson, but both are also relatives of Fielding. The quartet of tangled reception loyalties has affected, to some degree, the literary reputations of all involved.

Lady Montagu was Fielding's cousin and the source of many remarks, positive and negative, about Fielding's "aristocratic" family background. She was herself a woman of letters and apparently gave early encouragement and support to the fledgling Fielding. Montagu lived most of her adult life in Italy, however, and had left England permanently before Fielding published his first novel. It is doubtful she knew him very well, an unfortunate fact for both her (the many negative comments about Fielding's personality do not reflect well on her honesty or her family loyalty) and for Fielding's biographers (for whom she is, reluctantly, a primary source). Lady Mary never mentions Fielding's distinguished legal career, but she finds time to make several disparaging comments about Fielding's choice of an unaristocratic second wife. She did not care for Richardson, either, but has grudging praise for his novels. For example, Montagu is responsible for another strange moment in the history of the Richardson/Fielding opposition when two of Richardson's characters remind her of Fielding's ancestors:

> This Richardson is a strange fellow. I heartily despise him, and eagerly read him, nay, sob over his works in a most scandalous manner. The two first tomes of Clarissa touched me, as being very resembling to my maiden days; and I find in the pictures of Sir Thomas Grandison and his lady, what I have heard of my mother, and seen of my father.[175]

Sarah Fielding's position in relation to her friend Samuel and her brother Henry, and the up-and-down effect this has had on her canonicity, is a much more complex issue that cannot be dealt with fully here. Blanchard's patronizing comments may reveal much about her critical reception history in a short space:

> In spite of her generous early defense of her brother, was there a tinge of jealousy in her mind? We have already spoken of Richardson's praise, two years after Fielding's death, of the "finer springs and movements" which distinguish *not* the superficial Henry but the profound Sarah Fielding. Imagine the flutter of pride which she must have experienced to be thus praised by the man to whom she bowed down in worship![176]

Sarah Fielding has only recently emerged from the purgatory between her two rival literary patriarchs to be seen as a worthy novelist in her own right. In hindsight, Richardson ultimately did his friend the greatest service by contributing to the development of feminist literary criticism, which is largely responsible for her redis- covery.

Sarah's relationship with Richardson was not wholly literary. She was a member of Richardson's "inner circle" and was no doubt the go-between that allowed Richardson and Fielding to keep track of one another's work in progress and, possibly, to communicate mes- sages to one another. Her effect on Fielding's reputation has been much less significant than Fielding's effect upon hers, even though she makes polite allusions to several of Henry's characters in vari- ous prefaces to her works (mentioning Joseph Andrews alongside Sir Charles Grandison as ideal heroes in the preface to *The Lives of Cleopatra and Octavia*, for example). Sarah Fielding has affected Richardson's reputation more profoundly by simply being the sub- ject in one of Richardson's most tactless and embarrassing letters, written shortly after Henry Fielding's death:

> Had your bother, said I, been born in a stable, or been a runner at a sponging-house, we should have thought him a genius, and wished he had had the advantage of a liberal education, and of being admitted into good company; but it is beyond my conception, that a man of family, and who had some learning, and who really is a writer, should descend so excessively low, in all his pieces. Who can care for any of his people?[177]

The result of this letter, and ones like it, is a subject of chapter three.

Foreign Reception

I am not dealing with the German reception of Richardson and Fielding at length because it did not greatly influence their reputa- tions in England.[178] Richardson is the overwhelming favorite in eighteenth-century Germany for many of the same reasons he was popular in England: readers admired his sentimentality, morality, and didacticism. *Sir Charles Grandison* fared much better in Ger- many than in it did in England or France. Gotthold Lessing writes in a 1754 review that he dreads the thought of the novel coming to a close. Johann Gottsched calls *Grandison* the greatest novel ever written, and Christian Gellert says in 1755 that Richardson should be buried alongside Milton and the English kings.

Naturally there is also an isolated countermovement of those who prefer Fielding. Johann Musaeus, for example, satirized *Sir Charles Grandison*'s popularity in a Fieldingesque vein with *Grandison der Zwiete* (1760–62). By the 1770s, Richardson had lost ground in Germany partly because of his own idolatrous readers. McKillop writes, "Richardson was so strongly entrenched among the official critics as a conservative moralist that he held his ground on that side, but for this reason and others he did not command the unswerving allegiance of the younger generation."[179] There were others after the 1770s who felt constricted by sentimental didacticism and felt that Fielding offered a better model for the future of German literature. Germany needs humor to liberate the national spirit, they believed, and Germany lacks a native novel of manners. Friedreich Resewitz mocked German novelists as bookworms and aesthetes, "who would gladly turn from the task of writing a *Tom Jones* to the more congenial occupation of purveying 'sentiments'."[180] Also, Thomas Abbt argued against Richardsonian sentiment in favor of Fielding's doctrine of good heartedness.[181] By the 1780s and 1790s readers still respect Richardson as a canonical writer and several new editions of his novels appear, but he is seldom the subject of significant commentary.

The most pronounced audience for Richardson and Fielding in Germany is that of the creative writers. Reams of Richardsonian novels were produced throughout the century. "Richardson placed in the hands of weak aspirants for literary fame a precise and easy formula for the construction of a novel," writes Cross. "The plot—seduction or an abduction—ran on the simplest lines. The characters, with a little shading here and there into real life, were all villains or patterns of moral excellence. Consequently the number of Richardson's followers in Germany became endless."[182] Cross's estimate of the Fielding imitators is blunt: "[T]hey know little or nothing of life. The mere imitations of Fielding in Germany are beneath contempt; they are only tales of facetious adventure given the outward form of *Tom Jones* or *Joseph Andrews*."[183] There is at least one successful German novel in the Fieldingesque tradition, however: Goethe's *Wilhelm Meisters Lehrjahre*. Goethe fit Richardson and Fielding into the idealistic/realistic dichotomy, and *Wilhelm Meisters Lehrjahre* can be seen as a transition from Richardson's to Fielding's mode.[184]

In contrast to the energetic and imaginative responses of the type-one readers, German literary critics who discuss Richardson and Fielding as a pair find many of the same predictable dichotomies at work as their English peers did and do. J.W. von Archenholz (*England und Italien*, 1782) believes that *Tom Jones* is temporary while *Clarissa* is for the ages. C.F. von Blankenburg (*Versuch über den Roman*, 1774) advances *Tom Jones* over *Sir Charles Grandison* for the development of character. Johann Gottfried von Herder (*Über die Wirkung*, 1778) asks which is better, reflecting the world or trying to change it?; and Friedrich Schiller (*Kabale und Liebe ein bürgerliches Trauerspiel in füf Aufzugen*, 1784) states his preference for *Tom Jones* over *Sir Charles Grandison* for the way it engages the affections.

There are a number of lingering misconceptions about the reception of Richardson and Fielding in France.[185] Readers generally agreed with Margaret Calderwood when she writes in 1756 that "all Richardson's books are translated, and much admired abroad; but for Fielding's, the foreigners have no notion of them, and do not understand them, as the manners are so entirely English."[186] However, 1756 is early in the reception history of both novelists.

Tom Jones was translated into French, but the first translation (La Place, 1750) is terrible, omitting all of the introductory chapters, essays and narrative diversions. The omissions were not restored in other translations until the end of the century. The translation of *Amelia* by Mme. Riccoboni is likewise more of an adaptation. In contrast, it was commonly thought that Richardson's style improved, if anything, when translated into the elegance of French.

Fielding and Richardson were, at different times, both helped by their reputations of success in France, more so than by their reputations in Germany. Fielding did not live to see a good French translation of any of his works, but in 1796 a new and much better translation of *Tom Jones* was published by "le Citoyen Davaux" whose preface begins "BRAVO TOM JONES! . . . You know the amiable philosopher FIELDING, more gay, more sensible than RICHARDSON, and also the most profound."[187] Fielding also fit into certain aspects of the pre-existing French literary horizon. "Despite Fielding's Englishness, which was always commented on, his novel fitted into a French tradition, the *roman comique* or *satyrique* of Sorel, Scarron, Furetière, and Le Sage," write Paulson and Lockwood.[188] As a result, J.B. Defreval reports in 1750 that *Tom Jones* "has had a vast run here this good while."[189] Most influential, however, is the eulogy of Fielding by the codifier of neo-classical French taste, Jean-Francois de la Harpe, in 1786: *Tom Jones* is "the first novel of the world," the English have seen the faults of Richardson, their tastes are not as serious as the French, and "in general they all prefer Fielding."[190] La Harpe is still a bit premature to say Fielding had fully supplanted Richardson in England by 1786, but he was right to observe that this was the way the winds were starting to blow.

It remains true, however, that the literary horizon throughout most of eighteenth-century Europe was most conducive to a favorable reception of Richardson. Sentimentalism was the dominant trend, as it was in Germany, and the emotional psychology of Richardson's characters earned him the enthusiastic endorsement of Rousseau, Diderot, and many others. There was hardly any notice in France of Fielding's death in 1754, but fanatical panegyrics for Richardson poured in when Richardson died, most notably the famous eulogy by Diderot.[191]

The End of the Century: Expectations of Emerging Genres

Early reception of *Amelia* focuses on two main issues: Fielding loses sight of his true talent by writing in a sentimental mode, and he offends good taste with his realistic scenes of low life. In other words, readers criticized Fielding for attempting to solve the "problems" he was accused of having in the first place: his dangerous wit steers him away from true morality, and his superficial characters reflect badly on the gentry and aristocracy. Criticism of *Amelia*, from the eighteenth century to the present, is steeped in comparisons to Richardson. Fielding seems to be catching up with the horizon of expectations just in time for it to change around him. The reassessment of *Tom Jones* was just beginning, and the novel of sentiment was yet to become fully established. Richardson's *Sir Charles Grandison*, however, was the right novel at the right time to catch the first motions of a critical wave sweeping across Europe. The end of the century saw the evolution of new genres of fiction which sometimes helped and sometimes hurt Richardson and Fielding's reception but always put them back as a pair into active critical controversy.

Romanticism helps Richardson insofar as it places an emphasis on subjectivity and emotion, and it hurt him insofar as simplicity and directness became more important than didacticism and manners. People were admiring Richardson, but they were not reading him in large numbers. Literary philosophy often enters the popular horizon in the guise of fashion: the Richardsonian Anne Grant writes on 3 October 1778, "You can't think with what scorn I listen to little misses, and *very little* masters, who tell us in parrot phrase, 'Nobody reads Clarissa now. People *now* think it languid and tedious.' "[192] Richardson unfortunately did not live to hear his own eulogy. Diderot's exclamatory prose is remarkable for, among other things, its statement of Richardson's effectiveness as a Romantic writer:

> Oh, Richardson! in spite of ourselves we play a role in your works, we take part in the conversations, we approve, we blame, we marvel, we are angry and indignant. How often have I surprized myself, like a child taken to the theatre for the first time. . . . My mind was in perpetual excitement. How good I was! how just! how satisfied with myself![193]

Romanticism and the novel of sentiment together promoted Fielding by creating a taste for social realism during the 1770s and 1780s. The poetry of Crabbe, Wordsworth and others suggests there was a tolerance for scenes that readers quickly dismissed as "low" in Fielding's day. (Burney's portrayal of the Branghtons in *Evelina*, for example, received little of the scathing criticism which Fielding received for *Amelia*.) Bisset's "History of Literature and Science for the year 1799" offers this account of Fielding's characters, striking a distinct change of tone for Fielding's critics: "The materials for Fielding's novels were taken from a very extensive range of knowledge, which must have employed great attention to the human character, and exercised uncommon penetration and discernment."[194]

The primary comparative statement on Richardson and Fielding from a Romantic point of view comes from the Marquis de Sade in "Reflections on the Novel" (1800). Richardson and Fielding are the first two authors who come to mind when Sade considers the English novel. Both Richardson and Fielding are united, uncharacteristically, for their ability to portray the human heart. The sentimental novel, made possible in part by Richardson, is used as a point of contrast to the source itself. Sade appears more typically English than typically French, preferring the "robust and manly characters" of Richardson and Fielding to the usual "fastidious languours of love or the tedious conversations of the bedchamber." Sade's comments privilege the "masculine" over the "feminine," but he nevertheless credits both authors with teaching "the profound study of a man's heart—Nature's veritable labyrinth." Sade is at his most "sadistic" in this essay arguing that readers are most affected when characters are "subjected to the modifying influences of vice and the full impact of passion. . . . From these works we also learn that 'tis not always by making virtue triumph that a writer arouses interest."[195] Sade is unique in the Romanticism of his standard idealism/realism dichotomy. Richardson is allowed to share in Fielding's fame for realism, Fielding is allowed to share in Richardson's fame for emotional insight, and *both* are freed from the tyranny of didactic "virtue":

> 'Tis therefore Nature that must be seized when one labors in the field of fiction, 'tis the heart of man, the most remarkable of her works, and in no wise virtue, because virtue, however becoming, however necessary it may be, is yet but one of the many facets of this amazing heart.[196]

There is relatively little commentary on exactly how Richardson and Fielding do or do not compare to the Gothic novel, but Bisset for one is prepared to lay the responsibility for the entire negative, sloppy movement at Richardson's door: "The lower kind of novel-writers, a very numerous herd, have betaken themselves to the imitation of Richardson much more than Fielding; but are totally deficient in that lively genius which renders extravagance and improbability agreeable."[197] The *Monthly Review* of 1797 takes a similarly dim view of the new genre, but Richardson and Fielding are models for improvement rather than scapegoats for blame. In an unfavorable review of Ann Radcliffe's *The Italian*, an anonymous author writes:

> The most excellent, but at the same time the most difficult, species of novel-writing consists in an accurate and interesting representation of such manners and characters as society presents . . . they ought to be common characters, as to enable the reader to judge whether the copy be a free, faithful, and even improved sketch from Nature. Such is the Clarissa of Richardson, and such is the Tom Jones of Fielding.[198]

The author uses the familiar idealism/realism dichotomy which emerges again toward the end of the century. This may be because the Gothic novel, with its patent and unapologetic unrealism, brought the issue, and the Richardson/Fielding dichotomy which accompanies it, back into what people expect to find in the novel.

Conclusion

Richardson and Fielding entered the final years of the eighteenth century on more or less equal terms. The end of the eighteenth century finds readers interested in new genres of literature which seem to leave the older authors behind: Gothic and Romantic literature distracted critics from both Richardson and Fielding, and general readers expressed little interest in the best-sellers of their parents' generation. Still, sentimental literature keeps Richardson's name in circulation, and the distinguished critics James Beattie and John Ogilvie write enthusiastic praise of Fielding's novels in the 1770s.

In 1797, however, Fielding receives a crippling blow from an unnamed Richardsonian writing for the *Encyclopedia Britannica*. The contributer allots Fielding thirty-seven lines to Richardson's ninety-eight. Fielding's entry begins with a detailed account of his aristocratic lineage and privileges only to point out the severity of his decline: "[H]e married a young lady with 1500l. fortune, and inherited an estate of 200l. a-year from his mother: all which, though on the plan of retiring into the country, he contrived to dissipate in three years; and then applied himself to the study of the law for a maintenance." The contributor devotes only one sentence to Fielding's literary output: "He wrote a great number of fugitive pamphlets and periodical essays; but is chiefly distinguished by his Adventures of Joseph Andrews, and History of Tom Jones."[199]

The entry on Richardson, three times the length of Fielding's, claims Richardson "was bred to the business of a printer, which he exercised all his life with eminence." The contributor moves straight to commentary on Richardson's novels, which he says provide sensible readers with models of perfection. Richardson himself is "a man of fine parts, and a lover of virtue; which for aught we have ever heard to the contrary, he showed in his life and conversation as well as in his writings." The contributor then cites praise from Diderot, Warton, Johnson, and ends with Dr. Young's opinion: "I consider him . . . as a truly great natural genius; as great and supereminent in his way as Shakespeare and Milton were in theirs."[200] As Richardson and Fielding entered the nineteenth century, Richardson seemed unshakable.

Fielding would have to wait nearly a century for his vindication. Eighty-two years later the *Encyclopedia Britannica* had expanded Richardson's entry to an entire page—and allots Fielding five times as many.[201] What happens during those eighty-two years that makes this reversal possible is the subject of the next chapter.

3

The Nineteenth Century: Richardson's *Correspondence* to *The Saturday Review*, 1804–1893

Manners change from generation to generation, and with manners morals appear to change,—actually change with some, but appear to change with all but the abandoned.

—S.T. Coleridge, "Notes on *Tom Jones*"

"WHEN WE SEE FIELDING PARODYING PAMELA, AND RICHARDSON asserting, as he does in his letters, that the run of Tom Jones is over, and that it would be soon completely forgotten," writes Anna Barbauld in her preface to Richardson's *Correspondence* (1804), "we cannot but smile on seeing the two authors placed on the same shelf, and going quietly down to posterity together."[1] Richardson and Fielding are often smiled at in the nineteenth century and their place in posterity is confirmed by their readers, but "quietly" is not the first qualifier that comes to mind. The Richardson/Fielding opposition does not attract the same diversity of commentators that it did during the eighteenth century, but the debate advances during the century with a radically new intensity and tone.

These advancements reflect the differences between eighteenth- and nineteenth-century England. Victorians see themselves as having little in common with the Georgians. "There was little of the earnestness of life and quick invention and active benevolence which are the characteristics of our own age," writes William Forsyth in *The Novels and Novelists of the Eighteenth Century, in Illustration of the Manners and Moral of the Age* (1871). "The questions that have stirred the hearts of the present generation then slumbered in the womb of time. Reform, Free trade, Education, and Sanitary Laws, occupied no part of the thoughts of statesmen, and excited no interest in the people."[2] This chapter seeks to illustrate

93

not only how the nineteenth century continues to institutionalize the Richardson/Fielding opposition, but also how interpretations of the opposition often uncover the nineteenth century's interpretation of itself.

Richardson's *Correspondence*

Old arguments need new issues as a fire needs fuel. The nineteenth century might have come to see the Richardson/Fielding opposition as little more than a footnote in literary history but for the publication of *The Correspondence of Samuel Richardson* in 1804. The century begins with the opposition not only fully intact, but also renewed with fresh aggression. Most twentieth-century readers who are at all familiar with Richardson's novels are also familiar with his letters about Fielding: the Richardson/Fielding opposition is so much a part of our literary horizon that without even reading Richardson's correspondence we already know the kinds of topics and tone we will find there. It is sometimes difficult, therefore, to recover the alterity of how the *Correspondence* was received in 1804. Up to this point Richardson was seen as a kindly man with good intentions and a pure heart. As Frederic Blanchard puts it, "No doubt the virtues of Grandison had been as universally transferred to the author of that book as the faults of Tom Jones and Booth had been read into the character of Henry Fielding."[3]

Richardson's own image as a guru of good manners backfired. Richardson had spent great care cultivating a benevolent public persona, so readers were often shocked and disappointed to read Richardson's sharp and unforgiving comments on his rival. William Watson, for example, finds Richardson's opinions of Fielding "an instance of deplorable prejudice in a man, possessing the character of a highly cultivated and benevolent mind."[4] *The British Critic* notes that Richardson spoke "with an unbecoming contempt for Fielding, whose reputation as an author is at least equal to his own."[5] Decades later, *The Spectator* (6 October 1883), looking back to the *Correspondence*, writes of Richardson's bad judgment rather than his bad motives: "[Richardson] displays an irascibility of temper and an incapacity of discerning merit. . . . if we cannot expect Richardson to be pleased with *Joseph Andrews*, he ought, if not prompted by good-feeling, at least to have had the sagacity to write with justice of its author."[6] Even Richardson's supporters admitted his treatment of Fielding is at best "not graceful" and at worst "revolting."[7] Barbauld, the editor of the *Correspondence* and author of the long biographical preface, puts it delicately: "[Richardson] always speaks in his letters with a great deal of asperity of Tom Jones, more indeed than was quite graceful in a rival author."[8] Leslie Stephen, in his edition of *The Works of Samuel Richardson*, puts it bluntly: "It is painful to read this kind of stuff."[9] Robert Southey writes simply, "It is a most worthless book, more worthless than anything I ever saw."[10]

Other critics attempt to explain and excuse Richardson's treatment of Fielding. "Success evidently had nothing but a softening effect on him," writes Margaret Oliphant, using the references to Fielding to point out just how rarely the kind printer raised his temper. "The only bitterness in all the six, not over-lively, volumes of his correspondence is directed against Fielding, of whom he speaks with a certain acrid offence which is quite comprehensible, to say the least."[11] (Oliphant also points out the very dullness and simplicity of the man that emerges from the *Correspondence* makes his achievement in *Clarissa* all the more remarkable.) In the twentieth century Duncan Eaves and Ben Kimpel would write that they "believe that these remarks, one incident in his career, have been given too prominent a place in accounts of his character and that few men can bear to be judged by the worst incidents in their lives," but their comments only bear witness to the legacy of harsh character judgments which begin in 1804.[12]

The *Correspondence* had a mixed effect on Fielding's reputation. Richardson's decline does not necessarily guarantee Fielding's immediate rise. On the one hand, Richardson's comments elicited a degree of sympathy for the author who had been used so unfairly. On the other hand, the *Correspondence* put all of the rumors about Fielding back into circulation among readers who may not have been exposed to them otherwise. Barbauld's prefatory essay accentuated the latter effect, especially her often-repeated remark that Fielding's mind had received "a taint which spread itself in his works." Almost eighty years later the *Correspondence* and Barbauld's essay are still influential: Austin Dobson's biography of Fielding in 1883 attempts to clear Fielding's personal reputation by demonstrating that "the rancour of Richardson" has had "too much to do with the representation."[13]

Types of Readers

As I have stated in chapter two, the distance between implied readers and actual readers for Richardson's and Fielding's novels was relatively small during the eighteenth century. As their novels recede further into the past, however, the distance between implied and real readers naturally increases. Nineteenth-century critics are all too willing to point out the cultural differences that separate modern readers from (their perception of) the original audience. As the distance between assumed and actual audiences increases, different types of readers dominate the Richardson/Fielding debate at different times.

General readers tend to prioritize keeping up with the literature of the day over dipping deeply into the literature of the past. As a result, there is a significant shift in the Richardson/Fielding audience as the century progresses. In the first third of the century the novel achieves a new literary prestige as it enters a period of extraordinary popularity and energetic experimentation. Type-one readers, the creative writers, are the primary spokespersons on the Richardson/Fielding debate as they look back to evaluate the personalities, techniques and fame of their predecessors. In the middle third of the century the balance of the novelistic canon shifts with Walter Scott, and there is little commentary from any type of reader on Richardson or Fielding apart from biographical essays and brief comparisons with other authors. In the final third of the century, however, professional literary critics emerge as the dominant voice in the debate. Richardson and Fielding's novels were over one hundred years old at this point, and critics responded with an impressive variety of fresh interpretations of the novels to recover their relevance for an inquisitive and refined Victorian age. Because Richardson and Fielding's genre had aged along with their works, a long series of histories and critical surveys begin their as yet undiminished roll off the presses.

Type-One Readers: Creative Writers, Romantic and Victorian

Richardson and Fielding get more attention from their literary colleagues in the nineteenth century than from their colleagues in the eighteenth. While Johnson, Diderot, de Sade, Cumberland and Whitehead are the only major eighteenth-century writers to comment directly on the Richardson/Fielding opposition, the nineteenth-century contributors include Scott, William Makepeace Thackeray, Samuel Taylor Coleridge, Robert Louis Stevenson, George Eliot, and Thomas Hardy.[14]

Although creative writers offer a great deal of substantial commentary on Richardson and Fielding, there is little evidence that either of the rival novelists was "claimed" by the Romantics or the Victorians. Coleridge's evaluations, for example, do not hinge on any specific Romantic criteria, just as there is nothing particularly Victorian about Eliot's admiration of *Sir Charles Grandison*. Elizabeth Brophy finds this lack of period partisanship odd, at least in terms of Richardson's reception. As she writes in 1987, the Victorians could have easily appreciated "Richardson's not only moral but exemplary stance, which presents truly virtuous characters who . . . also exhibit a prudent grasp of the management of worldly concerns." The Romantics, on the other hand, could just as easily have promoted Richardson's theme of independence and self-worth in defiance of oppressive social structures, as well as promoting Richardson's "exploration of the 'divided heart' and his method of involving his reader in the struggles of the protagonist, fostering empathetic participation in psychological struggle."[15]

The Romantics may not have cared for Richardson because he did not fit their model of what an artist should be. Richardson was, after all, a respected middle-aged London printer rather than a conflicted, passionate, and visionary outcast. Lord Byron, for example, could not see Richardson's novels past Richardson the man. Byron, himself the consummate egoist, writes in his diary in 1821 mocking Richardson's vanity:

> I was out of spirits—read the papers—thought what *fame* was, on reading, in a case of murder, that 'Mr. Wych, grocer, at Tunbridge, sold some bacon, flour, cheese, and, it is believed, some plums, to some gipsy woman accused. He had on his counter (I quote faithfully) a *book*, the Life of *Pamela*, which he was *tearing* for *waste* paper, &c. &c. In the cheese was found, c., and a *leaf* of *Pamela wrapt round the bacon*.' What would Richardson, the vainest and luckiest of *living* authors (i.e. while alive)—he who, with Aaron Hill, used to prophesy and chuckle over the presumed fall of Fielding (the *prose* Homer of human nature) and of Pope (the most beautiful of poets)—what would he have said could he have traced his pages from their place on the French prince's toilets (see Boswell's Johnson) to the grocer's counter and the gipsy-murderess' bacon!!![16]

More thoughtful Romantic responses to Richardson and Fielding come from Coleridge and William Hazlitt.[17] When the primary criterion for each critic is the creative power of the imagination, they consistently privilege Richardson over Fielding. In his seventh lecture on Shakespeare and Milton, for example, Coleridge says of Fielding:

[I]n all his chief personages, Tom Jones for instance, where Fielding was not directed by observation, where he could not assist himself by the close copying of what he saw. . . . nothing can be more forced and unnatural: the language is without vivacity or spirit, the whole matter is incongruous, and totally destitute of psychological truth.[18]

Hazlitt agrees in "Standard Novels and Romances" that Fielding's characterization is strong, but Fielding lacks the imagination to follow it through when direct observation fails him. After repeating Samuel Johnson's dictum that Richardson knew more of the human heart than Fielding, Hazlitt writes, "Fielding . . . saw more of the practical results, and understood the principles as well; but he had not the same power of speculating upon their possible results, and combining them in certain ideal forms of passion and imagination." Richardson, on the contrary, "seemed to spin his materials entirely out of his own brain, as if there had been nothing existing in the world beyond the little room in which he sat writing. There is an artificial reality about his works. . . . They have the romantic air of a pure fiction." Unlike Coleridge, however, Hazlitt privileges Richardson for the best observation of character. "[A] very odd set of people they are," writes Hazlitt of the cast of *Sir Charles Grandison*, "but people whose real existence and personal identity you can no more dispute than your own senses, for you see and hear all that they do or say."[19]

Type-One Readers: Samuel Taylor Coleridge

Coleridge's role in the nineteenth-century Richardson/Fielding opposition is parallel to Samuel Johnson's and Ian Watt's roles in their respective centuries. Like Johnson, Coleridge spoke on Richardson and Fielding in strong partisan terms that were influential partially because they were so memorably expressed. Like Watt, Coleridge thought deeply about the issues and let his opinion evolve throughout his career by using the Richardson/Fielding dichotomy to illustrate other literary points. Most importantly, Coleridge parallels Johnson and Watt by using his literary authority to reinforce the oppositional connection of Richardson and Fielding's canonicity. Coleridge could not admire one author without simultaneously mentioning and devaluing the other, and by doing so, endorsed and renewed the debate for the next century. Up to the present day, the most frequently cited opinions on Richardson and Fielding seem to be from, respectively, Johnson and Coleridge.

We have a relatively complete record of the progression of Coleridge's opinions on Richardson and Fielding. His earliest mention of either author is the short poem "With Fielding's Amelia" (1792), praising the novel's characterization and sentiment. Fielding has ". . . here display'd / Each social duty and each social care; / With just yet vivid coloring portray'd / What every wife should be, what many are."[20] The next mention of Fielding is very different, however. Hazlitt discovers to his surprise in 1798 that Coleridge "liked Richardson, but not Fielding."[21] Coleridge was initially a somewhat reluctant Richardsonian. In a diary entry from 1805, after the publication of Richardson's *Correspondence*, Coleridge's tastes seem to run counter to his judgment: he is ambivalent about Richardson but settled about Fielding. The diary has the first traces of his later, more famous opinions on the two authors:

> I confess that it has cost, and still costs, my philosophy some exertion not to be vexed that I must admire, aye, greatly admire, Richardson. His mind is so very vile a mind, so oozy, hypocritical, praise-mad, canting, envious, concupiscent! . . . Richardson felt truly the defect of Fielding, or what was not his excellence, and made that his defect. . . . Fielding's talent was observation, not meditation. But Richardson was not philosopher enough to know the difference—say, rather, to understand and develop it.[22]

In later criticism Coleridge would build upon this dichotomy of meditation and observation. In his lectures on Shakespeare in 1813–14, he uses the Richardson/Fielding opposition to illustrate the comprehensiveness of Shakespeare. Richardson is still privileged, but again Coleridge seems suspicious about Richardson's psychological emphasis. Fielding has great excellence in "observations of living character," but "in drawing from his own heart, and depicting that species of character which no observation could teach, he failed in comparison with Richardson, who perpetually placed himself as it were in a day-dream. But Shakespeare excelled in both."[23]

Coleridge borrowed the dichotomy of meditation versus observation, but he eventually created his own metaphors of opposition. Throughout Coleridge's later criticism of Richardson and Fielding, Richardson is dark, hot, stuffy, and depraved; Fielding is bright, cool, breezy, and morally uplifting. The first appearance of the new opposition is in 1808: "The lower passions of our nature are kept through seven or eight volumes [of *Clarissa*], in a hot-bed of interest. Fielding's is far less pernicious; 'for the gusts of laughter drive away sensuality.' "[24]

Coleridge's note on *Tom Jones* follows a similar pattern. Coleridge's note may not be his most familiar statement on the Richardson/Fielding opposition, but it is possibly his most important. His preference is now firmly and unequivocally with Fielding (at Richardson's expense): "I do loathe the cant which can recommend Pamela and Clarissa Harlowe as strictly moral, though they poison the imagination of the young with continued doses of *tinct. lyttæ,* while Tom Jones is prohibited as loose," he writes. "There is a cheerful, sunshiny, breezy spirit that prevails everywhere, strongly contrasted with the close, hot, day-dreamy continuity of Richardson." Any honest young man who "consulted his heart and conscience only" without listening to what the "world would say" will inevitably rise from Fielding's novels "feeling himself a better man."[25] Blanchard writes of this note that "Coleridge ran counter to the still prevalent idea that it was Richardson and not Fielding who was the profound moralist. But the boldest stroke of all was his charge that the much-vaunted *Clarissa* was actually poisonous to the mind."[26] Coleridge's remark is the first strike in a particularly Victorian backlash against the eighteenth-century assumption that reading Richardson's novels is good for one's moral health.

Coleridge's comment on 5 July 1834 is now the most famous single statement from the nineteenth century on Richardson and Fielding and one of the most memorable statements in the history of the dichotomy. Like Johnson's comments, Coleridge's statement comes from secondhand casual conversation the speaker never intended for publication. "What a master of composition Fielding was! Upon my word, I think the Oedipus Tyrannus, the Alchemist, and Tom Jones the three most perfect plots ever planned," says Coleridge. "And how charming, how wholesome, Fielding always is! To take him up after Richardson, is like emerging from a sick room heated by stoves, into an open lawn, on a breezy day in May."[27]

Coleridge died three weeks after he made this statement, so he never saw any of the uncited allusions other critics would make to his words. It has become impossible to plagiarize Coleridge, since the phrase has become familiar enough to become the common property of Richardson and Fielding readers everywhere. To select just a few of the many examples, Thomas Shaw writes in 1849 that in reading Richardson "you seem to breathe the close and heated atmosphere of a city parlour; in the other you are tramping, a sturdy pedestrian, along an English high-road, inhaling a fresh, bracing, vigorous breeze."[28] In *The New Monthly Magazine* 13 (1 February 1820), T.N. Talfourd states that when "we read Fielding's novels after those of Richardson . . . [we] breathe the fresh air, and the common ways of this 'bright and breathing world.' "[29] As late as 1976, Russell Hunt marvels that Johnson rejected "the open, honest work of Henry Fielding and preferred to it the hothouse emotions created by Samuel Richardson."[30]

Other writers are perhaps more sensitive about being so obviously derivative. Individual parts of Coleridge's comment appear throughout the nineteenth century, as in an anonymous review of Stephen's edition of Richardson's *Works* in the 1883 *Spectator*: "For our part, we confess that we . . . feel stifled by dwelling in an unwholesome atmosphere."[31] Similarly, David Masson transforms Coleridge's metaphor for Richardson's novel into fact for Richardson's environment: Richardson is a "pompous little printer, cogitating his histories of virtue in his hot parlor at Parson's Green. . . ."[32] Fielding's portion of the metaphor is also used in isolation in passages postdating Coleridge's. "It would be as hard to criticise one of Fielding's novels as to criticise a fine day," writes a critic in the *North British Review* of 1885.[33] The anonymous critic in *Bentley's Miscellany* of 1856, however, is more wary, worrying that readers "may have too indiscriminately admired the healthy, bracing atmosphere in which Fielding breathes so *very* freely."[34]

Type-One Readers: Sir Walter Scott

Scott did more for the mass popularity and prestige of the novel than any author since Richardson. The only precedent for the *Waverley* craze is the early reception of *Pamela*. Scott brought new readers, new critical attention, and new commercial viability to his genre. His celebrity made him a natural choice in 1821 for a commission to write the introductory essays for a series of English novel reprints from Ballantyne Press, reprinted as *Lives of the Novelists*. As a result, Scott added the prestige and influence of his name to the Richardson/Fielding debate. Scott's opinions were particularly influential throughout the first half of the century while his novels were most popular. His quickly written essays on Richardson and Fielding were reprinted as standards in anthologies across England, France, Germany and America. His effect on each author was immense throughout the nineteenth century, but in ways Scott never foresaw nor intended. Like Coleridge, therefore, Scott may never have wished his casual opinions on Richardson and Fielding to be as influential and frequently cited as they came to be.

Scott is a major novelist, but he is a minor critic. One reason is that Scott praised everyone fairly indiscriminately, although this may be due to his conception of the "introductory essay" and its function for its publisher. In a review of *Ballantyne's Novelist's Library* in *Blackwood's*, April 1824, the writer expresses disdain for Richardson's prolixity and sentimentality and concludes that "Sir Walter Scott, we suspect, thinks much as we do about all these matters; although those who turn to his pages will find he has not ventured on much more than a *hint* of his real opinion."[35]

Scott generally preferred Jane Austen to Richardson, Richardson to Smollett, and Smollett to Fielding. Scott has strong praise for Richardson's detail, form, language, sentiment, and especially for his revolution in romance characterization:

> It will be Richardson's eternal praise, did he merit no more, that he tore from his personages those painted vizards, which concealed, under a clumsy and affected disguise, everything like the natural lineaments of the human countenance, and placed them before us barefaced, in all the actual changes of feature and complexion, and all the light and shade of human passion.[36]

It may come as a surprise, therefore, to find Blanchard claiming Richardson's reputation was "irreparably damaged" by Scott.[37] The reason is perhaps the clearest example of the distorting powers of the Richardson/Fielding dichotomy. Scott has more or less equal commendations for both Richardson and Fielding individually, but when he compares them side-by-side, Fielding always dominates. Because the Richardson/Fielding opposition is by now expected to infuse the horizon of criticism for either author, comparative statements on Richardson and Fielding tend to be more influential than individual accounts.

For example, Scott's approval of Richardson's gentle humor would have an entirely different tone if there had been no mention of Fielding. As it stands, however, Scott appears to damn Richardson with faint praise:

> His comedy is not overstrained, and never steps beyond the bounds of nature, and he never sacrifices truth and probability to brilliancy of effect. . . . [T]hough he is never, like his rival Fielding, irresistibly ludicrous, nor indeed, ever essays to be so, there is a fund of quaint drollery pervades his lighter sketches, which renders them very agreeable to the reader.[38]

Another example of the dichotomy's effect is the contrast of Scott's enthusiastic praise of Richardson's realistic characterization, quoted above, and Scott's criticism when Fielding is introduced. The difference of portraiture between Fielding and Richardson is analogous to "that which free, bold, and true sketches bear to paintings which have been very minutely laboured, and, amid their excellence, still exhibit some of the heaviness which almost always attends the highest degree of finishing."[39]

Scott helped Fielding's reputation the most by simply stating that Fielding is the "father of the English novel," a phrase actually borrowed from William Watson, but one which carried a particular emphasis coming from someone of Scott's literary prestige. It is fortunate for Fielding that Scott's biographical sketch was not quite as memorable. Scott did no original research and repeated the most negative and unsubstantiated rumors from Arthur Murphy's biographical sketch prefacing Fielding's *Works* of 1762, as well as the scandals reported by Watson, Montagu and Barbauld (the only biographical sources on Fielding available). Scott did deviate from received opinion, however, in his defense of *Tom Jones*'s morality. "The professed moral of a piece is usually what the reader is least interested in," begins Scott. Even so, the sins of Jones are those "which the world soon teaches to all who enter on the career of life . . . nor do we believe, that, in any one instance, the perusal of Fielding's Novel has added one libertine to the large list. . . ."[40]

Scott's comparisons of Richardson and Fielding implied a second comparison to his readers: Richardson and Fielding and Scott. The consensus during the period of *Waverley*'s popularity was that Scott was a greater artist than Richardson, Fielding, and virtually every other novelist. The *Blackwood's* reviewer claims that Scott himself has written as good or better novels than anything in the Ballantyne series he introduces. The single serious competitor is Fielding: "Grant that this nameless author has not produced any one novel so perfect in its shape, plot, and arrangement, as Tom Jones: grant this, and say what is it that any one of his predecessors has done which he has not equalled."[41] For the first time for an artist other than Richardson, comparisons with Fielding are read as an insult rather than as a compliment. Maria Edgeworth's reaction to the narrative technique in *Waverley* is indicative of readers' impatience with Fielding when a better contemporary novelist is available: "[W]e could not endure the occasional addresses from the author to the reader. They are like Fielding; but for that reason we cannot bear them, we cannot bear that an author of such high powers, of such original genius, should for a moment stoop to imitation."[42]

Scott's popularity had a mixed effect on the literary prestige of

Richardson and Fielding. On the positive side, Scott called serious critical attention to the history of the English novel. On the negative side, however, Scott's genre of historical romance became so popular that it correspondingly lowered the literary prestige of the epistolary and comic romance. R.S. Mackenzie, for example, writes in 1871 that Fielding "may rank as one of the inventors of the English novel, though not of its higher class,—the historical."[43] Of the two forms in which Richardson and Fielding wrote, however, critics considered Fielding's form to be the closest to Scott's spirit. Richardson's unflinching realism was seen as unimaginative and his epistolary form as vulgar. After the success of *Waverley*, Scott's humor, clever plotting, and firm narrative control established the popular novel as the progeny of Fielding, the "father of the English novel."

Type-One Readers: William Makepeace Thackeray

Thackeray is the primary Victorian spokesperson on the Richardson/Fielding opposition. His opinions on Fielding were particularly influential. Thackeray's lecture on Fielding (1851) was widely regarded as the definitive statement on the novelist between Coleridge and Dobson (1883). As with Scott, however, Thackeray has been a mixed blessing for Fielding and a curse for Richardson.

Just as the secondary critical rivalry between Smollett and Fielding invites another reception study for the eighteenth century, the rivalry between Thackeray and Fielding (and for that matter, Thackeray and Swift) invites another for the nineteenth. Their opposition provides a rich source of insight into the evolution of nineteenth-century tastes and even the mysteries of authorial psychology. Thackeray's career-long, hot-and-cold relationship with Fielding suggests he is working through his own "anxiety of influence," alternately supporting Fielding to legitimate the comic romance and rejecting him to affirm his contemporary superiority. Thackeray views Fielding not only as a father figure to be respected, but also as a child to be patronized. Thackeray's widely advertised public lecture on Fielding was part of a larger attempt to use Fielding's name to increase the fame of *both* novelists; Thackeray's expertise being earned at the expense of Fielding's notoriety.

Thackeray's 1851 lecture on Fielding, an expansion of what was to be published as an essay in *The English Humourists of the Eighteenth Century* (1853), did great help and harm to Fielding. The lecture includes not only heartfelt eulogies about the man and his spirit, but also damaging artistic criticism and disrespectful speculation passed off as biography. "I cannot offer or hope to make a hero of Harry Fielding. Why hide his faults? Why conceal his weaknesses in a cloud or periphrasis?" Thackeray writes.[44] Thackeray read all of the worst elements of Jones and Booth into Fielding's own personality: "He is himself the hero of his books: he is wild Tom Jones, he is wild Captain Booth."[45] Other relationships between biography and criticism are entirely fabricated. For example, Thackeray assumes Fielding probably smoked and drank, so for no other reason he writes that "when Mr. Jones enters Sophia's drawing room, the pure air there is rather tainted with the young gentleman's tobacco-pipe and punch."[46] Wilbur Cross says of this and other passages, "By his little fabrications and subtle interplay between Tom Jones, his author, and himself, Thackeray readily did more than any other man has ever done to stain the memory of Fielding."[47] There have certainly been highly creative biographical readings of *Tom Jones* in the past, but Thackeray's statements were cited as authoritative in Frederick Lawrence's *Life of Fielding* (1855) and circulated extensively from there. As Thackeray himself writes, "[E]very author must lay his account not only to misrepresentation, but to honest enmity among critics, and to being hated and abused for good as well as for bad reasons."[48]

As Richardson is not an English Humorist, he receives no extensive treatment in Thackeray's formal criticism. Thackeray introduces Richardson only to promote the masculine superiority of Fielding. Thackeray's evaluation of Richardson's novels is also informed with a highly speculative approach to biography. His criticism here recalls the harsh, satiric tone found in parts of his novels, and his remarks on Richardson are blunt, childish, and cruel:

[Fielding] could not do otherwise than laugh at the puny, cockney bookseller, pouring out endless volumes of sentimental twaddle, and hold him up to scorn as a moll-coddle and a milksop. *His* genius had been nursed on sack-posset, and not on dishes of tea. . . . 'Milksop!' roars Harry Fielding, clattering at the timid shop-shutters. 'Wretch! Monster! Mohock!' shrieks the sentimental author of 'Pamela;' and all the ladies of his court cackle out an affrighted chorus. . . . [Richardson's] squeamish [stomach] sickened at the rough fare and the rough guests assembled at Fielding's jolly revel. Indeed the cloth might have been cleaner: and the dinner and the company were scarce such as suited a dandy.[49]

Type-One Readers: The Minor Commentators

Maria Edgeworth, like Austen, is a "domestic satirist" whose probable influence from Richardson and Fielding makes it disappointing that she leaves only a few scattered references to her predecessors. Edgeworth's only comparison of Richardson and Fielding is delightful, however, and would have thrilled the eighteenth-century advocates of Richardson's redemptive morality. In Edgeworth's *Ormond* (1817), Harry Ormond is an easily-influenced young man who is corrupted from a reading of *Tom Jones*, a novel which "seized" his attention. He comes across a copy of *Sir Charles Grandison* and is slow to commit himself: "He hated moralizing and reflections; and there was here an abundance both of reflections and morality. . . . [A]t first he detested Sir Charles Grandison—he was so different from the . . . heroes he had admired in books." Eventually, however, the act of reading Grandison works the magic dreamed of by the most idealistic of moralists worried about Fielding's effect upon impressionable youth:

> The character of Sir Charles Grandison, in spite of his ceremonious bowing on the hand, touched the nobler feelings of our young hero's mind, inspired him with virtuous emulation, made him ambitious to be a *gentleman* in the best and highest sense of the word. In short, it completely counteracted in his mind the effect of Tom Jones—all the generous feelings which were so congenial to his own nature, and which he had seen combined in Tom Jones . . . he now saw united with high moral and religious principles, in the character of a man of virtue, as well as a man of honour. . . . Ormond has often declared, that Sir Charles Grandison did him more good, than any fiction he ever read in his life.[50]

There is no evidence that Edgeworth contributed to any significant upswing or downswing in the reputation of either Richardson or Fielding. Her view of Richardson's wholesome morality probably would have seemed quaint and slightly antiquated to her 1817 audience. It is perhaps enough, however, that we record *Sir Charles Grandison*'s perfect moment of unqualified triumph in his ongoing duel with *Tom Jones*.

George Eliot (along with George Meredith) helped make realism fashionable again in the 1870s, marking a significant change in the literary horizon after the more fantastic novels of Scott, Thackeray, and Charles Dickens. The shift was potentially amenable to both Richardson and Fielding, but with the full weight of Eliot's considerable reputation behind an endorsement, Fielding perhaps benefited most. Eliot's influence as a serious, thoughtful writer contributed to Fielding's reputation as a major figure in the history of the novel just as the cottage industry of literary histories was beginning. Ironically, Eliot was a Richardsonian. Eliot's private letters forcefully support Richardson, whereas her only brief comment on Fielding reached, and still reaches, a vastly wider audience as a narrative aside in *Middlemarch* (1771–72).

"I had no idea that Richardson was worth so much," writes Eliot to Sara Hennell on 12 October 1847. "The morality is perfect—there is nothing for the new lights to correct."[51] Although she felt Harriet Byron to be "too proper and insipid," she writes to Bessie Parkes on 30 October 1852, "Like Sir Charles Grandison? I should be sorry to be the heathen that did not like that book."[52] *Sir Charles Grandison* is clearly Eliot's favorite of Richardson's novels, and she writes to Mrs. Charles Bray on 21 December 1876 that she is "sorry that the long novel was not longer. . . . We have fallen on an evil generation who would not read 'Clarissa' even in abridged form."[53]

Eliot notably does not praise Richardson's morality by criticizing Fielding's. She also does not praise Fielding's narrative style by criticizing Richardson's epistolary form. Instead, in *Middlemarch*, her original image of Fielding the man and Fielding the narrator is one of the happier nineteenth-century fusions of nostalgia, biography, and literary criticism:

> [Fielding] had the great happiness to be dead a hundred and twenty years ago, and so to take his place among the colossi whose huge legs our living pettiness is observed to walk under, glories in his copious remarks and digressions as the least imitable part of his work, and especially in those initial chapters to the successive books of his history, where he seems to bring his arm-chair to the proscenium and chat with us in all the lusty ease of his fine English. But Fielding lived when the days were longer . . . when summer afternoons were spacious, and the clock ticked slowly in the winter evenings.[54]

Robert Louis Stevenson, the author of *Kidnapped* and *Treasure Island*, did not care for *Robinson Crusoe*. "[N]othing can more strongly illustrate the necessity for marking incident than to compare the living fame of *Robinson Crusoe* with the discredit of *Clarissa Harlowe*," Stevenson writes in 1882. "And yet a little story of a shipwrecked sailor, with not a tenth part of the style nor a thousandth part of the wisdom, exploring none of the arcana of humanity . . . goes on from edition to edition, ever young, while *Clarissa* lies upon the shelves unread."[55] Stevenson's comments on Richardson and Fielding are one of the great curiosities of nineteenth-century criticism.[56] While the tide was definitely turning in Fielding's favor during the 1880s, Stevenson begged his friends to assist him in locating out-of-print copies of Richardson's novels. He writes to a friend in December 1877 to "search in all Melbourne for one of the rarest and certainly one of the best books—*Clarissa Harlowe*."[57]

Moreover, Stevenson used the inherited tools of the Richardson/Fielding opposition to launch an attack on Fielding in the *Scribner's Magazine* for June 1888. Stevenson's article is unique, however, for its reversal of many of the opposition's critical commonplaces. In "Some Gentlemen in Fiction" he begins by outlining the conventional social distinctions between the two novelists and links their backgrounds with their underlying temperaments:

> [O]ne descended from a great house, easy, generous, witty, debauched, a favourite in the tap-room and the hunting field, yet withal a man of a high practical intelligence, a distinguished public servant, an ornament of the bench: the other, sprung from I know not whence—but not from kings—buzzed about by second-rate women, and their fit companion, a tea-bibber in parlours, a man of painful propriety, with all the narrowness and much of the animosity of the backshop and the dissenting chapel. Take the pair, they seem like types: Fielding, with all his faults, was undeniably a gentleman; Richardson, with all his genius and his virtues, as undeniably was not.[58]

Stevenson's unique stroke, however, is to oddly foreshadow much twentieth-century political criticism by giving more attention to the social positions of the characters than to the morality they exhibit. He can admire Richardson's villains, therefore, more than Fielding's heroes: "Lovelace—in spite of his abominable misbehaviour—Colonel Morden and my Lord M—are all gentlemen of undisputed quality. They more than pass muster, they excel," writes Stevenson. "The best of Fielding's gentlemen had scarce been at their ease in M——Hall; Dr. Harrison had seemed a plain, honest man, a trifle below his company. . . ."[59]

Thomas Hardy makes a subtle aesthetic argument in "The Profitable Reading of Fiction" (1888) that "a story should be an organism." He claims, surprisingly, "the art of novel-writing is as yet in its tentative stage only," but echoes Coleridge by naming *Tom Jones* as one of those novels which approaches formal perfection. "Speaking for myself, I do not perceive its great superiority in artistic form over some other novels of lower reputation," Hardy writes, citing *The Bride of Lammermoor* and *Vanity Fair*.[60] Richardson's "claim to be placed on a level with Fielding" is not found in the portrayal of female characters, the psychological detail, or the casuistic study of moral dilemmas, all of which we might expect from Hardy's criticism. To the contrary, Clarissa and her companions are "cold, even artificial" compared to "the figures animated by Fielding." Richardson's equality with Fielding lies instead with the "artist spirit that he everywhere displays in the structural parts of his work and in the interaction of the personages." Hardy does not define the "artist spirit," but writes that it is a quality which "so few non-professional readers enjoy and appreciate without some kind of preliminary direction. It is usually the latest to be discerned by the novel consumer, and it is often never discerned by him or her at all."[61]

Type-Two Readers: Critics and the Critical Perspective

The line between type-one and type-two readers is sometimes hazy in the nineteenth century. Not only are there a number of poets who double as essayists, such as Coleridge and Charles Lamb, but there are also essayists who approach their genre as an art, such as Hazlitt and Leigh Hunt. Literary criticism flourished throughout the nineteenth century, although the range of people calling themselves "critics" is more narrow than it was during the previous century. Criticism increasingly becomes a matter of profession rather than inspiration, and it becomes almost exclusively the profession of university-educated males.

The trivializing tone of most nineteenth-century criticism on Richardson and Fielding may have something to do with the fact that educated males wrote it, or it may be a part of a larger literary horizon which encouraged an aristocratic, detached, and sharply-etched perspective. (Oscar Wilde did not contribute to the Richardson/Fielding debate, but after surveying the comments of those who did, it is not difficult to imagine the content and style of what he would have said.) There is evidence that the Richardson/Fielding opposition had become a kind of amusement for the critics, a contest of wit between urbane men of letters. As Brophy writes of the nineteenth century, "A kind of parlor game can be played, surveying the novels of the nineteenth century and declaring them 'Richardsonian' or 'Fieldingesque.' "[62] Hazlitt provides a contemporary example in his description of the parties at Lamb's home on Thursday evenings in 1810. The group of literati had "many lively skirmishes" on "the old everlasting set," including Richardson and Fielding:

> What a keen, laughing, hair-brained vein of home-felt truth! What choice venom! How often did we cut into the haunch of letters, while we discussed the haunch of mutton on the table! How we skimmed the cream of criticism! How we got into the heart of controversy! How we picked out the marrow of authors![63]

The problem is not that critics *enjoy* what they do to Richardson and Fielding, but that their game of "picking the marrow out of authors" often passes for the history of the English novel.[64]

The Richardson/Fielding opposition and the issues it represents are not always trivial interests for the critics. To the contrary, the sometimes violent language they use to denounce one author vividly reveals the ferocity of their commitment to the rival. Richardson and Fielding had been dead for generations by the time these critics came to write. They were writing after the polished rhetoric of the Augustan age and before the objective historical research of the modern age; apparently they felt their personal attacks and name-calling would do no harm.

Byron's glee at a gipsy-murderess's bacon being wrapped in pages of *Pamela* is recorded above (pp. 97), in addition to Thackeray's description of Richardson as a "mollcoddle and a milksop" (pg. 105). Other examples of personal attacks are found throughout this chapter from all types of readers, although it is the critics who make them most unapologetically and vindictively. Among the most egregious are Christopher North's description of Richardson as "a sort of idiot, who had a strange insight into some parts of human nature, and a tolerable acquaintance with most parts of speech"; John Ruskin's image of Fielding and Smollett licking their chops like dogs; Stephen's reference to Richardson's "second-rate eighteenth-century priggishness and his twopenny-tract morality"; Masson's portrait of "the nervous, tea-drinking, pompous little printer, coddled as he was by a bevy of admiring women, who nursed his vanity"; and the usually relatively objective Dobson, who alludes to Richardson as "a middle-aged London printer, a vegetarian and water-drinker, a worthy, domesticated, fussy, and highly-nervous little man."[65]

Type-Two Readers: The Art of Form, the Form of Art, and the Nineteenth-Century Critical Imagination

As in the eighteenth century, the obvious differences in Richardson's epistolary and Fielding's omniscient narrative forms are frequent points of contrast for nineteenth-century critics. The author who set the standard for literary form in the early nineteenth-century was neither Richardson nor Fielding nor Scott, but Jane Austen. Her novels established the horizon of expectation for what many critics saw as the formal perfection possible in a novel. The critical opinion that the novel could be considered a genre of high art arguably began with Austen and was confirmed with Scott, Dickens, and especially Eliot. The reevaluation of the eighteenth-century novel therefore tended to see the epistolary mode as distastefully intimate and loosely structured, while Fielding's all-controlling narrative voice was seen as sophisticated and carefully disciplined. Critics throughout the century affirm Coleridge's remark that *Tom Jones* has one of the three most perfect plots. "However opinions may differ as to the other merits of 'Tom Jones,' they are unanimous as to its harmony of design and masterliness of structure," writes James Russell Lowell.[66]

There is not a single critic in the nineteenth century who prefers the epistolary when comparing Richardson's form to Fielding's. An anonymous reviewer in the *Spectator* (October 1883) bluntly declares that the "interminable letters" of Richardson's narrative style form "the worst method a novelist could select."[67] The *Quarterly Review* of July 1886 agrees, emphasizing the carelessness of Richardson's structure to claim new relevance for Fielding's:

> Letters enable each actor to describe his own feelings for himself: but a story told in this form inevitably becomes tedious, disjointed, and crowded with superfluous matter. Both in form and style the novels of Fielding and Smollett approximate to the modern type more closely than those of Defoe and Richardson.[68]

In the 1830s more attention was being paid to Fielding's essays. This contributed to his growing reputation as a prose stylist as well as a narrative craftsman. Even John Stuart Mill, a writer who has virtually nothing in common with Fielding stylistically, improved his writing by studying Fielding.[69] In the middle of the century criticism of Fielding turns to other issues, but by the 1880s there is a renewed appreciation for Fielding's style from George Saintsbury, Andrew Lang, Edmund Gosse and others. The forum for this new appreciation is often the literary anthologies which began to appear around the turn of the century, featuring brief critical introductions and representative selections of prose styles not unlike the "readers" designed for introductory literature classes today. Henry Craik's *English Prose Selections* (1893) is typical in its format and in its privileging of Fielding's technique. John Hepburn Millar writes in his introduction to Richardson's excerpt, "We are not, indeed, to look to Richardson for that nameless quality of style which is the property of a scholar and a gentleman such as Fielding was; for Richardson belonged to neither category."[70]

Perhaps appreciations of artistic form and style contribute to a curious and isolated phenomenon in nineteenth-century criticism of Richardson and Fielding: the frequency of painting and sketchwork metaphors for literary technique. The use of the art metaphor throughout the nineteenth century, far outstripping the use of any other single critical focus, suggests there must be something in the cultural climate encouraging it. The cause may be the emphasis on the style rather than content of novels, the historical distance of the novels requiring a more active visual imagination, the participation of working artists in the critical conversation, or the crosspollination from the debate between naturalism and impressionism. Of course it could also be an enormous coincidence. Whatever the reason, the art metaphor provides a useful common thread uniting a diversity of opinions about the Richardson/Fielding opposition.

I am not aware of any practicing artists who publish a comparative opinion on Richardson or Fielding in the eighteenth or twentieth centuries, but there are at least four during the nineteenth.[71] Ruskin was a devout Richardsonian who writes that *Sir Charles Grandison* is "above all other works of fiction I know. It is very, very grand; and has, I think, a greater practical effect on me for good than anything I ever read in my life"; whereas he vividly imagines Fielding and Smollett "gloating and licking their chops over nastiness, like hungry dogs over ordure; founding one half of the laughable matter of their volumes in innuendoes of abomination."[72] The painter W.P. Frith also reads Richardson with a visual imagination: "Though I cannot agree with Dr. Johnson that Richardson is a greater writer than Fielding, I am a great admirer and constant reader of his works, and had always a desire to try my hand on a picture of 'Pamela.' "[73] (Frith did paint one picture of Pamela writing a letter home and one picture of Tom Jones showing Sophia her image in a mirror.) Benjamin Robert Haydon, the painter and partial inspiration for Harold Skimpole in *Bleak House*, compared them to painters. He writes in 1823 that *Tom Jones* prepares us for the imperfections of human nature while *Clarissa* points toward the salvation necessary to correct them. "Fielding painted men as they are, Richardson as they ought to be. The characters of Fielding are the result of observation, those of Richardson of imagination and observation," Haydon writes. "Fielding is the Hogarth of novelists and something higher. Richardson may be called the Raphael of domestic life."[74]

Finally, Hazlitt preserves a considerable amount of opinion on Richardson and Fielding in his *Conversations of James Northcote* (1830). Northcote's words, as recorded and probably elaborated on by Hazlitt, are a casual, cantankerous, and loosely conversational series of critical epigrams. Northcote seems familiar with Richardson and Fielding's works as well as with the recurring dichotomies which mark their critical reception. "We are amused with *Tom Jones*; but we rise from the perusal of *Clarissa* with higher feelings and better resolutions than we had before," he writes.[75] Later in the same conversation Northcote inserts his own imagery into the familiar critical opposition of Richardson and Fielding's morality:

> Fielding did not know what virtue or refinement meant. As Richardson said, he should have thought his books were written by an ostler; or Sir John Hawkins has expressed it still better, that the virtues of his heroes are the virtues of dogs and horses—he does not go beyond that—nor indeed so far, for his *Tom Jones* is not so good as Lord Byron's Newfoundland dog. I have known Newfoundland dogs with twenty times his understanding and good-nature. That is where Richardson has the advantage over Fielding—the virtues of *his* characters are not the virtues of animals—*Clarissa* holds her head in the skies, a 'bright particular star;' for whatever may be said, we have such *ideas*—and thanks to those who sustain and nourish them, and woe to those critics who would confound them with the dirt under our feet and Grub-street jargon![76]

Non-artists are more likely to use the art metaphor than the artists themselves. The metaphors range from simplistic similes to elaborate conceits. Beginning with the most basic examples, John Dunlop contrasts Richardson's "delineation of character" and Fielding's position as "a painter of manners"; James Mackintosh writes, "I acknowledge and admire the extraordinary talent of Richardson for *truth* in painting"; and Scott compliments Richardson by titling him the "Rubens of fiction."[77] Stephen compares Fielding with an artist and then uses the metaphor for Richardson: "In Fielding and his beloved Hogarth we have the 'prosai-comi-epos' . . . of the middle class of the time. Richardson, though a greater artist, is far inferior in sheer intellectual vigor, and Smollett is comparatively but a caricaturist."[78]

Other uses of the art metaphor are more elaborate if not especially original. "The painter dissects, fills his room with models, and takes every limb and joint from the living figure, and the novelist must bestow no less pains on the details of his pen pictures," writes a critic in the *Westminster Review* of October 1853.[79] Scott's essay "Richardson" contains a related treatment of the authors' "pen pictures," comparing the analogy between Fielding and Richardson to "that which free, bold, and true sketches bear to paintings which have been very minutely laboured, and, amid their excellence, still exhibit some of the heaviness which almost always attends the highest degree of finishing."[80] Robert Chambers reverses Scott's interpretation, citing Richardson as the quick sketch artist and Fielding as the minute realist:

> Perhaps Richardson stretches . . . too violently and too continuously; his portraits are in slashes, full charged with the peculiarities of their master. Fielding has a broader canvas, more light than shade, a clear and genial atmosphere, and groups of characters finely and naturally diversified. . . . [Fielding creates] genuine pictures of human nature without romance, and the most perfect art in the arrangement of his plot and incidents.[81]

The *Quarterly Review* reverses the dichotomy yet again, making Fielding the "slashing" artist: "[T]he broader, more vigorous touch of Fielding is the style of a greater master; the one gives a minute inventory, the other a striking epitome of nature; a microscope is needed for the pictures of the one: those of the other are best seen at distance." Later in the same article the anonymous writer makes one of the more imaginative and subtle art comparisons to Richardson and Fielding (also reversing Chambers' opinion): "It is the difference between the first and subsequent proofs of an engraving. Richardson's are first impressions; Fielding's pictures were taken when the plate, blunted and worn, was no longer capable of producing lights and shades."[82] J.J. Jusserand also makes Richardson the more detailed (and superior) artist, playing Fra Angelico to Fielding's Hogarth.[83]

Art metaphors are a part of a larger nineteenth-century critical phenomenon. The language of nineteenth-century criticism is markedly different from the language of the eighteenth and mid-twentieth century: it is more conversational, emotional, and, in many ways, more imaginative. The eighteenth century is not the only period in which "wit" is a valued, perhaps even overvalued, part of literary criticism. In the Richardson/Fielding debate, for example, the most famous eighteenth century witticism is Johnson's ingenious and pointed comparison: "there was as great a difference between [Richardson and Fielding] as between a man who knew how a watch was made, and a man who could tell the hour by looking on the dial-plate."[84] In the nineteenth century the most famous single statement on Richardson and Fielding is from Coleridge: "To take [Fielding] up after Richardson, is like emerging from a sick room heated by stoves, into an open lawn, on a breezy day in May."[85] Nineteenth-century critics seem to have learned that witty and epigrammatic critical utterances are a key to fame.

Epigrams are not only memorable, but they are also convenient ways to make sharp distinctions and categorize information. Oppositions are a tempting target, as they have always been sources for humor and invention—to this day wits hold forth on men and women, democrats and republicans, northerners and southerners, adults and children, black and white. In terms of the Richardson/Fielding opposition, the result of epigrammatic and witty criticism is often a gross oversimplification of a complex network of aesthetic issues, reinforcing the impression that Richardson and Fielding are essential opposites. Nineteenth-century criticism of Richardson and Fielding is often entertaining to read, but it is not always subtle or terribly insightful. Sounding good is often more important than being fair or accurate. Leslie Stephen, for example, writes that Richardson did "more good every week of his life" than "Fielding was ever able to do throughout the whole of his."[86]

Epigrammatic examples of Richardson/Fielding criticism will be found throughout this chapter, but it is important to note that Richardson in particular is the target of most of the caustic wit. Hippolyte Taine, for example, writes of Sir Charles Grandison, "His conscience and his wig are unsullied. Amen! Let us canonise him, and stuff him with straw."[87] Oliphant writes another unforgettable phrase about Richardson and the eighteenth century: "It was a prosaic age, and Richardson was prose itself."[88] Finally, on a more positive note, Thomas Shaw writes a striking impression which may include a tongue-in-cheek reference to Richardson's prolixity: "If our great modern works of creative fiction may be compared to the rapid colossal agency of volcanic fire, the productions of Richardson may resemble the slow and gradual formation of an alluvial continent. . . ."[89]

Type-Two Readers: Biography and Fiction

We have seen how the nineteenth-century critical horizon promotes a trivializing, epigrammatic, imaginative, and metaphorical style of criticism. When all of these influences are combined with the necessity of critical introductions (one could never assume Richardson or Fielding would be instantly familiar to general readers), there is a tendency for critics to get excessively creative with Richardson and Fielding's biographies. "Regarded merely as writers, there can, I suppose, be no real rivalry between Fielding and Richardson," writes Augustine Birrell in 1892.[90] In order to keep the rivalry alive, therefore, critics often focused their attention on everything *except* the novels. Bad information on these authors snowballs from one biographer to another, beginning in 1804 with Barbauld's life of Richardson (or arguably Murphy's essay on Fielding in 1762), and not ending until 1883 with Dobson's biography (or arguably with Eaves and Kimpel in 1971 and Battestin in 1989). The narrative qualities of these nineteenth-century biographical essays sometimes rival the romantic improbabilities of the authors they discuss.

Fielding has it especially hard. Lady Mary Wortley Montagu's letters were published in 1803, providing the root source for many of the stories about Fielding's supposedly decadent life and volatile personality. Barbauld's prefatory life of Richardson in the *Correspondence*, portraying Richardson as a natural genius and Fielding as a conniving rival, followed one year later. Watson's life of Fielding was published in 1807, emphasizing scandal even more than Murphy's essay, and Scott's *Lives of the Novelists* capped the string of biographical essays that did Fielding no good in the first two decades of the century. Thackeray's lecture was the midcentury lowpoint for Fielding in 1851 ("I cannot offer or hope to make a hero of Harry Fielding"). By the end of the century Fielding was enjoying something of a biographical renaissance, as Thomas Keightley (1858), Saintsbury (1893), Gosse (1898), and William Ernest Henley (1903) all attempted new and somewhat more impartial biographies. James P. Browne's introduction to his edition of Fielding's works (1871) was a setback, as he put the essentials of Murphy's essay back into circulation with little new information.

Dobson's *Fielding* (1883) is a nineteenth-century turning point. Several critics of the book thought it missed the opportunity to draw a moral from Fielding's life, but that is precisely the kind of biography-as-novel Dobson attempts to avoid. "[T]here can be no doubt that the new scientific spirit, with its desire for facts, was clearly manifesting itself in the general attitude," writes Blanchard of Dobson's book. "Criticism was passing into the hands of specialists."[91] Richardson attracts less professional biographical attention. The length and depth of Barbauld's biographical essay on Richardson in 1804 is not surpassed until Alan D. McKillop's biography in 1936.

The biographical fallacy was apparently not yet a fallacy throughout most of the nineteenth-century. It was perfectly acceptable to make assumptions about what kind of man Richardson or Fielding was and then scan their novels for supporting "evidence." If the assumptions and the evidence did not always fit together, the next step was to invent biographical data, preferably negative, to make the details fit. Biographers "felt that anything said in one sentence to the credit of Fielding must be withdrawn not later than the next," writes Cross, whose biography of Fielding was published in the twentieth century but researched in the nineteenth. "Few [of Fielding's nineteenth-century critics] have given evidence of possessing that kind of judgment which the world describes as common sense. Many of them, when they touched upon Fielding, appear to have lost their minds completely."[92]

Leslie Stephen is widely regarded as the preeminent Victorian biographer. His biographical introduction to Fielding's works (1882), however, is a model of irresponsible scholarship. Appearing in his essay for the first time are the stories of Fielding using his wife's relatives as false police informers, his sponging off Lady Mary Wortley Montagu, and his gullibility about quack doctors. As Stephen freely confesses, the facts of Fielding's life are so sketchy that "anyone may fill up more minutely by such colouring as pleases his fancy."[93] Even more extreme is William Collier, who writes in the opening sentence of *A History of English Literature* (1881), "This History of English Literature is essentially biographical, for true criticism cannot separate the author from his book," and who also invents a lively scene of the original reception of *Pamela*. In one stroke Collier transforms the Bow-Street Justice into someone who randomly assaults senior citizens:

> [T]here rang a mocking laugh from the crowd of scamps and fast men, who ran riot in London streets, beating the feeble old watchmen, and frightening timid wayfarers out of their wits. To such men virtue was a jest; and among the loudest was a careless, good-humoured, very clever lawyer of thirty-five, called Harry Fielding.[94]

George Curtis, the editor of *Harper's Magazine*, concludes in the February 1860 issue that Fielding has such a "cheerful, robust, sensible mind" and that he "beyond doubt" referred to the "sanctimonious Puritan" as "Sammy."[95] George Barnett Smith claims Fielding was such a profligate with money that he once tried to borrow money from no less than Samuel Johnson.[96] William Mudford tells us Fielding did not write his plays "until his door is besieged by bailiffs" and he died of diseases "which he had entailed upon himself by a youth of folly and dissipation."[97] Other examples from the *Encyclopedia Britannica* and from Thackeray are cited above; the most interesting imaginative biography of Richardson comes from Oliphant and will be dealt with separately below.

The impulse toward narrative fiction in critical accounts of Richardson and Fielding reaches something of a climax in two of the most delightful essays of the period, Henry Duff Traill's "Richardson and Fielding" from *Dialogues of the Dead* (1884) and Hunt's "A Novel Party" (1847). Traill's essay is an imaginary dialogue between Richardson and Fielding in the afterlife, surveying their eighteenth- and nineteenth-century reception. Traill's dialogue is true to the voices of Fielding's narrator in *Tom Jones* and Richardson in the *Correspondence*, and it reveals a great deal about nineteenth-century views of the aesthetic and moral opposition in their works. For example, Richardson is said to appeal to women and Fielding to men.[98] In contrast of their readerships, Richardson says, "A work of morality is not to be judged by its effects on the rakehells of Covent Garden." Fielding replies, "No; nor by its acceptance among the precise spinsters of Fleet Street. If the one be beyond the reach of reform, the others are beyond the need of it."[99] The wittiest exchange about the traditional opposition concerns the difference between idealism and realism of characterization:

> F: You did not study from the life, though perhaps you thought you did, but you had a certain power of imagining types. . . . I should like to say the same of Pamela, but I cannot. She is neither an ideal waiting-maid nor a real one.
> R: I know not why a squire or a waiting-maid should not comport themselves as they do in *Pamela*.
> F: Then take the word of a squire who has had some experience of waiting-maids, that they would not.[100]

The most in-depth discussion in Trail's dialogue is reserved for the most contentious issue in Richardson's and Fielding's reception history. Richardson defends the morality of his novels by arguing that the author must play God: "His judgment-say is in his last chapter, and the good must be rewarded and the evil punished before he pens his 'Finis,' or not at all." Fielding responds with a different interpretation of the author's omniscient role: "He also, if I may say it without irreverence, is a creator: and none can know so well as he what allowances are to be made for the infirmities of his creatures."[101] As for the morality of Fielding's trial-and-reward plot in *Tom Jones*, Richardson says, "Why teach young men that vice may escape punishment . . . while yet hoping to be rewarded with a Sophia Western at last?" Fielding responds, "Well, Mr. Richardson, and why teach waiting-maids that virtue will always be rewarded by £10,000 a year and a couple of country houses?"[102] Richardson is nevertheless undaunted about the moral duty of the novelist. "It is his duty sir to put [readers] upon contemplating only what is good, and to encourage them to the pursuit of it by showing what advantages it brings." Fielding's response is grounded in his customary realism:

> Is that his duty? Then egad, let him throw aside his pen and quit his closet, clap on a cassock and bands and get him to the pulpit, for that, sir, is the proper place for him. . . . That, Mr. Richardson, is his business—the business of a man whose concern is with the future world, and not like my own, as I conceived it, with the present.[103]

Fielding outwits and outargues Richardson on every point, revealing Traill's sympathies. Fielding has most of the dialogue, and Richardson generally stays on the defensive. In this respect Traill's essay is an accurate (as well as entertaining) encapsulation of the nineteenth-century Richardson/Fielding reception.

Rather than reading Richardson and Fielding themselves as fictional characters and passing it off as biography, Hunt reads the characters of their novels as real people and invites them to dinner. The part-time poet and dramatist's "A Novel Party" is a fantasy about what would happen if characters from eighteenth-century novels were all to converge at once for an elegant party. Hunt's criticisms of Richardson and Fielding are subtle and mostly limited to the motivations and affectations of character. Fielding generally emerges as the more moral and engaging of the two, with Tom Jones besting Sir Charles Grandison as the least pretentious gentleman and Sophia surpassing Pamela for charm.

Other interpretations of Hunt's opinions are left to the ingenuity of the reader in a delightful quiz of literary history and exercise in expectation. Captain and Mrs. Booth are seated next to Sir and Lady Charles Grandison. (Lady Grandison asks the speaker for his opinion of Amelia's nose, but he declines to comment.)[104] When Squire and Lady Booby arrive, Captain Booth catches Pamela's wandering eye ("[T]here is no knowing these precise people," writes the narrator.)[105] When the Grandisons and the Harlowes

strike up a conversation full of "long and curious gossip," the narrator observes, "we could perceive they were not so admired by the
rest of the company as by one another."[106] Grandison's "female
friends . . . were eternally repeating and deprecating their own
praises," while Peregrine Pickle "said something about Pamela and
Covent-Garden which we do not choose to repeat."[107] Tom Jones is
not amused at the coarseness of Roderick Random's conversation,
especially before the ladies, but Squire Western loves it.[108]

The party then breaks into two groups which reflect the Richard-
son/Fielding conflict. "We are afraid, from what we saw this evening, that poor Joseph is not as well as he would be with his sister
Pamela," writes the narrator in a *Shamela* tone. "When the re-
freshments came in, we observed her blush at his handing a plate
of sandwiches to Mr. Adams. She called him to her in a whisper;
and asked him, whether he had forgotten that there was a footman
in the room?"[109] Grandison nobly intervenes to prevent a quarrel
between Mrs. Clinker and Mrs. Slipslop about the jellies. Hunt's
commentary on the female characters is superficial: Clarissa stays
at home to coach her morally reformed husband Lovelace, Sophia
Western "was all ease and good-nature, and had a charming
shape," Lady Grandison "was a regular beauty; but did not become
the cloak. She was best in full dress," and Pamela "had something
in the corner of her eye, which told you that you had better take
care how you behaved yourself. . . . Pamela was not so splendidly
dressed as her friend Lady Grandison; but her clothes were as
costly."[110] In conclusion, the narrator is thankful for the variety of
the English novel and for the fact that none of these characters are
likely to have much impact outside the imagination:

> The conclusion of the company seemed to be, that if the world were to
> be made different from what it is, the change would be effected rather
> by the philosophies of these gentlemen [Grandison and company] than
> the seraphics of the other party [Jones's]; but the general opinion was,
> that it would be altered by neither, and that in the meantime, 'variety
> was charming'; a sentiment which the Vicar of Wakefield took care to
> explain to his wife.[111]

Type-Two Readers:
Questions & Answers, Alterity, and Expectations

The horizon of expectation which governs nineteenth-century
criticism of Richardson and Fielding offers little to refute the ste-

reotypes of the prim, nationalistic, and snobbish Victorian era. If the primary questions to which Richardson and Fielding were the answer in the eighteenth century were "Does the author have my loyalty? How will his novels affect the minds of young readers? Does he reflect or improve upon nature?", then the primary questions in the nineteenth century seem to be "Did the author lead a refined life? Do his novels portray good manners? Does he have imagination?"

The eighteenth century did not often look far back into seventeenth-century culture to find its own identity. Nineteenth-century critics, however, frequently discuss the eighteenth century as a way to identify the areas of "progress" in their own lives. The fact that Richardson and Fielding were by this point historically distant meant the horizon of the original audience had to be reconstructed in order to measure any subsequent change. Finding "alterity" with the eighteenth century was not at all difficult for nineteenth-century critics.

Eighteenth-century novels were often read as documents of social history rather than as works of art, then as now. As Hazlitt writes, *Joseph Andrews* is a "perfect piece of statistics."[112] Rather than using the comparative dichotomy of ideal versus real portraits of nature, therefore, nineteenth-century critics more frequently evaluate Richardson and Fielding according to which one best reflects (what the critic perceives to be) the times. Stephen's *History of English Thought in the Eighteenth Century* (1876) is an excellent example of an attempt to recreate the full eighteenth-century world view from a nineteenth-century perspective. He values Fielding for his historical perception in an implied comparison to Richardson:

[F]or insight into the motives of his contemporaries; for a power of seeing things as they are; for sympathy with homely virtues; and contempt for shams and hypocrites, Fielding is as superior to some later writers of equal imaginative force as they are superior to him in width of sympathy and delicacy of perception. His art is thus the most faithful representative of his age. . . .

Fielding's significance as a historian makes Richardson redundant. Fielding is so much the representative of his culture that

a complete criticism of the English artistic literature of the eighteenth century would place Fielding at the center, and measure the completeness of other representatives pretty much as they recede from an approach to his work. . . . Fielding, more than anyone, gives the essential—the very form and pressure of the time.[113]

Fielding meets approval for reflecting his age, but this should not be confused with a Victorian approval for the age itself. Nineteenth-century critics' disapprobation of the eighteenth century carries over into their vindictive criticism of Richardson, Fielding, and other eighteenth-century authors. Their image of a barbarous, chaotic century would be more recognizable to Swift or Smollett than to Addison or Burney. If one believes Collier, it is a wonder people read at all (at least those who could keep their eyeballs):

> The life described in Fielding's books was—let us be thankful for the change—totally unlike the life we now live. Much of the fun was of the roughest physical kind—practical jokes that would now-a-days fill our courts of law with actions for assault and battery, and violent altercations in road-side inns, which generally ended in a row, involving everybody present, to the serious detriment of eyes and limbs. The *mêlée* of fishwives, cabbage-mongers, and policemen, which enlivens every second or third scene of the comic business in our Christmas pantomimes, affords us a specimen of the same boisterous humour.[114]

One might mistake the subtitles for the eighteenth-century sections in Bayard Tuckerman's *A History of English Prose Fiction* (1882) for the kinds of subtitles we might just as easily expect to find in a twentieth-century book about the nineteenth (or, perhaps, a twenty-first century book about the twentieth): "Indifference to Poetry," "Indifference to Religion," "Political Corruption," "Social Corruption," "Contempt for Marriage," "Disrespect Toward Women," "Coarseness of Taste," "Highwaymen," "Prevalence of Crime," "Police Inefficiency," "Condition of the Prisons," and "State of Society."

Reconstructions of the age vary according to the author being discussed. If Fielding is the author in question, as he is for Lowell, the eighteenth century is "a generation whose sense of smell was undisturbed by odors that would now evoke a sanitary commission, and its moral nostrils were of an equally masculine temper."[115] If the subject is Richardson, the eighteenth century is, in the words of Gosse, "the age of tears" which "meditated with Young and Blair among the tombs, that combined the lachrymose with the sentimental, that wrapped itself, sighing, in the genteel mantle of melancholy."[116] Although Richardson and Fielding were contemporaries, their opposition is nevertheless projected onto different conceptions of the era: "Diatribes against hypocrisy and cant in an age most insincere, set in sun-lighted pictures of realistic brilliancy in an age that preferred to see everything through a moonlit mist, these were the novels of Fielding," writes Gosse, "and who can wonder that their author was misconsidered by his contemporaries?"[117]

The audience that appreciated Fielding is portrayed, as we have seen with Collier, as coarse and uncivilized. The audience that appreciated Richardson is completely different, although no more attractive. As Stephen writes,

[T]ime hung heavier, and letter-writing was a more serious business. . . . [Richardson's novels] are a fearful indication of the *ennui* from which the perpetrators must have suffered. We pity those who endured the toil as we pity the prisoners whose patient ingenuity has carved a passage through a stone wall with a rusty nail.[118]

The perception of time moving more slowly in the eighteenth century (an image to which Eliot gives a positive connotation in regard to Fielding) perhaps suggests readers felt time was moving too quickly in the nineteenth. "We have so many good novels which do not require the attention and labor exacted by him," writes Tuckerman of Richardson's works. "We live so fast that we cannot spare the time for so much sentiment. These novels, like the elaborate embroideries of the last century, belong to a period when life was less full, and books less abundant."[119] Masson agrees, revealing exactly what it is about the plotting of nineteenth-century novels that has altered the horizon of expectation:

We do not read Richardson's novels much now; and it cannot be helped that we do not. There are the novels of a hundred years between us and him; time is short; and novels of eight or ten volumes, written in the tedious form of letters, and recording conversations and meditations in which the story creeps on inch by inch, without so much as an unexpected pistol-shot or a trick of Harlequin and Pantaloon to relieve the attention, have little chance against the brisker and broader fictions to which we have been accustomed.[120]

The last phrase in Masson's passage, "fictions to which we have become accustomed," demonstrates the general lack of "negative capability" in nineteenth-century readers. Modern readers are trained to exercise a certain double-mindedness about reading older texts, often bracketing off comparisons with contemporary life and literature as extraneous to an understanding of the text itself. Nineteenth-century readers of Richardson and Fielding, however, rarely make such a distinction. (In Jaussian terms, the twentieth-century tendency toward *theoria* has overtaken the nineteenth-century tendency toward *poiesis*.) Victorian evaluations of older novels frequently contain references to how the works fit into the radically different contemporary horizon, one which Richardson or Fielding never could have foreseen.

As late as 1882, Tuckerman has concerns about how Fielding's novels will affect the morality of young readers. "His novels are coarse to a degree which may nullify their merits in the eyes of some readers of the present day, and may unfit them for the perusal of very young people," he writes. This is not necessarily Fielding's fault, however, since "their coarseness was adapted to the lack of refinement in thought and speech characteristic of the time."[121] Or, as the *Westminster Review* of October 1853 puts it, the characters in Richardson's and Fielding's novels appear "as if they had lived in the days of King Alfred. . . . The greater refinement of manners in modern days may render Richardson's pictures of life revolting to our more fastidious tastes."[122] Perhaps most tellingly (and graphically), the publisher Alexander Macmillan writes a letter to a colleague in 1866 thinking of bringing out a series of eighteenth-century novels: "The difficulty is the selection. You begin with Richardson, Fielding, Smollett, Sterne. But what are you to do with their dirt? Modern taste won't stand it. I don't particularly think they *ought* to stand it. Still less would they stand castration."[123] The project was dropped.

Perhaps the book most revealing of how a reader's horizon of expectation is informed by his conception of the period, and also the most obnoxious, is William Forsyth's *The Novels and Novelists of the Eighteenth Century, in Illustration of the Manners and Morals of the Age* (1871). Forsyth's book is one long sneer at the eighteenth century, full of congratulation for the nineteenth and its polished civilization. Drenched in sexism and class prejudice, it is a pre-Darwinist, -Marxist and -Feminist dinosaur. Selecting representative quotes is essentially arbitrary: "We have to face an amount of coarseness which is in the highest degree repulsive," writes Forsyth. "[S]ociety was accustomed to actions and language which would not be tolerated now."[124] Forsyth has harshly critical words for Richardson, Fielding, and every other novelist in the eighteenth century. "To me, I confess, 'Clarissa Harlowe' is an unpleasant, not to say odious, book," he writes. "The key-note of the whole composition is libertine pursuit, and we are wearied and disgusted by volume after volume devoted to the single subject of attack on a woman's chastity." The tradition of spiritual autobiography which informs Richardson's novels is long-forgotten by 1871. Forsyth can only read *Clarissa* through contemporary eyes:

> If any book deserved the charge of 'sickly sentimentality,' it is this, and that it should have once been so widely popular, and thought admirably adapted to instruct young women in lessons of virtue and religion, shows a strange and perverted state of the public taste, not to say public morals. . . . It is nauseous to find religion thus mixed up with such a story.[125]

Forsyth at least brings himself to *summarize* Richardson's novel, which is more than he does for *Tom Jones*. "The truth is, that it would be impossible to give an analysis of the novel, or even describe the plot except in the most meager terms, without offending against the respect due to female delicacy now."[126] Surprisingly, of the two novelists, Forsyth prefers Fielding. "I think that of all the novels of that period, 'Amelia' is the one which gives the most generally truthful idea of the manners and habits of middle-class society then."[127]

Only Dickens, perhaps because he is a realist author himself, defends Richardson and Fielding from the critics who would object to their works out of Victorian self-satisfaction. In the preface to *Oliver Twist* (1837–38) he defends his own practice by citing eighteenth-century precedents:

> I am not aware of any writer in our language having a respect for himself, or held in any respect by his posterity, who ever has descended to the taste of the fastidious classes. . . . Fielding, De Foe, Goldsmith, Smollett, Richardson . . . all these for wise purposes, and especially the two first, brought upon the scene the very scum and refuse of the land . . . and yet, if I turn back . . . I find the same reproach levelled against them every one, each in his turn, by the insects of the hour who raised their little hum, and died, and were forgotten.[128]

The last word on the issue of reconstructing social horizons, however, should go to Stephen: "We can hardly fancy a genuine hero with a pigtail, or a heroine in a hoop and high-heeled shoes, nor believe that persons who wore those articles of costume could possess any very exalted virtues," he writes in "Richardson's Novels." "Perhaps our grandchildren may have the same difficulty about the race which wears crinolines and chimney-pot hats."[129]

Type-Two Readers: Morality

Eighteenth-century criticism of Richardson and Fielding is largely based on theological and moral criteria. Richardson's enthusiastic early reception comes mostly from readers who found the morality of his novels inspiring. (Many of those same readers found the opposite traits in Fielding's novels, of course.) Critics of every generation think they have discovered higher ethical truths hidden to previous generations, but eighteenth-century critics brought morality to literary criticism with a pervasiveness not seen since the medieval period. The nineteenth century—infamous for its unyielding "Victorian morality"—is surprisingly flexible with its ethical criticism. Moral evaluations of Richardson and Fielding persist after the eighteenth century, but they do so in different directions with different emphases for different reasons.

As I have discussed in chapter two, Paul Hunter claims that personal improvement was a primary motive for reading in the early eighteenth century. Both the supply and the demand of eighteenth-century novels promoted didacticism. With Sentimentalism, the Gothic, and Romanticism, however, a more passive entertainment (*aesthesis*) gradually displaces the motive of didacticism (*catharsis*). The nineteenth-century reception of Richardson and Fielding proves that the transformation is complete in the post-Scott era. Stephen writes that by 1874 literary didacticism has changed from a necessity to a disadvantage. "[A] direct intention to prove that men ought not to steal or get drunk, or commit any other atrocities, is generally considered to be beside the novelist's purpose, and its introduction to be a fault of art," Stephen writes.[130] Sydney Smith writes as early as 1809 that appeal is a stronger motive for readers than moral improvement: "Sir Charles Grandison is less agreeable than Tom Jones; but it is more agreeable than Sherlock and Tillotson; and teaches religion and morality to many who would not seek it in the productions of these professional writers."[131]

Smith is typical of several nineteenth-century critics insofar as his moral criticism emphasizes aesthetic appeal. Readers still champion Richardson's morality over Fielding's, but their evaluations often include an aesthetic perception missing in much eighteenth-century criticism. Francis Jeffrey, for example, worries that Richardson's considerable artistic talents are misapplied. Jeffrey speaks in terms of mood and meanings rather than behavior and spirituality: "[T]here is a certain air of irksome regularity, gloominess and pedantry, attached to most of his virtuous characters which is apt to encourage more unfortunate associations than the engaging qualities with which he has invested some of his vicious ones."[132]

There are still scattered instances of librarians and clergymen banning Fielding throughout the 1830s and 1840s.[133] The Reverend Edward Mangin, who had probably not read *Tom Jones*, warns his parishioners in 1808 that it teaches young men they may "riot in security amidst illicit enjoyments, and ultimately reap a richer harvest than tame and timid prudence can hope for!", and believes the novel is an extended exposition on "the whole craft and mystery relating to the generation and breeding of illegitimate children."[134] William H. Brown's preface to his novel *Ira and Isabella* (1807) lists novelists who "allure the untutored mind to the practice of virtue . . . and to deter it from vice," citing Richardson along with Defoe, Smollett and Sterne. Fielding is noticeably absent, perhaps for the first and only time losing his place as a moralist to Smollett.[135] Hugh Blair represents a more parochial conservatism in 1835 in his *Lectures on Rhetoric* written for young students. One of the questions on which pupils are to be catechized is "Who is the most moral of our novel writers?". The correct answer is "Samuel Richardson."[136] Blair would not have been proud of Richardson's mid-century critics, many of whom were quite possibly drilled with Blair's popular textbook.

Fielding's morality is not only dubious to some critics, it is also unfashionable. "What an impression [Fielding's] novels leave of low sentiment, coarse habits, and the prevalence of gross vice everywhere," writes the *Westminster Review*.[137] Tuckerman likewise believes "Fielding's novels are now considered unfit for general perusal. . . . His novels are coarse to a degree which may nullify their merits in the eyes of some readers of the present day, and may unfit them for the perusal of very young people." Fielding's novels provide bad moral examples not from any fault of his own, but because the "standard in such matters has changed" and their "coarseness was adapted to the lack of refinement in thought and speech characteristic of the time."[138]

Almost everything Johnson did for Richardson's moral reputation was undone by Coleridge. Whereas Johnson said Richardson taught the passions to move at the command of virtue, Coleridge said Richardson poisons the imagination. Few nineteenth-century critics cite Coleridge as a specific inspiration, but many share his belief in the contagion of Richardson's diseased mind. Southey's opinion of Richardson is "that for a man of decorous life he had a most impure imagination, and that the immorality of [Restoration] drama is far less mischievous than his moral stories of Pamela and Squire Booby. . . ."[139] William Roscoe finds Mr. B. (not even Lovelace) more pernicious than Shakespeare's Iago: "We rightly think Richardson's *Pamela*, unfit reading, on account of its prurient minute details . . . [but] Iago and Blifil leave no stain on the mind."[140] *The Quarterly Review* also finds Richardson more prurient than Fielding. Speaking of how the two authors deal with love, the critic writes, "In this respect Fielding, in our opinion, sins least offensively. There is a mawkishness about Richardson's sentiment which would be prurient but for his simplicity."[141]

Type-Two Readers: Critical Dichotomies, Tragedy vs. Comedy

Many of the critical dichotomies used to discuss Richardson and Fielding in the eighteenth century recur in the nineteenth century, although necessarily altered to fit the times. Other dichotomies are unique to the nineteenth century and mark a clean break with eighteenth-century concerns.

The most basic and popular of the dichotomies is that of tragedy and comedy. As Masson writes, making the dichotomy as inescapable as biology itself, "[A]nything whatever may be looked at and considered in two ways—gravely and seriously, or . . . comical; . . . some minds tend constitutionally to the one mode of thought, and others to the other."[142] Not all writers are as content as Dunlop in *The History of Prose Fiction* (1814) to make such obvious and sweeping classifications as "serious" for Richardson and "comic" for Fielding.[143] Barbauld is more typical, as she locates the tragedy/comedy polarity in the nature of the creative imagination itself: "Fielding had all the ease which Richardson wanted, a genuine flow of humour, and a rich variety of comic character . . . but he could not describe a consistently virtuous character, and in deep pathos he was far excelled by his rival."[144]

The nineteenth-century connotations of tragedy and comedy are very different from those of the eighteenth century, however. Tragedy tended to be seen by the Augustans as the more heroic, didactic, idealistic, and moral of the two modes, whereas the chief virtue of comedy seemed to be realism and satire. The Richardson versus Fielding framework puts Coleridge into a position that produces an alternate approach to both genres, however. As he writes in 1808 of Richardson, "The lower passions of our nature are kept through seven or eight volumes, in a hot-bed of interest. Fielding's is far less pernicious; 'for the gusts of laughter drive away sensuality.' "[145] Tragedy is "pernicious" rather than moral, and comedy produces laughter as the corrective. Meredith agrees that Fielding's comedy "corrects" Richardson's tragedy: "The look of Fielding upon Richardson is essentially comic. His method of correcting the sentimental writer is a mixture of the comic and the humorous."[146]

The preference for Fielding throughout the century is therefore related to the preference for comedy. The novels of Thackeray and Dickens no doubt contribute to the predominance of this particular expectation, at least by mid-century when the taste for Scott's style of historical romance begins to fade. "[C]omic literature seems to be in the ascendancy among us, and . . . even our men of greatest talent find it necessary to wear the cap and bells," writes Masson in 1859, shortly before the appearance of Eliot's and Hardy's first works. "Perhaps could we wish . . . for the appearance among us of a great soul that could not or would not laugh at all; whose every tone and syllable should be serious. . . ."[147] Tuckerman is unique in the century for acknowledging that both comedy and tragedy are necessary twins, and that Richardson and Fielding "cannot be fairly compared, nor should they be considered as rivals. . . . Each has a high place in English literature, which the greatness of the other cannot depress. Richardson is best able to make his reader weep, and Fielding to make him laugh."[148]

Type-Two Readers: Critical Dichotomies, Ideal vs. Real

Another common dichotomy critics use throughout the eighteenth century is the opposition between the ideal and the real. Nineteenth-century critics offer no variation on the direction in which the dichotomy is traditionally applied to Richardson and Fielding. The century's overall distaste for Richardson reveals the *extent* of Richardson's idealism, however, and adds a negative connotation to didactic reform that is missing in the eighteenth century. As Dobson writes of *Tom Jones*, "Its relation to . . . Richardson, [is] that of the real to the ideal—one might also add, the impossible."[149] Mudford, likewise, has a subtle distaste for Richardson's idealism: "The admirers of human perfection, as displayed in the faultless delineation of Richardson, were necessarily irritated by those exhibitions of Nature which Fielding delighted to hold up to the eyes of mankind."[150] The *North British Review* (November 1855) applies the dichotomy specifically to Parson Adams and Sir Charles Grandison: "Fielding, unlike the sentimental Richardson, drew things as he saw them . . . [Adams] as far surpasses in beauty the perfect heroes of his fellow-novelist, as a natural rose, with its slight irregularities, does its mathematically correct prototype in wax. . . ."[151] Northcote also uses an art metaphor. His evaluation of the two authors appears fairly balanced and neutral to modern eyes, but that is just a sign of our different expectations of idealism and realism. "Fielding painted men as they are, Richardson as they ought to be," but, Northcote says, "you relinquish Fielding with hope, [and] Richardson leaves you in a gloomy agitation."[152] Dickens is the only writer in the period who finds both Richardson and Fielding to be realists.[153]

Type-Two Readers:
Critical Dichotomies, Internal versus External

The most frequently repeated dichotomy in the long history of the Richardson and Fielding rivalry, internal versus external observation, persists well into the nineteenth century. Nineteenth-century culture made it more difficult for critics of the period to simply parrot the standard polarity, however. Writing long after sentimental and romantic literature had been absorbed into the literary consciousness, it is seldom enough for a critic to remark upon internal and external experience as competitive traits of a genre trying to shake its way clear of the Romance. The internal/external dichotomy is therefore used less frequently than it is in other periods, and it usually serves some larger critique.

Like Johnson's before him, Coleridge's words renewed the validity of the distinction. Fielding's observations of diverse "living" characters have "great excellence," but "in drawing from his own heart, and depicting that species of character which no observation could teach, he failed in comparison with Richardson, who perpetually placed himself as it were in a day-dream," writes Coleridge in his Bristol lectures. The dichotomized talents of Richardson and Fielding are used as illustrations of a problem which Shakespeare does not have. Fielding has living characters, Richardson has heart, "but Shakespeare excelled in both."[154] T.B. Macaulay also compares the internal/external dichotomy of Richardson and Fielding to the lack of it in Shakespeare, but does so as part of a speech to Parliament about a proposed copyright bill in 1841. "Take Richardson's novels," Macaulay writes. "No writings are more deeply pathetic. No writings, those of Shakespeare excepted, show more profound knowledge of the human heart."[155]

Other critics unimaginatively repeat the cliché as it has been handed down to them. Speaking of the power to "see things as they are," Stephen writes, "Fielding is as superior to some later writers of equal imaginative force as they are superior to him in width of sympathy and delicacy of perception."[156] Masson cites Johnson's evaluation of Richardson and Fielding, asserting Fielding to be "broader . . . more rich, more various, more interesting" than his rival. Richardson conversely works "according to the method of ideal development from within outwards."[157]

There are also critics in the period who use the dichotomy more creatively or who find a deeper insight into the precise techniques of Richardson and Fielding. Jane West, for example, imagines a hypothetically perfect novelist who would unify the Jekyll-and-Hyde personalities of Richardson and Fielding. "Fielding . . . preferred the exhibition of the grotesque and depraved part of our species," West writes. "Such almost intuitive knowledge of the human heart as the former possessed, combined with the morality and pathos of Richardson, *would* have formed the desideratum in this class of literature."[158] The *Quarterly Review* uses the internal/external dichotomy to make a three-way comparison between Richardson, Fielding, and Smollett, with Fielding parallel to West's imaginary perfect author:

> In their delineations of character Richardson knows only the principles; Smollett insists on the practical results; Fielding . . . treats character as a living whole. Richardson dreams men only from within, Smollett only from without, Fielding from both.[159]

Finally, in *The Development of the English Novel*, Cross makes an intellectual distinction that replaces the oversimplifications of the standard dichotomy with a subtle reading of Richardson and Fielding's temperaments and literary sources. Prefiguring Ian Watt's own intellectualized account, Cross claims the novel is essentially about realism. As in Watt's book, Richardson takes highest honors: "The novel as Richardson left it was a sober dissection of the heart. With Fielding, it was perhaps a no less serious effort, though its purpose was clouded by extravagant wit and humor." Cross breaks with tradition by saying that both Richardson and Fielding write of the inner life, but Richardson's background in the romance leads him to reach internal experience with sentimentalism, while Fielding's background in the fabliau, picaresque, burlesque, and adventure genres leads him to reach it with "vices and follies." Rather than using the standard tragedy/comedy distinction for Richardson and Fielding, Cross sees *both* novelists as comic (due to Richardson's roots in the romance). The distinction between Richardson and Fielding is that of two different types of comedy: "Richardson turned to Steele's 'Conscious Lovers'—a moral disquisition ar-

ranged in dialogue . . . Fielding turned to the light, gay, and burlesque comedy of Molière and Congreve."[160]

Type-Two Readers:
Critical Dichotomies, "Feminine" versus "Masculine"

One of the most frequent dichotomies to make its debut in the
period goes on to affect criticism of Richardson and Fielding deep
into the twentieth century: "feminine" versus "masculine." Victorians were anything but ambiguous about the traditional domestic
roles of women and men, and the Richardson/Fielding opposition
is fueled by the relative values these (mostly) educated males
placed upon "femininity" and "masculinity."

Great interpretive insight into the hidden Freudian subtleties of
language are rarely necessary in nineteenth-century pronouncements on Richardson and Fielding.[161] The assignments of "femininity" and "masculinity" to Richardson and Fielding are clear,
stated plainly, and there is no question about the superiority of the
"masculine" temperament. The connection between the distaste
for "feminine" literature and Richardson's critical neglect is just as
clear. "The Victorians, who might have respected Richardson's
strict morality, were probably influenced . . . by a certain suspicion,
in an era of vigorously masculine energy, of a man who was, according to biographical legend, constantly in the company of females,"
writes Brophy.[162]

Richardson is always assumed to be the "feminine" author. A
wide range of characteristics is called upon to support the claim,
ranging from Richardson's early childhood associations with
women to his taste for tea. Stephen takes Richardson's "femininity" as a matter of course and assumes it is part of an unnatural
deviation from the balance of a healthy human character. "That
Richardson was, as we have said, something of the milksop is obvious," Stephen writes. "Every man should have in him some considerable infusion of feminine though not of effeminate character."
Richardson's tendencies, writes Stephen, make him as imperfect a
woman as he is an imperfect man. Richardson's strength is "the
sensibility to emotion, and the interest in small details, which only
women exhibit in perfection."[163] The *Spectator's* review of Stephen's *Works of Samuel Richardson* (October 1883) similarly finds
both Richardson's faults and virtues to be "feminine," and his
"opinion of books is as worthless as that of an enthusiastic but ignorant school-girl, and in writing of his great rival Fielding he displays

an irascibility of temper and an incapacity of discerning merit only to be tolerated in affairs of the heart." Even Richardson's antipathy for Fielding stems from his "feminine" temperament: "A fond girl who has lost her lover may be excused for speaking contemptuously of the woman who takes her place," but Richardson should have at least "had the sagacity to write with justice of its author."[164]

Fielding, on the other hand, has shed his eighteenth-century image as a sentimental, large-hearted man who doted on his children with a mother-like affection. Fielding is a Victorian man's man, a Crusoe forging his way through the wilderness of the early novel. "From the fatal effects of that sentimental disease which infected Richardson, England was saved by the sturdy common-sense of men like Fielding," writes the *Quarterly Review*.[165] Thackeray expands the heroic metaphor in *English Humourists*, discussing "A Voyage to Lisbon" and comparing Fielding with

> a wounded captain, when the vessel founders, who never loses his heart, who eyes the danger steadily, and has a cheery word for all, until the inevitable fate overwhelms him, and the gallant ship goes down. Such a brave and gentle heart, such an intrepid and courageous spirit, I love to recognise in the manly, the English Harry Fielding.[166]

Lowell puts the same basic idea in direct language: "If we seek for a single characteristic which more than any other would sum him up, we should say that it was his absolute manliness, a manliness in its type English from top to toe. . . ."[167]

There are many examples of direct "feminine" and "masculine" comparisons. Jeffrey's comment on the language of Richardson's *Correspondence* implies a comparison with Fielding: "The gaiety of all his characters is extremely girlish and silly, and is much more like the prattle of spoiled children, then the wit and pleasantry of persons acquainted with the world."[168] Gosse takes the same position from the opposite angle, commenting on Fielding's characterization and implying Richardson. Tom Jones is "one young gentleman who continues to be the type of the healthy and red-blooded Englishman who puts forward no pretension to a priggish faultlessness, but who makes the best fight he can for virtue in the rough horse-play of his instincts."[169] (Note that the connotations associated with childhood—"prattle" and "horse-play"—vary according to gender.) Masson contributes a simpering portrait of the publication of *Clarissa*, grudgingly allowing Richardson the temporary victory:

> The nervous, tea-drinking, pompous little printer, coddled as he was by a bevy of admiring women, who nursed his vanity, as Johnson thought,

by keeping him all to themselves, and letting nothing but praise come near him, had beaten, for the moment, the stalwart Fielding, roughing it never so manfully among companions of the other sex, and invigorating his views of things with club-dinners and claret.[170]

The "feminine"/"masculine" dichotomy naturally leads to discussions of how each author portrays highly gendered characters. Then, as now, the women characters provide one of the few areas in which Richardson often bests Fielding in direct comparisons. Nineteenth-century critics usually see women characters as the weak link in Fielding's "masculine mastery" of the art. Conversely, critics tend to see Richardson's characterization as his primary talent. One of the many things that separates these rather trite observations from modern feminist analyses is the passive nature of the nineteenth-century criticism: the portrayal of women characters is a matter of artistic technique, only one element among others, and the criticism rarely carries any suggestion that characterization has any social or political implications for the lives of real women. In terms of the "feminine"/"masculine" dichotomy, Richardson's technical strength comes from his personal weakness, and Fielding's personal strength leads to his technical weakness.

"Sophia Western was, as we have seen, a comely girl enough," writes Birrell epigrammatically. "[B]ut she was as much like Clarissa as a ship in dock is like a ship at sea and on fire. . . . When you have dug Tom Jones in the ribs, and called him a lucky dog, and wished her happy, you turn away with a yawn; but Clarissa is immense."[171] Sophia often seems two-dimensional when compared to Clarissa. "Sophia Western is a pretty creature, a sweet sketch of the surface and outside of a woman," writes Oliphant. Clarissa, however, lives "in the island, owing nothing to earth and all to heaven."[172] The Quarterly Review (1886), too, finds Richardson's female characters the most authentic. Fielding's women are "matter-of-fact, commonplace, healthy young women, with nothing characteristically feminine in their composition. . . . Sophia Western is a far less subtle study that Clarissa Harlowe."[173] Richardson's women characters are superior to Fielding's because Richardson has "an advantage over him both in training and temperament," and for once Fielding's talent for "observation" fails him:

Till [Fielding's] marriage he formed no conception of the inner mind of women. Richardson, on the other hand, was, as we have seen, peculiarly fitted to portray female character. His idea of the inmost nature of women was a primitive ingredient, an essential element of his mental constitution. . . . It was not pieced together from the results of experience, but it was a constituent part of his mind. . . . Fielding drew from observation, Richardson from intuition.[174]

Fielding's nineteenth-century critical reception was so much more favorable than Richardson's that a number of critics, even if they are in the minority, can still find excuses for praising his female characters over Richardson's. Fielding's women are sometimes seen as down-to-earth and entertaining, compared to Richardson's who are self-important and solemn. At Hunt's metaphorical dinner party, as we have seen, Sophia Western "was all ease and good-nature, and had a charming shape. Lady Grandison was a regular beauty; but did not become the cloak. She was best in full dress."[175] One of the few women critics of the period, Clara Thomson, defends Sophia and Amelia as a "man's ideal" and attributes them with a "manly honour" as an addition to their "tenderness and kindness."[176] Haydon, writing in 1823, gives Fielding the credit usually reserved for Richardson for portraying the subtleties of the female mind: *Tom Jones* "lets you into all the little follies and amiable weaknesses of nature; it shows you that the most virtuous, the most pure and innocent woman may have little imperfections, little vanities, in fact, perfectly natural feelings, without corrupting her heart."[177] Fielding has come far since the Reverend James Fordyce said in 1764 that a woman who reads Fieldingesque novels "must in her soul be a prostitute, let her reputation in life be what it will."[178]

Type-Two Readers: Margaret Oliphant

The most insightful and original use of the "feminine"/"masculine" dichotomy in the period comes from the novelist and biographer Margaret Oliphant.[179] Her essay "Historical Sketches of the Reign of George II. No. X—the Novelist" from *Blackwood's Edinburgh Magazine* (March 1869) holds its own with the best of nineteenth-century literary criticism and is ripe for rediscovery. Her essay is certainly more original than Scott's *Lives of the Novelists*, more sensitive than Coleridge's "Lectures on Shakespeare," more carefully reasoned than Thackeray's *English Humourists*, less academic than Hazlitt's "Standard Novels and Romances," and as well-written as any of them.

Oliphant's long article on Richardson, with passing references to Fielding along the way, is easily a hundred years ahead of its time.

It is essentially the first major feminist statement on *Clarissa*, and Oliphant's perspective, politics, and writing style may seem to us the most "modern" of all the nineteenth-century statements on Richardson. Her central position, that Victorian women's domestic spheres are sources of power separate but equal to men's greater social mobility, was innovative when Nancy Armstrong published *Desire and Domestic Fiction* in 1987.

Oliphant, who lived from 1828 to 1897, was widowed early and left with a large dependent family. She supported herself, her children and her relatives by writing ninety-eight novels, over fifty short stories, and over three hundred articles. She has been called "easily the most prolific writer of the nineteenth century," and this is in an *age* of prolific authors.[180] She is perhaps best remembered for her "Chronicles of Carlingford" series, including the novels *Salem Chapel* (1863), *The Perpetual Curate* (1864), *Miss Majoribanks* (1866), and *Phoebe Junior* (1876). She admits in her autobiography that a majority of her novels are formulaic romances written only for the money. Most of her articles were published in *Blackwood's* magazine, where she was also an editor and proofreader (although never a salaried employee). Subsequent generations have given her novels little serious attention and her criticism even less. Today, academic interest in women's autobiographies has made Oliphant most familiar for her diary, which relates in detailed honesty the personal and professional pressures placed on a busy nineteenth-century woman writer. She describes herself in the diary as

> very small, very obscure . . . rather a failure all round, never securing any small affection, and throughout my life, though I have had all the usual experiences of women, never impressing anybody,—what a droll little complaint! . . . I acknowledge that there is nothing in me—a fat, little, commonplace woman, rather tongue-tied—to impress any one.[181]

There is certainly nothing "commonplace" or "tongue-tied" about her essay on Richardson. Beginning with the conventional comparison of Richardson to Fielding, Oliphant quickly moves on to contrast the masculine attractiveness of Lovelace and Tom Jones. Oliphant reverses generations of critical cliché by finding Richardson's conniving and self-interested villain to be an *attractive* model of social behavior. Finding a vicious rapist to be seductive is not necessarily a great step forward for feminism, of course, but Oliphant's methods here are more important than her conclusions. Oliphant sees Lovelace first and foremost as a rebel, a ruthless Machiavellian who uses all the tools at his disposal to assert his independence. Lovelace is described as a "woman's hero" not because he is a rapist, but ironically because his methods for overcoming limitations are the same as those offered to Victorian women limited to a repressive domestic lifestyle. She writes:

> Vice has to [Lovelace] all the attraction of intrigue, all the charm of sentiment and emotion, and that irresistible temptation of universal conquest which is so strong in a woman. Lovelace, like a true woman's hero, will not allow himself to be beat. . . . He is bent upon making himself the object of everybody's attentive admiration, wonder, or horror, as the case may be. . . . Society gazes and averts its eyes with a flutter of horror, yet is continually dazzled by the courageous front he bears. . . .[182]

Rather than following other critics and claiming that Tom Jones's good-heartedness is better than Lovelace's corruption, Oliphant claims that Jones's crude youthfulness pales beside Lovelace's sparkling vices. For the first time in Richardson criticism, a *woman* says what women find attractive in men, and Oliphant is scandalously honest. As she writes in some wonderfully descriptive prose, Tom Jones is

> infinitely nastier and infinitely more innocent than the subtle seducer. . . . To women, vice of the Tom Jones development is abhorrent and incomprehensible; while vice like that of Lovelace, which sets all the powers to work—which is full of plot and contrivance, of insatiable love of approbation and necessity for conquest, of emotion and mental excitement, and remorse and passion—is something which they can understand and realise.[183]

Oliphant now plays a trick based upon the sexual assumptions of her readers. She puts a new spin on the Victorian cultural assumptions that the "masculine" is always privileged over the "feminine," and questions the standard masculine assumption that academic learning is always privileged over domestic experience. For example, while Fielding was a young man at Eton learning the classics, Richardson spent his adolescence sharing secrets and writing love letters with a circle of needlepointing ladies, learning things much more useful to the early development of the novel. Oliphant writes of Richardson by writing ostensibly about Fielding:

> [S]o far as talk is concerned, the sisters of the boy upon whom we are spending heaps of money at Eton and Oxford, are not only much pleasanter to talk to, but very much more ready and better qualified in many

instances to take a part in those mild intellectual encounters, those little incursions over the borders of metaphysics, discussions of motives,
sentiments, cases of conscience, points of social honour, which are the
most prolific subjects of conversation, than—not only their brother, but
their brother's tutor, and all the learned community to which he belongs.[184]

Oliphant's urbane, conversational, and coolly ironic tone in these
passages looks far forward to the language of Virginia Woolf's essays
and *A Room of One's Own.*

Since Oliphant is among the first of Richardson's readers to reject the simplistic condemnation of Lovelace by rejecting moralistic
criticism and embracing a personalized reader-response, she is
unique in her century for being able to respect *both* Clarissa and
Lovelace. Oliphant bases her unqualified admiration of Clarissa on
the sophistication, feminine insight, and inexplicable inspiration of
her portrait, as opposed to the male Victorian critics who usually
scoff at Richardson's crude and prurient epistolary technique. Her
appreciation of Lovelace, on the other hand, is based on a frank
acknowledgment of perhaps the ultimate Victorian taboo: a woman's irrational, amorous, and amoral desire.

The achievement is all the more impressive when we remember
the Victorian habit of padding the authors' biographies, as we have
seen in the work of Thackeray, Collier, Stephen, and others. Oliphant subtly inverts the technique to her own rhetorical advantage.
The essay begins by drawing contrasting biographical portraits of
Richardson and Fielding as contemporaries. She portrays a delicate, dull, and domestic Richardson who prefers the company of
women and settles into the moderately profitable tedium of the
printing business. The younger and more worldly Fielding, by contrast, is a born gentleman, makes many friends, and performs brilliantly at Eton. "Fielding has a thousand advantages to start with
over our homely forefather. . . . And then his knowledge of the
world!" she writes. "Richardson's knowledge was only of good sort
of people, and secondary *litterateurs*, and—women, who are not
the world, as everybody knows."[185]

Not only is the "feminine" privileged over the "masculine," but
along with it come domestic experience over academic learning,
meditation over action, and Richardson over Fielding. Up to this
early point in her essay Oliphant has offered nothing to seriously
challenge the expectations of her readers. But she continues:

[T]he observers of the present day might be tempted, in the spirit of an
age which inquires into everything, to ask why Covent Garden should

teach knowledge of the world more effectually than Salisbury Court, and whether players and debauchees throw more light upon the workings of human nature than honest and reasonable souls,—this is so entirely taken for granted by critics, that it would be vain to make any stand against so all-prevailing a theory. . . . The triumph of the old fogey over the splendid young adventurer is complete in every particular. It may be said that Richardson did not mean it, but that in no way detracts from the glory of his originality. Shakespeare probably did not mean it either.[186]

Using the Richardson versus Fielding debate as her springboard, Oliphant then turns to attack other relative values traditionally assigned to the "feminine"/"masculine" dichotomy, quoting Thackeray specifically, and exposing the connection between sexism and Richardson's critical downslide: "the society and confidence of women has an irresistible charm," and a man who can appreciate it "is by no means of necessity a milksop, as society in general is good enough to suppose."[187]

So, to summarize briefly, Oliphant is the first critic of *Clarissa* to write from a woman's emotional perspective, claim that women have a greater source of novelistic power than men, admit that Lovelace is attractive, and assert that Richardson's masculinity is not at stake simply because he has an appreciation for the subtleties of female society. This is enough to give the article its historical significance, but not quite enough to make it brilliant. Oliphant's *coup de gras*, the twist of the knife that allows the piece to undercut cultural assumptions even while it makes them, is her narrative method: the entire essay is written from the persona of a man.

Oliphant published this essay anonymously. In her autobiography she describes *Blackwood's* magazine as the "most manly and masculine of magazines."[188] It is safe to assume, therefore, that *Blackwood's* readers would believe the articles to be written by a man unless specifically told otherwise. Oliphant did not *always* write anonymously, however, and her reasons in this case may have been to protect her career and her employer. In a letter to her friend and publisher John Blackwood (one of her only two surviving references to this article), Oliphant writes, "I suppose I ought to be ashamed that . . . as a matter of taste I actually prefer Lovelace to Tom Jones! . . . Pray don't tell of me; if I betray my sentiments in public they shall be laid upon the heavily burdened shoulders of what Clarissa would call 'my sex,' and your contributor shall sneer at them as in duty bound."[189] Whatever the reason Oliphant chose to publish anonymously, she nevertheless uses the default assumption of a male authorship as the source for the irony that drives her point home. According to Elisabeth Jay,

> [S]he uses her disguise for an act of sabotage. Encoded in this overtly male essay are the highest terms of praise her critical vocabulary knows: the words that are on the face of it terms of abuse, such as 'ordinary', or 'commonplace', are . . . the precise source of interest to the discerning novel reader. By the time she reaches a discussion of the individual novels she has contrived to shake the conventional critical vocabulary so free of its normal pejorative associations that she can afford to claim that the greatness of *Clarissa* resides partly in Richardson's creation of Lovelace as 'a feminine ideal'. . . . In this article Mrs Oliphant appropriated the male voice to educate male readers into an understanding of the woman's point of view.[190]

In other words, this female reviewer uses a male voice to praise a male author who uses a female voice.

Oliphant's article is significant not only for what it tells us about Richardson and his novel, but also for what it tells us about Oliphant and her novels. For example, when Oliphant reverses critical expectations by asserting that Richardson's early experiences with the "needlepointing ladies" make him a more qualified novelist than Fielding's distinguished experiences at Eton, it is worth remembering that Oliphant herself, the author of ninety-eight novels and three hundred nonfiction articles, was largely self-educated. From a personal point of view, however, Oliphant's attraction to Lovelace is completely unexpected. She seemed to have little "desire" of her own. Oliphant was widowed after a very short marriage and spent the rest of her life self-consciously playing the role of a dour Victorian matron. For all her hundreds of essays and books, a friend of her sons remembered her as "always a gracious lady, apparently occupied with nothing more serious than some piece of delicate needlework, always ready to pour out tea and listen patiently to my selfish confidences."[191] Oliphant even writes of herself in the autobiography as primarily a housekeeper and mother. But behind the tea parties and the gossip expected of a nineteenth-century woman of station was an ambitious, creative, and passionate imagination.[192] If it was taboo for a nineteenth-century woman book reviewer to admit this about herself, then she could praise it in the work of a *another* author of a *different* century and a *different* sex. Oliphant writes of Richardson:

> He had lived half a century in the commonplace world before any one suspected him of the possession of genius. Ordinary duties, common-

place labour, had filled up his fifty years. He had gone through what it was natural to suppose would be the hardest affliction of a man conscious of an original gift of his own, the printing and publication of much rubbish of other people's with the greatest patience, and had, to all appearance, occupied himself with his own life without any thought of reproducing its mysteries for the edification of others. He had been respectable and helpful and friendly from his cradle. . . . None of those irregularities which are supposed to belong to genius, existed in this homely man. . . . And yet, strangely enough, when the late blossom came, it was not a humble specimen of a class already known, but something entirely new and original.[193]

Oliphant had never written anything quite like this before, and she would never write anything quite like this again. Those few critics who give serious attention to Oliphant's book reviews inexplicably tend to agree with John Stock Clarke: "When Mrs. Oliphant chooses to voice an opinion she expresses orthodox Victorian views. . . ."[194] Oliphant was against women's suffrage, firmly rejected all radical feminist views in a series of articles on the "Condition of Women" in 1856 and 1858, and did not particularly care for women's fiction. Oddly enough, two years before her review of Richardson, she objects to the plots of novels often written by and for women where the heroines "marry their grooms in fits of sensual passion" and "pray their lovers to carry them off from husbands and homes they hate," or in other words, plots which have a great deal in common with *Clarissa*. In her own novels she often expresses a gentle irony about men and their attraction to decorative women, but she creates no Lovelaces or Clarissas.

The final irony is that Oliphant's most famous review is not the one presently under discussion, but a notorious 1894 review of Hardy's *Jude the Obscure*, which she accused of being immoral and against the holy institution of marriage. Margarete Rubik writes, "The havoc caused by this attack can hardly be overestimated. Her literary work fell into oblivion, not, however, this unfortunate article, which reinforced the wide-spread impression that Oliphant was nothing but an outraged Victorian matron."[195] The source of Oliphant's displeasure is Hardy's heroine, Sue Bridehead. She represents for Oliphant a tendency, largely promoted by female novelists like George Eliot, of women having a mysterious moral influence "capable of subduing men by the sheer force of their high-minded convictions."[196] This is, of course, exactly the same situation between Pamela and Mr. B, as well as between Clarissa and Lovelace. Of *Clarissa*, however, Oliphant writes movingly,

The conception stands by itself amid all the conceptions of genius. . . .
Neither ancient nor modern woman has ever stood before us thus pale
and splendid in the shame which is not hers, sweet soul, though it kills
her. . . . Not a woman of her generation is half so true to nature; and
now that most of the women of her generation are dead and buried,
Clarissa lives, still surprising the warm tears of youth out of world-worn
eyes.[197]

Oliphant is not strictly a "Richardsonian." Her critical independence rests not only in her views of gender, but also in her resistance to commit to a blanket condemnation of her favorite author's rival. "Richardson has nothing which can compare with the conception of Parson Adams," writes Oliphant, crediting the Richardson/Fielding rivalry as the impetus for a literary masterpiece. "A greater compliment could not have been paid to Pamela."[198] Oliphant may find Richardson the more profound artist, but she finds Fielding in many ways the better writer. Oliphant reverses the critical trend of juxtaposing one author's strengths with the rival author's weaknesses. In Oliphant's criticism, Fielding's skill ultimately serves to highlight Richardson's genius:

In power and subtlety of conception [Lovelace] is as far superior to
[Jones] as he is inferior in execution. Perhaps the very inferiority of execution, indeed—the long-windedness, the wearisome prolixity, as contrasted with the incisive brilliant brevity and clearness of the rival moralist—does but bring out the more, the extraordinary advantage, in point of elevation and depth, which the one has over the other.[199]

Oliphant herself did not seem to think much of her essay, and there is little evidence it had any impact on the prevailing criticism of the day. Her only comment on it after the fact is a letter to Blackwood saying "I am very glad you like the paper on Richardson: I hoped you would."[200] Other reaction to the essay, when there is any, is usually just as blunt. There are only brief references in Sarah Smith's and Richard Hannaford's annotated Richardson bibliographies (Hannaford's is quite misleading), it is not mentioned at all in Eaves and Kimpel's biography, and Blanchard has only one evaluative comment: "Truly there is no accounting for tastes!"[201] An anonymous article called "Growth of the English Novel" in *The Quarterly Review*, however, draws directly on Oliphant's essay and plagiarizes a few of her statements.[202] Rubik refers to Oliphant's article in a footnote, but misses the point entirely by claiming that Oliphant's ironic style is probably borrowed from Henry Fielding! The only serious attention to this article has come only recently, when Elisabeth Jay devotes a page to it in her book *Mrs Oliphant: 'A Fiction to Herself': A Literary Life*. Jay briefly summarizes the article and comments on the satiric properties of the male persona, but she does not seem to recognize the uniqueness and significance of the article in the full context of Richardson's reception history.

Type-Two Readers: William Hazlitt

Since the nineteenth century is the time when creative writers are most active in the Richardson/Fielding debate, it is appropriate that the most influential single comments come from Coleridge, Scott and Thackeray. It is also fitting, therefore, that the most influential critic on the issue in general is Hazlitt, an essayist who crossed that vague line between literary criticism and literature itself. Hazlitt has restrained, intelligent praise for both rivals. Fielding, however, seems to be not only his favorite author of the two, but also his favorite author of all. After Hazlitt's longstanding argument with Lamb over the comparative merits of Fielding and Smollett (Hazlitt won), Hazlitt began a Richardson/Fielding debate with Coleridge (which Hazlitt also obviously won). Looking back on how their debates have informed ours, Hazlitt's primary contribution to Fielding's long-term reputation may turn out to be, in fact, his conversion of Coleridge.

According to the index of Hazlitt's *Works*, there is some allusion to Fielding during every year from 1814–30. As Blanchard writes, "Fielding had passed into the very texture of Hazlitt's mind."[203] The frequency of allusions to Fielding may lead us to overlook Hazlitt's appreciations of Richardson, however. (As with most other readers, thoughts of one author usually bring to mind thoughts of the other.) Blanchard claims that Hazlitt "never tried to set Richardson above Fielding," but in direct comparisons the opposite is true.[204] Hazlitt is, along with Scott, one of the nineteenth century's best examples of how appreciations of Richardson or Fielding individually are significantly transformed when they are read as a pair, and read as answers to one another's questions.

Hazlitt is the antithesis of Scott in terms of the Richardson/Fielding opposition. Whereas Scott was a great admirer of Richardson whose direct comparisons always ended up promoting Fielding, Hazlitt is a great admirer of Fielding whose direct comparisons always end up promoting Richardson.[205] In "Standard Novels and Romances" (1815), an essay largely devoted to the enthusiastic praise of Fielding, Hazlitt finds Fielding derivative when compared to Richardson's original genius: "Fielding is more like Don Quixote than Gil Blas. . . . Richardson can scarcely be called an imitator of any one." [206] Later in the essay Hazlitt writes that Fielding understands the principles of the human heart, "but he had not the same power of speculating upon their possible results, and combining them in certain ideal forms of passion and imagination, which was Richardson's real excellence." In other words, Fielding "has none of the fine pathos of Richardson."[207] Finally, it is only a powerful Fielding bias that could lead Blanchard to misread the following passage from "Standard Novels and Romances" so thoroughly that he could claim Hazlitt "never tried to set Richardson above Fielding":

> It is no a very difficult undertaking to class Fielding or Smollett;—the one as an observer of the characters of human life, the other as a describer of its various eccentricities. But it is by no means so easy to dispose of Richardson, who was neither an observer of the one, nor a describer of the other; but who seemed to spin his materials entirely out of his own brain, as if there had been nothing existing in the world beyond the little room in which he sat writing. . . . This kind of high finishing from imagination is an anomaly in the history of human genius; and certainly nothing so fine was ever produced by the same accumulation of minute parts.[208]

The only essay in which Hazlitt appears equally magnanimous about both Richardson and Fielding is "On Reading Old Books." Hazlitt turns for "solace" to random pages of *Peregrine Pickle* or *Tom Jones*. Everywhere he reads he finds "the same delightful, busy, bustling scene as ever, and feel myself the same as when I was first introduced into the midst of it."[209] In the same essay he makes the exceptionally iconoclastic statement that he likes "the longest of [Richardson's] novels best, and think no part of them tedious; nor should I ask to have any thing better to do than to read them from beginning to end." As with Fielding's novels, re-reading always brings back the original pleasant reader responses: Hazlitt looks forward to reading Richardson's novels until "every word and syllable relating to the bright Clarissa, the divine Clementina, the beautiful Pamela, 'with every trick and line of their sweet favour,' were once more 'graven in my heart's tables.' "[210]

Type-Three Readers

Lady Bradshaigh writes a letter to Richardson on 10 October 1748, threatening to cast a spell his way if he did not give *Clarissa* a happy ending: "May the hatred of all the young, beautiful and virtuous for ever be your portion! and may your eyes never behold anything but age and deformity! May you meet with applause only from envious old maids, surly bachelors, and tyrannical parents!"[211] Richardson's nineteenth-century reception among general readers may lead one to suspect Lady Bradshaigh's curse had come true. As the history of literature became more a strictly academic pursuit and as contemporary novelists captured the lion's share of the reading public with their own demanding novels, Richardson and Fielding found fewer general readers as the century progressed.

Richardson fares particularly badly. Nineteenth-century criticism of Richardson's novels almost always includes plot summaries, indicating that Richardson was less familiar to general readers. (Plot summaries invariably take away space from intellectually engaging criticism, another element contributing to Fielding's more positive critical reception.) According to Smith's and Hannaford's bibliographies, there are no comparisons of Richardson to Fielding from 1859 to 1868, and no references to Richardson at all from 1839 to 1840, in 1864, and from 1866 to 1867. When there are comments about Richardson, many of them include the observation that Richardson, despite his unquestioned canonical position, does not retain a significant readership. Tuckerman writes, "Samuel Richardson will take his place among the great authors who are much admired and little read, whose works every educated person should have heard of, but upon which very few would like to be examined."[212] Or, as Stephen observes, "Every one knows the names of Sir Charles Grandison and Clarissa Harlowe. They are amongst the established types which serve to point a paragraph. . . . [B]ut the volumes in which they are described remain for the most part in undisturbed repose, sleeping peacefully."[213] Stephen's lament that Richardson remains unread also contains a foreshadowing of a new kind of reader who emerges at the end of the century—the overburdened undergraduate. Unlike Lady Bradshaigh, Stephen would no doubt be pleased that his wish *did* come true:

We should like to see a return of the number of persons who have fairly read to the end of the *Faery Queen*, or of *Paradise Lost*, who could pass an examination off-hand even in books of greater claims to popularity. . . . Richardson's slumber may be deeper than that of most men of equal fame, but it is not quite unprecedented.[214]

Testimony of Richardson's peaceful repose is not limited to any single part of the century. Scott writes in 1821 that Richardson "may, in the present generation, be only paying, by comparative neglect, the price of the very high reputation which he enjoyed during his own age."[215] (As I argue in chapter two, some readers ironically reject Richardson or Fielding precisely because of their popularity.) "Who reads Richardson?" asks an anonymous reviewer in *Blackwood's* magazine, April 1824. "[H]ow few, now-a-days, will wade, or ought to wade, through such a heap of lumber as Clarissa Harlowe . . . or to endure the interminable prosing of the Cedar Parlour in Grandison?"[216] Whitwell Elwin, a critic who is also a member of the Anglican ministry which once advocated Richardson's works so strongly, writes in 1855, "[F]ew now wipe away the dust which has gathered [on Richardson's] voluminous stories, or else, repelled by the tedious trivialities and mawkish prosings [they] prematurely close the book."[217] In 1868 Edward Fitzgerald writes to W.F. Pollock that critics still allude to Richardson, but few have actually read him and probably never will: "[I] am sure I could (with a pair of Scissors) launch old Richardson again: we shouldn't go off the stocks easy . . . amid the jeers of Reviewers who had never read the original."[218]

Fielding is often linked with Richardson when critics mention the overall neglect of eighteenth-century novels. As Traill has Fielding whisper to Richardson in the afterlife, "They have raised a statue to me, and for aught I know they may raise one to you, but— *they do not read either of us.*"[219] Despite Fielding's relative popularity with the critics, general readers are often pressured to feel embarrassed about reading Fielding. Hazlitt states as early as 1828, "You are asked if you like Fielding as if it were a statuteable offence."[220] By 1843 the situation is not much better, according to the theologian George Borrow. It has "long been the fashion" to reject Fielding "in public" while reading him "in secret."[221] Lady Louisa Stuart, Lady Mary Wortley Montagu's granddaughter, writes in an 1831 letter, "Mrs. S. and I have been quite alone these . . . days, and are not at all tired of one another, nor of a wicked book we have been reading (TOM JONES if you won't tell)."[222] Finally, as Thackeray has Colonel Newcome say in *The Newcomes* (1854), "'Tom Jones,' sir; 'Joseph Andrews!' sir, he cried, twirling his mustachios. 'I read them when I was a boy, when I kept other bad company, and did other low and disgraceful things, of which I'm ashamed now.' "[223]

There are very few surviving primary sources for general readers reacting to Richardson and Fielding as a dichotomized pair. The comments of four painters—Ruskin, Haydon, Frith and North-cote—are cited above, and there is also Lady Louisa Stuart's letter. Other records of general readers comparing Richardson or Fielding come from other novelists or from critics. These second-hand reports of general readers are still valuable, however, as they can demonstrate the social positions of the general readers, the availability of the novels, the prejudices of the critics, and the horizon of expectation for the literary culture at large.

For example, Birrell provides an extremely rare account, worth quoting at length, of a general reader encountering *Pamela* in 1892. Richardson's novel was not in print in 1892 and was available only in used bookshops. Birrell's patronizing, sexist, and satiric attitude toward Richardson's reader goes a long way toward illuminating the expectations which many critics brought to Richardson's texts and passed on to general readers. If we can believe his account, Richardson's hypnotic power over general readers, especially *Pamela*'s originally intended audience of domestic servant girls, is still intact:

> Two months ago a cook in a family of my acquaintance, one Saturday evening, when like old Caspar 'her work was done,' suddenly bethought herself of *Pamela*, a book she had not read since girlhood. Rest was impossible—get it forthwith she must. . . . The spell of *Pamela* was upon her, and out she sallied, arrayed in her majesty, to gratify the soul's desire. Had she been a victim of what is called 'Higher Education of Women,' and therefore in the habit of frequenting orthodox bookshops, she would doubtless have found the quest at so late an hour as hopeless as that of the *Holy Grail*; but she was not that sort of person, and the shop she had in mind, and whither she straightway bent her steps, was a small stationer's where are vended *Family Heralds* and *Ballads* and *Pamelas*; for the latter, in cheap sixpenny guise . . . is a book which is constantly reprinted for sale amongst the poor. The cook, having secured her prize, returned home in triumph, nor was a dinner worthy of the name to be had until Pamela's virtue was rewarded.[224]

With employers like Birrell, we can perhaps sympathize with the cook's feeling that Pamela's struggle against Mr. B is more important than cooking dinners worthy of the name.

Birrell states that *Pamela* was available only in "cheap sixpenny guise" and only in shops where "victims of Higher Education of Women" would never go. The unavailability of texts to educated readers, the ones most likely to record their receptions, is a contributing factor in Richardson's nineteenth-century critical decline. Since Richardson's novels *were* "constantly reprinted for sale amongst the poor," however, we should not assume that Richardson's rejection by the critics necessarily means there was a proportional rejection from general readers. To the contrary, only "the poor" seem to have access to them by 1892, with the obvious implication being that Richardson must have had at least some measure of general readership. Richard Altick's research on the nineteenth-century second-hand book trade supports Birrell's account of the cook's purchase: "A regular practice in the middle of the century . . . was to break up sets of the collected *Spectator* papers or of a multi-volumed old novel like *Pamela*; sold a volume at a time, these went more quickly, and at better prices, than in sets."[225]

Earlier in the century, general readers had the lending libraries as their main channel of access to Richardson and Fielding. Altick describes these institutions expanding into the lower classes of society as the "fashion" for leisure reading spread: "Usually charging a rental of a penny a volume, they were conducted in both London and the provincial towns as side lines to the barbering, confectionery, news-vending, stationery, and tobacco trades."[226] The London Statistical Society did a survey of the numbers and types of books in ten circulating libraries in 1838. Their report is as good a portrait of general readers' subject matter in the 1830s as we are likely to get, and the categories themselves reveal much about early nineteenth-century literary expectations:

Novels by Walter Scott, and Novels in imitation of him; Galt, etc. (166)

Novels by Theodore Hook, Lytton Bulwer, etc. (41)

Novels by Captain Marryat, Cooper, Washington Irving, etc. (115)

Voyages, Travels, History, and Biography (136)

Novels by Miss Edgeworth, and Moral and Religious Novels (49)

Works of a Good Character, Dr. Johnson, Goldsmith, etc. (27)

Romances, Castle of Otranto, etc. (76)

Fashionable Novels, well known (439)

Novels of the lowest character, being chiefly imitations of Fashionable Novels, containing no good, although probably nothing decidedly bad (1008)

Miscellaneous Old Books, Newgate Calendar, etc. (86)

Lord Byron's Works, Smollett's do., Fielding's do., Gil Blas, etc. (39)

Books decidedly bad (10)[227]

Richardson is not mentioned specifically (but would possibly fall into the "Works of a Good Character" category). Fielding falls into a dubious category which must have been self-explanatory at the time, perhaps suggesting the picaresque (if we can assume Byron's "Don Juan"). Fielding's association with Le Sage and others is a step up in his critical reputation: fifty years earlier any official government agency would have filed his works under "Books decidedly bad."

The only secondhand example I have found of general readers enjoying Fielding is from William Chambers. Chambers recalls his years as a bookseller's apprentice in Edinburgh in 1820, when, for the payment of a hot roll, he would stop by a baker's shop each morning from 5:00 to 7:30 A.M. and read to the cook and his two sons while they kneaded dough. "The baker was not particular as to subject. All he stipulated for was something droll and laughable." Chambers read them Smollett and Fielding, and the cooks reported "unqualified satisfaction."[228]

Foreign Reaction

There is no better gauge of Richardson's nineteenth-century decline than the lack of commentary on his novels in Germany. As I have shown in chapter two, Richardson's eighteenth-century reception in Germany was even more enthusiastic than his early reception in England. In the nineteenth century Richardson began to seem, in the words of Friedrich Schelling, "diffuse and pedantic." Fielding's novels, when they are noticed at all, seem a mere "picture of manners."[229] German Idealism was a powerful force in the period, partly as a reaction to the rationality and objectivity of the eighteenth century. This Idealism is reflected in the 1818 lectures of the major Romantic critic of the period, August Schlegel. Richardson's descent was so rapid that Schlegel has only mild praise for Richardson's imagination and dislikes the entire secular spirit which produced novels like *Tom Jones*.[230]

The critic Abraham Kästner is the last of the great German Richardsonians. After reading *Pamela* in German, French, and English, as well as translating *Sir Charles Grandison*, he compares Amelia's virtues unfavorably to Pamela's. F.C. Schlosser's *History of the Eighteenth Century* (1843) balances Kästner's praise of Richardson, giving the laurels to Fielding and claiming that the sentimental craze for which Richardson is partly responsible only served to delay Fielding's German popularity.[231]

"The French have been its most enthusiastic admirers, but I don't know whether their present admiration is more than traditional, like their set phrases about their own classics," writes George Eliot.[232] Eliot had good reason to be skeptical about Richardson's nineteenth-century French reception. Richardson's canonical position is secure as the French romance continues to flourish, but his works become frequent targets for casual criticism. Richardson's readership declined sharply (*Journal des Débats* 2 September 1831), and even Balzac found *Sir Charles Grandison* too long.[233]

Taine's *Histoire de la littérature anglaise* (1863) contains nineteenth-century France's most lengthy analysis of the Richardson and Fielding opposition, and it is in many ways typical of French consensus on Richardson and Fielding's contrasting temperaments. Taine is in line with the English instinct for creative biography, finding Fielding a high-living, passionate, impetuous man, someone who is "sure to dislike Richardson. He who loves expansive and liberal nature, drives from him like foes the solemnity, sadness, and pruderies of the Puritans."[234] Taine's vivid and superfluous descriptions of what he imagines to go on in *Tom Jones* reveal not only nineteenth-century impressions of the eighteenth century, but also French impressions of the hearty English. Taine's critical language is unusual for the nineteenth (or any other) century, more "literary" than Thackeray's, more Romantic than Hazlitt's, and close to the overt narrative fiction of Traill and Hunt:

> It is a pleasure to observe these potent stomachs; roast-beef goes down into them as to its natural place. . . . Fielding, turning his back on Richardson, opens up a domain as wide as that of his rival. What we call nature is this brood of secret passions, often malicious, generally vulgar, always blind, which tremble and fret within us. . . . [The characters] are so many, so strong, so interwoven, so ready to rise, break forth, be carried away, that their movements elude all our reasoning and our grasp.[235]

The precise point of Taine's high-flown language also, at times, eludes all our reasoning and our grasp. His criticism of Fielding becomes epistolary, an exercise in idealistic pre-Freudian psychology which sounds better than it enlightens:

> You are rendered heavy by your conscience, which drags you along step by step and low on the ground; you are afraid of your genius; you rein it in. . . . You flounder into emphatic and well-written phrases; you will not show nature as it is, as Shakspeare shows it, when, stung by passion

as by a hot iron, it cries out, rears, and plunges over your barriers. You cannot love it, and your punishment is that you cannot see it.[236]

Taine's second address finds Fielding just as insensible to delicate feeling, making the scenes of love "unnatural" and full of only "author's phrases."[237]

Another French critic of Richardson and Fielding who likewise finds both good and bad in each author is Anne Louise de Staël-Holstein. She asserts Richardson stands "first in rank" in English fiction, but she is also prepared to concede that *Tom Jones* "cannot be considered simply as a novel: the abundance of philosophical ideas, the hypocrisy of society, and the contrast of natural qualities are brought into action with an infinity of art."[238] For lengthy analysis and unqualified support, Richardson's French allies have narrowed to one: the distinguished historian J.J. Jusserand consistently prefers Richardson's sentiment, characterization, and resonant literary influence to Fielding's coarse and shallow narratives. Jusserand is quick to admit, however, that history has a way of reversing its opinions on Richardson and Fielding, and that Gibbon's prediction that Fielding may outlive the Austrian empire may indeed come true.[239] (It has.)

Richardson's works fared better in Spain. At the turn of the century, *Clarissa* was reincarnated in several novelistic, dramatic, and operatic adaptations. The Richardson revival, perhaps spurred by Jules Janin's adaptation of *Clarissa* in France, culminated with a drama which ran for one hundred performances in 1847.[240] An anonymous author in *Memorial Literario* (1801) goes so far as to place Richardson above Fielding, and Fielding above the great Spanish literary hero himself: "Fielding can be compared very well to Cervantes, and even surpass him. But which novelist can be compared to Richardson, the Homer (so to speak) of the novel?"[241]

The most prominent nineteenth-century American critics on Richardson and Fielding are Wilbur Cross, Bayard Tuckerman, and Sidney Lanier. Cross wrote sporadically on Richardson and Fielding before 1894, but his primary contributions begin with works which will be discussed in the next chapter. Tuckerman's various comments on the coarseness of the eighteenth century, its slow-moving time, Fielding's effects on young readers, comedy and tragedy, and Richardson's lack of readership (all from *A History of Prose Fiction*, 1882) are discussed above. I have saved Lanier's *The English Novel* (1881) for individual consideration, however, because his is the only American work which betrays signs of a specifically American conception. Lanier's comments on Richardson and Fielding demonstrate a class-based criticism which is relatively rare even in high-Victorian England. Perhaps Lanier is not writing from his own personal literary horizon, but in exaggerated imitation of what he imagines to be the *British* horizon: "It may be that the high birth of Fielding . . . had something to do with his opposition to Richardson, who was the son of a joiner."[242] Lanier finds *Clarissa* "hideous," *Grandison* less so, but finds Squire Allworthy appealing for his suspiciously American moral capitalism. Allworthy performs his good deeds so he might "obtain the largest possible credit which he found himself forced to buy against the inevitable journey into those foreign parts lying beyond the waters of death."[243] Generally, though, Lanier is not overly sympathetic with Richardson, Fielding, or any other eighteenth-century novelist. "I cannot help believing that much of the praise is simply well-meaning ignorance," Lanier writes. "I protest that I can read none of these books without feeling as if my soul had been in the rain, draggled, muddy, miserable."[244]

Conclusion

This chapter ends with G. B. Hill's *Writers and Readers*, Augustine Birrell's lecture on Richardson (in *Res Judicatæ*), and an edition of the *Saturday Review*, all published in 1892 and 1893. There are several reasons, practical and symbolic, why Richardson and Fielding's nineteenth century ends shortly before everyone else's. Practically, a new type of reader and a new type of literary criticism were emerging. Birrell's book is one of the last of a breed. Loose collections of lectures and essays written by magazine contributors begin to be replaced with methodical, chronological, and opinionated literary textbooks written by professional academics. The next substantial criticism of Richardson and Fielding after 1892 comes from Walter Raleigh's *The English Novel* (1894), a survey written primarily for a new type of reader: the inexperienced, full-time university student taking survey courses in English literature.

Symbolically, this chapter ends with the near appearance of several statements that summarize how far Fielding has eclipsed Richardson since the days when his novels were blamed for earthquakes. George B. Hill, a committed Richardsonian and editor of Johnson, admits, "For one reader of [Richardson's] novels there are perhaps ten readers of his rival's, neglected though Fielding is."[245] The *Saturday Review* of 22 April 1893 runs an entire article on "The Morals of Fielding," looking back with confident ease over the entire history of the controversy and finding it wrong-headed and laughable. "Fielding's real position is manifestly this—a prodigious pother, he says, is made about one single point of conduct; that saved, all the rest—generosity, kindness, charity, goodness of heart—are almost neglected," the author writes, seeing beyond the horizon of the Victorian era and peering into the twentieth century looming ahead. "So he draws characters who have his favourite and noble virtues, but who are decidedly lax just where the other moralists are stringent. . . . He leaves the world to judge between them and the verjuice virgins who now write novels of Purity." The fact that Robert Louis Stevenson once said that *Tom Jones* is "dull and dirty" now makes the "eyes of amazement to open wide."[246]

Birrell has the final question which brings us to an answer in the next chapter: "Regarded merely as writers, there can, I suppose, be no real rivalry between Fielding and Richardson. . . . No wonder *Tom Jones* is still running; where, I should like to know, is the man bold enough to stop him?"[247]

4

The Twentieth Century: Raleigh's *The English Novel* to Watt's *The Rise of the Novel*, 1894–1957

> *To the eighteenth century writer the critic was a noxious worm, a venomous reptile, between whom and the novelist was enmity unquenchable. Now the relations have changed; no longer does the critic bruise the heels of the fathers of the English novel, but the head of him who finds fault. Even that perhaps is allowing him too much dignity. He is not so much the champion proving the love of his master on the body of his opponent, as an humble "barker" standing at the gangplank of the three-decker, begging idlers on the quay to embark on the voyage.*
>
> —R.A.P. Utter, "On the Alleged Tediousness
> of Defoe and Richardson"

"IT IS THE TASK OF THE LITERARY HISTORIAN TO WORK HIS WAY BEYOND the events of authorship, publication, and reception to some estimate of fundamental values," writes Alan D. McKillop in 1956. McKillop claims that twentieth-century readers are in a better position than their eighteenth-century counterparts to appreciate the novels of Richardson and Fielding "without exaggeration" of their differences.[1] Criticism of Richardson and Fielding in the first half of the twentieth century certainly makes many estimates of "fundamental values," but it makes no significant departure from eighteenth- and nineteenth-century criticism in working its way "beyond the events of authorship, publication, and reception." Twentieth-century readers do tend to view Richardson and Fielding as very different kinds of moralists, but it is still very premature to claim that readers judge the novelists "without exaggeration."

In terms of the rise-and-fall of the literary rivalry, the early twentieth century makes a smooth transition from the late nineteenth century. Readers admire Fielding much more widely and enthusiastically than they admire Richardson. The *Saturday Review* of 20

April 1907 indicates the times, declaring an unqualified "victory" for Fielding and stating that there has been a complete reversal in the Richardson/Fielding opposition since the eighteenth century. Early twentieth-century readers may arrive at many of the same pro-Fielding conclusions as late nineteenth-century readers, but they do so for some very different reasons.

As I have stated in the previous chapters, the distance between implied readers and actual readers increases as Richardson's and Fielding's novels recede into the past. One reason for Fielding's rise and Richardson's fall between 1894 and 1957 may be the amount of negative capability required for modern readers to assume the personas of Richardson and Fielding's implied readers: while educated, urbane gentlemen-critics still exist in large numbers for Fielding, it is safe to say that the early twentieth century produced fewer anxious servant girls and dowered virgins (and those that remained did not, as far as we can tell, turn in large numbers to Richardson's novels). When Richardson and Fielding became required rather than recommended reading in the early days of English departments, readers for *both* authors tended to be educated, urbane gentlemen-critics (or at least gentlemen-critics-in-training).

While Richardson and Fielding's literary status remains fairly secure during the transition from the nineteenth century to the twentieth, what changes most is their types of readers and the channels through which the readers carry their influence. If general readers of Richardson and Fielding had their greatest impact in the eighteenth century and creative writers their greatest impact in the nineteenth, then critics have their greatest impact as Richardson and Fielding become canonized by the twentieth-century academy. Keeping with Jauss's order of readers, however, it is important to acknowledge from the beginning the significant critical contributions made by Richardson and Fielding's fellow novelists.

Type-One Readers: Creative Writers

Novelists still read Richardson and Fielding in the first half of the century, but there were no ongoing debates such as the one between Coleridge and Lamb to keep the dichotomy alive and relevant. Seldom are Richardson and Fielding mentioned in a direct comparison. Just as the dominance of Scott and Dickens often distracted nineteenth-century novelists from Richardson and Fielding, early twentieth-century novelists apparently felt other, more pressing influences in the innovative early years of high modernism.

Judging by the number of allusions to each author, Fielding is more influential than Richardson. Authors who have positive, negative or mixed reactions to Fielding without mentioning Richardson include Samuel Butler (1897, neg.), George Bernard Shaw (1898, pos.), Henry James (1899, mixed), Algernon C. Swinburne (1902, pos.), George Moore (1903, neg.), Clement Shorter (1907, pos.), G.K. Chesterton (1908 and 1913, pos.), Owen Wister (1908, pos.), Bret Hart (1910, pos.), H.G. Wells (1911 and 1912, pos.), John Galsworthy (1912, pos.), Mary Sinclair (1912, neg.), John B. Yeats (1914 and 1921, pos.), Eden Phillpotts (1915, pos.), W.L. George (1918, mixed), Frank Norris (pos., 1924), E.M. Forster (1927, mixed), George Orwell (1944, pos.) and Graham Greene (1951, pos.). Writers who allude to Richardson without mentioning Fielding make a much smaller coalition, including Alfred, Lord Tennyson (1897, pos.), W.H. Hudson (1915, neg.), and E.M. Forster (1927, pos.). Elizabeth Bowen has brief, conventional entries on each novelist as part of her *English Novelists* (1942), referring to Richardson at one point as "a pursy, not interesting little man."[2]

In stark contrast to the forceful and colorful comments of Johnson, Coleridge and Thackeray, the comments of twentieth-century creative writers about either author tend to be passing references serving as illustrations of something else. There are a few notable exceptions, such as W.H. Hudson's animated essay on Richardson in *A Quiet Corner in a Library* where *Sir Charles Grandison* is found desperately dull and much praise of the "nauseating" *Clarissa* is judged "wild talk, reckless and absurd."[3] The statement that has surprised the most readers, however, comes from the distinguished drama critic George Bernard Shaw in 1898. Whereas Fielding's dramas traditionally receive little serious critical attention, Shaw thinks Fielding is "the greatest dramatist, with the single exception of Shakespear, produced by England between the Middle Ages and the nineteenth-century." Ever since the Licensing Act drove Fielding to switch genres, Shaw believes, "the English novel has been one of the glories of literature, whilst the English drama has been its disgrace."[4] (No doubt Shaw felt that a Fielding-esque satiric dramatist would soon emerge to restore English drama to its former glory—someone that the public might recognize as Shaw himself, for example.)

Only two novelists have offered substantial, extended contributions to the Richardson/Fielding debate. The first of these, Sir Arthur Conan Doyle, famous for the intricacies of his plotting and the guest speaker at the Fielding bicentennial celebration in 1907, was a devoted Richardsonian. (One is perhaps reminded of the paradox that Robert Louis Stevenson, the author of pirate adventures, found it inconceivable that anyone could prefer Defoe to Richardson.) Doyle's *Through the Magic Door* (1907) compares Richardson and Fielding at length and states "There indeed is a competition of giants."[5]

Doyle's criticism is partial to Richardson, but it is not partisan: he freely admits the areas in which Fielding is Richardson's superior or equal. Doyle finds Richardson's epistolary style improbable but finds Fielding's omniscient narrative breaking "all the fetters which bound his rival," giving the novel a new "freedom and personal authority."[6] Fielding is Richardson's equal in an area where no one but Doyle has ever pronounced a draw: the characterization of women. "In this respect our rival authors may claim a tie, for I could not give a preference to one set of these perfect creatures over another," Doyle writes.[7] Where Richardson and Fielding begin to differ, however, is in their portrayal of men. Fielding's men lack even "one touch of distinction, of spirituality, of nobility," and when Doyle compares Tom Jones to the "high-souled" Sir Charles Grandison, Doyle finds that "the plebeian printer has done very much better than the aristocrat."[8] Doyle's preference for Grandison leads him to challenge the "realistic" school of criticism inherited from the late nineteenth century. "But 'you must draw the world as it is,'" writes Doyle, recalling the real versus ideal dichotomy commonly used to privilege Fielding over Richardson. "Why must you? Surely it is just in selection and restraint that the artist is shown."[9]

Doyle's best-known character, the insightful and sophisticated Sherlock Holmes, offers some valuable clues to Doyle's motives for preferring Richardson to Fielding. Richardson is a careful investigator whereas Fielding is a crude entertainer: "He concerns himself with fine consistent character-drawing, and with a very searching analysis of the human heart," Doyle writes. "He condescends to none of those scuffles and buffetings and pantomime rallies which enliven, but cheapen, many of Fielding's pages."[10] Doyle imagines an eighteenth-century horizon conducive to Richardson, one that modern readers would do well to recover. The impression is not unlike the setting of many Victorian mystery stories: "In the lonely country-house, with few letters and fewer papers, do you suppose that the readers ever complained of the length of a book?"[11]

The second creative writer to make extensive observations on

Richardson and Fielding is the enduring British man of letters, Victor Sawdon Pritchett, best known for his broad and ironic short stories in *Cornhill Magazine* and *The New Statesman* in the 1920s, as well as for his editorial work for *The Oxford Book of Short Stories* (1981). In *The Living Novel* (1946), Pritchett finds little to say in favor of either novelist. Both are alike in "attacking the criminal violence and corruption that underlay the elegance of the time," but that is where the similarities end.[12] Richardson and Fielding differ sharply with their treatments of the two dominant early twentieth-century critical obsessions: sexuality and psychology.

The "muscular Christians" of the 1910s gave way to "a generation with a feminine preoccupation with sex and the fortune-telling scene of psychology," writes Pritchett. "If one was going to read the eighteenth-century novelists at all, Richardson was your man and the masculine tradition of Fielding was less congenial."[13] Richardson may have been "the man" for these new readers, but not for Pritchett. Richardson's masculinity is dubious at best: "[T]he author himself is a monster. . . . The smug, juicy, pedestrian little printer from Derbyshire, more or less unlettered, sits down at the age of fifty and instructs young girls in the art of managing their virtue to the best advantage." Richardson is, simply put, a dirty old man. "Is there not some other strain in this dull and prodigiously painstaking little man? There is. Samuel Richardson was mad. . . . Richardson is mad about sex." Pritchett at this point coins a critical phrase that recurs in various forms in subsequent Richardson criticism, recalling the impact of Coleridge's epigrammatic dichotomy of the sick room versus the open lawn in May. *Clarissa* is "a novel written about the world as one sees it through the keyhole."[14] Atypically, however, the negative connotation attached to Richardson's perceived "femininity" does not translate into a positive connotation for Fielding's perceived "masculinity." Speaking of Lovelace's "feminine" traits of intrigue and vanity, and perhaps borrowing a line from Margaret Oliphant, Pritchett writes that "a very masculine novelist like Fielding is too much a moralist, and too confidently a man, to catch a strain like that."[15] Pritchett dislikes Richardson's "madness," but Fielding is apparently not "mad" enough ("too confidently a man") to suit twentieth-century critics' hunt for the hidden, rebellious sexual subconscious of the artist.

Other critics take their cue from Fielding himself and pass their judgments on Richardson through parody and burlesque. Katharine Tynan's "The Romance of a Bookseller" in *The Cornhill Magazine* (1907) is particularly vicious. "Mr. R.," the author of *Clorinda*, is a pathetic middle-class novelist who loves his beautiful correspondent Dulcinea. Dulcinea eventually rejects Mr. R. in favor of the more generous and masculine Mr. F. The rest of the town hears the news, and they all agree that it was a mistake to admire *Clorinda* in the first place. Tynan's piece is remarkable not so much for its hackneyed opinions, but for its timing. If "The Romance of a Bookseller" had appeared one hundred years earlier while the Richardson backlash in the wake of the *Correspondence* was in full force, it no doubt would have reached a wider and more appreciative audience. In 1907, however, one wonders how many readers caught the allusions, and, of those, how many still found it necessary to use the strong medicine of satire to ridicule an author long dead and rarely read.

Type-Two Readers: Richardson and Fielding Go to College

In 1777 Hester Chapone predicted that the subtle "strokes of nature" in Richardson's novels which make their way into the heart will one day be "lost, or at least weakened, by the restraints of critical elegance."[16] Chapone was prophetic. The novels of both Richardson and Fielding increasingly become the domain of sophisticated and highly trained critics for whom "strokes of nature" and sentiment are, at least at first, of little significance.

As I have discussed in chapter two, James Beattie was among the very first to treat Fielding seriously as a literary artist. Effusive praise of Fielding's novels from a professor of Moral Philosophy came as a surprise to the original eighteenth-century audience. Augustan readers did not see popular novels, particularly *Fielding's* novels, as objects worthy of serious academic attention. By the mid-twentieth century, however, Fielding's novels (as well as Richardson's) are the subject of almost nothing else *but* academic attention. By the 1890s, community colleges and universities throughout England and America began to establish "English Studies" in their curricula.[17] A new genre of criticism begins a reciprocal relationship with a new kind of reader: undergraduates require general textbooks, and general textbooks in turn shape undergraduates' academic and literary tastes.

The new dynamic between critic and reader has its impact on the reception of both Richardson and Fielding. "The overwhelming ovation which Richardson received in his own century has subsided into the critical appreciation of the student of literature, and the number of his readers must be few," Williams can write as early as 1911.[18] For Fielding, "To speak of a twentieth-century view . . .

we must distinguish at the outset between readers and scholar-critics," writes Ronald Paulson. "Readers have never deviated from enjoyment of Fielding's novels. The critics are another matter."[19] According to Austin Dobson, however, the popular/critical opposition operating with Richardson's audience works the other way around: "Richardson's popularity with the public of the circulating library is never likely to revive again. . . . He must always find readers . . . with the students of literature."[20] D.J. Palmer argues that the expansion of English departments in universities has made literature and literary criticism commodities, leading to an ever-widening gap between type-two and type-three readers.[21] It is still not clear, however, which type of reader ultimately most influences the other.

The transformation of Richardson and Fielding's audience from creative writers and general readers into professional critics is virtually complete by mid-century. What readers remain from the first two types take on the critical posture of the latter: creative writers publish books of criticism, and student readers write formal argumentative essays. Rawson points out that the only non-critics to publish on Fielding between 1945 and 1962 are George Orwell, Kingsly Amis, and Rebecca West (Rawson overlooks Graham Greene in 1951). "Of these . . . Amis was, at the time, a university teacher anyway; and Rebecca West's essay was part of a series of lectures delivered at Yale." Rawson concludes, "One of the disadvantages of scholarly specialization . . . has been a partial loss of the broader perspectives of the cultivated amateur."[22] This "cultivated amateur" is precisely the type of reader most vocal on Richardson and Fielding throughout the eighteenth and up to the mid-nineteenth centuries.

The age of increasing academic specialization among professional readers has served at times both to undermine and reinforce the Richardson/Fielding opposition. Increasingly thorough and responsible biographical criticism provides clearer pictures of both Richardson and Fielding, presenting the two novelists as neither complete saints nor complete sinners; neither natural geniuses nor lucky hack-writers who stumbled across innovation. On the other hand, academia tends to pigeonhole authors into particular narratives of literary history that it preserves more for convenience than for accuracy. As Rawson writes of specialist criticism, there are risks of

> a false equation of the work of art with its ideological content, of undue systematizing, with its desire for a ship-shape coherence and its ten-

dency to resist the notion that authors, like other human beings, are sometimes inconsistent, moody, or ambiguous in their feelings.[23]

Nowhere is this more true than with the history of readers' reactions to Richardson and Fielding (or, for that matter, with the reactions of Richardson and Fielding to one another).

"The great fame of *Tom Jones* begins with later times, when neither private friendship nor malice nor envy could warp the reader's judgment," writes Wilbur Cross, as if literary critics are themselves no longer inconsistent, moody or ambiguous.[24] Literary judgments, including Cross's, are often still overtly subjective and opinionated despite admirable movement toward a more objective scholarly distance. If anything, the scholarly tone in most twentieth-century criticism only serves to highlight the occasional personal insults and imaginative biography familiar from the nineteenth century. Biases, loyalty, and the group mentality can be found between the lines of critics' works, even in statements that protest to the contrary. Cross's words cited above, for example, tell us that the age of biased Fielding criticism is over—but the very same passage implies that it is only natural that Fielding should rise to the top when the obstacles disappear. Even articles devoted to topics as concrete as sales figures are not free from the subjectivity of the Richardson/Fielding dichotomy. Frederic S. Dickson, in the 1917 *Notes and Queries*, titles his article "Fielding and Richardson on the Continent" but introduces it by writing, "Let me give Fielding's record, and let some devotee of Richardson give the record for his favorite."[25]

Type-Two Readers: Sources of Opinion

By the 1930s the volume of literary criticism began to multiply rapidly. Periodicals running commentary on Richardson and Fielding change from names like *Blackwood's* or *Harper's* to *Illinois Studies in Language and Literature* and *Philological Quarterly*. Titles of articles change from names like "On Reading Old Books" to "*Clarissa*: A Study in the Nature of Convention." Along with the proliferation of English departments and the professionalization of criticism comes at least one new genre: doctoral dissertations, which from the 1920s onward, account for approximately 10 percent of the commentary on Richardson and Fielding.[26] A much higher percentage of this critical explosion comes from textbooks and reference works aimed at the ever-expanding body of college students (due in part to the G.I. bill and, later, the Baby Boom). "[I]t was not until 1945 that the academic floodgates opened, releasing many important additions to the factual record and some of the best-informed academic criticism, along with unprecedented quantities of lugubrious rubbish," writes Rawson.[27]

As early as the 1930s, however, a new dichotomy created by these academic texts begins to transform Richardson and Fielding criticism. Literary criticism had become a disciplined professional industry, but critics also found themselves in the roles of teachers who had to entertain and inspire undergraduates. Literary history was undergoing an identity crisis in the wake of Leslie Stephen, attempting to balance the relative objectivity of traditional literary biography with the acknowledged subjectivity of evaluative literary criticism. (The work of F.R. Leavis reveals many of the tensions of the period: Leavis codifies his own personal opinions as if they are stable and self-evident literary categories.) The Richardson/Fielding opposition fits naturally into the network of other dichotomies operating in the twentieth-century academic horizon. As literature becomes a source of academic study, bringing older works to readers who may never have read them otherwise, it also becomes simplified for introductory literature courses.[28] The resulting compromise is the debate on the literary canon, dominated in turns by Leslie Stephen, T.S. Eliot, F.R. Leavis, Walter Allen, Ian Watt and many others, which still affects and often outrages literary critics to the present day. Because Richardson and Fielding's early reception history conditioned them to be eternal rivals for that Coy Mrs. Fame, very few critics are willing to defend them both as equally qualified candidates for canonization. Hence another odd transformation in Richardson and Fielding criticism—readers who will admit enjoying an author but will not recommend him to others, or who will recommend an author to others without enjoying him.

A perfect example of the dichotomized, compromising trend is William Otis and Morriss Needleman's *A Survey History of English Literature* (1938). It is perhaps the pinnacle of the early twentieth-century textbook mentality and its tendency to reinforce the Richardson/Fielding opposition. One author is never discussed without the context of the other, and the differences between the two are neatly laid out in parallel columns. Table 4.1 reflects the state of the Richardson/Fielding opposition in 1938.

Table 4.1.

FIELDING	RICHARDSON
1. Characters alive with super-abundant life. Superior in	1. Great genius in portraying female character. Hence he is

characterizing the robustness of men.	called the "Apostle of Feminism."
2. Healthful morality.	2. Smug sentimentality.
3. Truth-plumbing content.	3. Falsely-commonplace content.
4. Rambling, picaresque-structured stories, effective in their very plotlessness; yet possibly surpasses Richardson in ability to construct a plot.	4. Novels in letter-form often charged with clumsiness in handling of construction and technique, while, possibly, stricter in the selection of incidents.
5. Excellent sense of humor.	5. Almost total absence of humor.
6. Virile satire and coarse fun—the objective method.	6. Sentimentality and analysis—the subjective method.

The authors neatly categorize Richardson and Fielding for the benefit of the student who does not have the time to read the originals. Richardson, for example, is the "first psychological-analytical-sentimental novelist," invents the novel of character, writes the first novel to "profess a moral purpose," and contributes four new character types: "the polished rake, the pure gentleman, the chaste woman, and the Protestant martyr."[29] Despite Richardson's canonical significance, Otis and Needleman do not suggest that anyone should actually read his novels. Side by side with their scientific language of typology and first causes is their evaluation of Richardson's subjective appeal: Pamela is "neither delicate in feeling nor pure-minded, but rather vulgar in her view of honor and dishonor; her business-like, adventurous view of morality is warped," while *Clarissa* is a novel of "long-winded letters, redundant detail, improbabilities of plot, irrelevantly interminable gossip, and obtruding judgments." *Sir Charles Grandison* is simply "a distinct failure, even in its own day."[30]

Even the physical layout of textbooks like Otis and Needleman's affect the Richardson/Fielding opposition. The repetitive nature of these textbooks is such that the chapter on the eighteenth-century novel invariably begins with Richardson and uses "Shamela" as a transition to Fielding. The pattern is logical if not especially creative, but the end result is that critics almost always use Richardson as a context for Fielding, and Fielding is almost never used as a context for Richardson. Richardson therefore can appear to be innovative where Fielding is derivative, or, depending upon the proclivities of the critic, Fielding can appear to build upon and correct the stumbling first steps of Richardson. Richard Church writes in the preface of his 1951 textbook, for example, "What Shakespeare was to the whole of life and literature, Fielding was to the English novel. . . . But first we have to consider Richardson, because his activity and achievement further prepared the way for Fielding. . . ."[31] When critics introduce Fielding after Richardson, they usually highlight the comic and satiric in Fielding's novels at the expense of the moralistic and the epic. Bruce McCullogh's *Representative English Novelists* (1946) is indeed representative. The preceding evaluation of Richardson informs McCullogh's evaluation of Fielding, to the point that Fielding is everything Richardson is not: "[Fielding] does not preach too much and is not too grave. He is clearly on the side of virtue without being a prig. He moves easily through a wide range of comedy without becoming tiresomely facetious. His style is graceful and fluent without being shoddy or bombastic."[32]

College textbooks were the newest and probably most influential sources of twentieth-century opinion on Richardson and Fielding, but they were not the only sources. Academics wrote for one another as well as for their students. Scholarly books and articles naturally increased along with the number and size of university English departments (although the explosion within the explosion of scholarship produced for the "tenure race" is a more recent phenomenon). The multiplication is not anywhere near equal on both sides of the Richardson/Fielding equation, however. Garland Press has issued two bibliographies, one for Richardson and one for Fielding, both identical in format and editorial policy, citing criticism on each author from 1900 to 1978. Richardson's entries total 940, and Fielding's total 1453. Whole years go by with no references to Richardson at all. The numbers can be slightly misleading for Fielding, because a great deal of his references in the early years of the century are largely the work of a small body of extremely prolific scholars: Austin Dobson, Leslie Stephen, Andrew Lang, Edmund Gosse, Wilbur Cross, and George Saintsbury.

Periodical literature on Richardson and Fielding addresses topics which readers scarcely could have imagined publishable in the eighteenth and nineteenth centuries. A great deal of the criticism is historical, textual, and genre based rather than personal, moral, and emotional. Whereas a typical nineteenth-century article would contrast the ethics and sentiments of Clarissa and Sophia, Watt contrasts the origins and connotations of their names ("The Naming of Characters in Defoe, Richardson, and Fielding," 1949).[33] *Notes and Queries* became a particularly fertile field for the arcane, particularly for Fielding and much of it by Frederick Dickson in the

1910s (including a note in June 1916 pointing out that Tom Jones buys his sword in book seven and does not use it until book sixteen). There are also ongoing critical exchanges through the 1930s on whether 6 August 1754 is the date Fielding arrived or disembarked in Portugal, and whether it was Goldwyre or Barker who set Charlotte Cradock's broken nose.[34] Comparable articles are noticeably missing for Richardson, apart from a brief exchange of information about Richardson's London address and his true birthday.[35]

Richardson's critical high point before Watt came not from the textbooks or the periodicals, but from biography. McKillop's *Samuel Richardson, Printer and Novelist* (1936) portrays Richardson as an eminently sensible businessman whose literary talents stem more fron. experience and hard work than from perverse genius. As with Scott, however, no amount of respect for Richardson prevents negative direct comparisons to Fielding. "[Richardson's] intelligence was no. strong or free enough, his sympathies were too narrow and his sense of humor too feeble, to initiate him in that art of life of which Henry Fielding was the master and the chronicler," writes McKillop.[36]

Earlier twentieth-century biographies of Richardson can be positively hostile, begging the question of exactly why the authors chose to begin the project in the first place. Dobson, the only scholar to write separate biographies of both Richardson and Fielding, is clearly a Fieldingite in *Samuel Richardson* (1902). Dobson is much kinder to Richardson the man than to Richardson the novelist, claiming that Richardson's books are far too long, suffer from their epistolary form, and are not due for a twentieth-century revival. Clara Thomson is another scholar who seems out of place working on Richardson. *Samuel Richardson: A Biographical and Critical Study* (1900) opens and closes with comparisons to Fielding and leans heavily on the dichotomy throughout. Fielding possesses twice Richardson's "knowledge of the world," has "perfectly refined" women characters where Pamela makes "capital out of her virtue," and has "large, loving sympathy" in contrast to Richardson's "young lady's horror of anything approaching farce."[37]

Fielding appears to have made a full recovery from Murphy's essay in 1762 and the various biographical works which it subsequently informed. Negative assumptions of Fielding's personal parallels with the lives of Jones and Booth are generally replaced with a fondness, even a nostalgia, for the literary roast beef of olde England. Fielding is "one of the most humanly attractive personalities in the biographical history of literature," writes Williams. "He falls into his natural place with some of the great creative minds of the world's history, Chaucer, Shakespeare, Cervantes, and Scott, for whom we instinctively conceive a feeling of personal friendship, and know that we should feel at our ease with them if they were to appear suddenly in the room."[38] If Fielding suffered little in biographical accounts of his rival, the same cannot be claimed for Richardson. Cross's three-volume biography in 1918 spoke powerfully for Fielding's contemporary popularity and canonization, although reviewers complained of a "whitewash" of Fielding's faults.[39] Despite his avowed intention of freeing Fielding from the irrational slander of his former biographers, Cross does not hesitate to do for Richardson what Arthur Murphy did for Fielding. Cross refers to Richardson as "the little fat printer" and generally makes no pretense of keeping a balanced, scholarly tone when mentioning Richardson and Fielding side by side. "A word in praise of *Tom Jones* set [Richardson's] shrunken heart boiling with rage and envy; a word in disparagement of the novel set it beating at a happy pace," Cross writes.[40] Williams claims in a set of biographical essays that even those critics who believe Richardson is the better novelist must acknowledge that Fielding is the better *man*.[41]

Type-Two Readers: The Old Oppositions

Early twentieth-century critics, for all their innovative approaches, still make use of the standard Richardson/Fielding dichotomies: internal/external, subjective/objective, ideal/real, and "feminine"/"masculine." Even when the readers take new perspectives on the old oppositions, the fact that the old dichotomies are still being used after two hundred years is in itself a significant phenomenon in the history of Richardson/Fielding criticism.

The first of these inherited dichotomies is internal versus external. Unlike nineteenth-century critics who value these elements for their moral potential, twentieth-century critics tend to see characterization and social representation as parts of the novelist's overall technique. Whether or not Fielding's broad social canvas provides incentive for readers to examine the delicate workings of their own hearts, for example, is less important than whether or not the episodic nature of *Tom Jones*'s structure creates a sense of aesthetic closure. "It is doubtful whether Fielding always surpassed his predecessors—Defoe and Richardson, for instance—in character portrayal," writes Carl Holliday in 1912, "but never before in English prose had been seen such complexity and intricacy of plot."[42] Other critics carry on the debate about which author is internal and which is external, or, to use Frederic Blanchard's terms, which represents "conduct" and which represents "character."[43] A preference for one novelist over the other often hinges on a reader's opinion about which of these elements is most central to the novelistic tradition. Richard Burton privileges Richardson, for example, because he believes that character, rather than incident and realism, is the true source of the novel.[44] Charles F. Horne, on the other hand, complains that in Richardson's novels "the outer physical life is hardly noted as it passes by," whereas Fielding "gives a broad picture of the actual, external world."[45]

Closely related to the internal/external dichotomy is the subjective/objective dichotomy. Twentieth-century critics are generally happy to overturn traditional opinions on Richardson and Fielding, but no one is prepared to go so far as to argue that Fielding is subjective and Richardson is objective.[46] It is common for twentieth-century readers to link subjectivity with sentiment and sentiment with tragedy, a uniquely modern association which would have puzzled eighteenth-century readers familiar with *The Man of Feeling*, *David Simple*, and *Tristram Shandy*. Twentieth-century fiction and criticism affects expectations for Richardson and Fielding in such a way that sentiment, subjectivity, seriousness, tragedy, and realism become related concepts, all of which are opposed to rationality, objectivity, humor, satire, and imagination. Dobson, for example, believes that the traditional assignments of the subjective/objective dichotomy are central to the Richardson/Fielding opposition and contain the essence of what separates their temperaments and techniques. In "Richardson at Home" (1892), Dobson writes that Richardson is mainly a *"spectator ab intra"* who is the Father of the Novel of Sentiment, while Fielding is mainly a *"spectator ab extra"* who is the Father of the Novel of Manners.[47] Burton, too, associates subjectivity with sentiment and objectivity with action. Each author reaches their triumph in different ways: "Richardson by sensibility often degenerating into sentimentality, and by analysis—the subjective method; Fielding by satire and humor (often coarse, sometimes bitter) and the wide envisagement of action and scene—the method objective," writes Burton in high academic style.[48]

The traditional critical opposition of idealism and realism has evoked the most varied, intense and partisan responses from readers of Richardson and Fielding, and it continues to create controversy in the twentieth century. The idealism/realism dichotomy, like the internal/external dichotomy, is stripped of much of its moral significance in favor of more formalistic concerns. A few readers, such as Cross, continue to use the dichotomy to oversimplify Richardson and Fielding's technique: Richardson's characters have "nothing to offer but portraits of ideal goodness and villainy" whereas Fielding's are "drawn from his own observation" and "rarely was there any idealizing."[49] Generally, however, twentieth-century readers succeed in complicating and problematizing the dichotomy, replacing the black-and-white didacticism of the last two centuries with more academic concerns for the subtleties of aesthetic effect.

Archibald Shepperson's *The Novel in Motley* (1936) is typical of the academic perspective that makes a network of associations for each side of the idealistic/realistic dichotomy rather than accepting it at its simplistic face value. Shepperson opposes Richardson's realism with Fielding's satire, giving Richardson the initial advantage: "[R]ealism has this advantage over satire, that it sets up something else in place of that which is torn down." Fielding first attacks Richardson with satire in "Shamela," then as *Joseph Andrews* progresses, counters with a realism that out-realizes Richardson's and makes *Pamela* seem more like an idealistic fantasy.[50] Maynard Mack's influential introduction to his edition of *Joseph Andrews* (1948) is very similar to Shepperson's, claiming that Fielding's most effective satire of Richardson's idealism comes not from burlesque, but from an alternate and superior realism. "[I]t is a more inclusive world than Richardson's, and also a more profoundly familiar one, being motivated not by sex alone but also by the humdrum motions of avarice, stupidity, vanity, courage, and love," writes Mack of *Joseph Andrews*.[51] Realism becomes increasingly important as academic criticism moves more toward historical investigation and further away from close readings of individual texts. The critical predilection for realism tends, traditionally, to favor Fielding. The climax of the mid-century academic discussion of realism and the early novel is, however, Watt's *The Rise of the Novel* (a full discussion of Watt's work follows below). Watt complicates the idealism/realism dichotomy by associating idealism with the romance and elevating "formal realism" into the very definition of the novel. Part of the controversy in the reception of Watt's work was due to his seemingly paradoxical defense of formal realism and simultaneous attack on Fielding. By 1957 Watt was running counter to almost two centuries of Richardson and Fielding criticism that first valued (moral) idealism over (scandalous) realism and then valued (Fielding's candid) realism over (Richardson's pompous and perverse) idealism.

The one critical opposition inherited from the nineteenth cen-

tury that remains just as extreme, personal, and resolutely "unaca-
demic" in the early twentieth century is the "feminine"/
"masculine" dichotomy. Even those critics who express outrage at
Fielding's slanderous biographers have no qualms about assigning
Richardson all the worst traits of their own highly subjective sexism. No disciplined academic mode of response—New Criticism,
Structuralism, Psychoanalysis, or Marxism—makes the slightest
difference in the negative associations placed on Richardson's supposedly "feminine" sensibility. "The difference between the two
men's experiences and view-points is at once recognized. Richardson was acquainted with women and a world of feminine emotions;
Fielding with men and a world of masculine activities," writes Holliday with the certainty of a chemist. When Holliday moves to evaluate those gendered traits, however, his language changes:

> The little fat book-printer, moreover was never in the best of health,
> and often complained of his nerves; Fielding was a healthy animal, and
> never knew he had nerves until near the day of his death. The result is
> that his books are full of healthy animal activity.[52]

The academic distance and formal tone informing Church's textbook also disappears whenever sexuality becomes the point of contrast. "To watch [Richardson] writing a book is like watching a
woman buying a new hat," Church writes. "And for a man, it can
sometimes be just as embarrassing, with its indecisions, its touches
of acidity with attendants, its holding up of the more urgent and
important matters of life (from a male point of view)."[53]

Church is willing to acknowledge (albeit in parentheses) that
there may be alternatives to the "male point of view." Even those
critics who find femininity an advantage in the novel have difficulty
applauding Richardson. "In spite of being a husband and a father,
he remained an old maid," Church writes.[54] The tendency is even
more pronounced when critics read Richardson side by side with
Fielding. Robert Etheridge Moore, who calls Fielding "a man, and
what is more, a man's man," does the best he can in 1951 to balance his preference for Fielding and do justice to the feminine tradition in the novel. The intended flattery, however, does not quite
work: "Richardson may be called, in all seriousness, one of our
great women."[55]

The "feminine"/"masculine" dichotomy may not have produced
exciting new advancements in the discussion of Richardson and
Fielding's alleged personalities, but the case is very different for the
discussion of gender in their characters. The period 1894–1957

saw radical shifts for women in society, and readers often reflect their attitudes toward these changes in their reading of Richardson and Fielding. Both novelists present antiquated views of women which leave modern readers with a great deal of alterity to recover before developing a working conception of the original eighteenth-century horizon.

Frederick C. Green, a Canadian Fieldingite, is fairly typical of male critics who find an imaginative reconstruction of eighteenth-century social mores more trouble than it is worth. "Few novelists have yawned more bowelfully over the purity and sanctity of woman than Samuel Richardson in *Pamela*," he writes in *Minuet* (1935). Green then makes the familiar nineteenth-century connection of the novelist's characterization with what he supposes to be the novelist's biography: "Richardson's idea of the perfect household makes the traditional picture of the mid-Victorian home seem like a feminine paradise, and we know from his biography that, in his quiet way, this fat little sultan of North End was a tyrant of the worst description."[56] Aurélien Digeon also cannot see past his own 1925 expectations. Sophia is a sensible modern woman who makes brave decisions based on a rational evaluation of the facts, whereas Clarissa ten times "has the advantage over Lovelace and ten times, for the most trifling reasons, she loses the opportunity of ending the whole matter and marrying."[57] William Henley is no less crassly insensitive in 1902:

> [Fielding] knew the worth of a wench's humour, and for another how the noble Mr. B. should have done by Pamela, and would assuredly have done by Pamela, had he not been the creation of a Vegetarian, who knew nothing of life, and wrote of women only from their own report of themselves.[58]

Even those twentieth-century male critics who do not appear sexist still have difficulty appreciating Richardson's women. "The heroine of contemporary fiction is seldom meek, scarcely unsophisticated, far from submissive, and dubiously chaste," writes Grant C. Knight in 1931. "She governs machines, overcomes nature, tames man, conquers all but herself. Compared with her, Richardson's virtuous ladies are as rain water to Tokay."[59]

Other male critics find better things to say about Richardson's female characters, but even when they do, the tone and perspective of their comments often differ sharply from similar evaluations made by female critics. "Each could draw the most delightful women—the most perfect women, I think, in the whole range of our literature," writes Doyle of both Richardson and Fielding. "They had such a charming little dignity of their own, such good sense, and yet such dear, pretty, dainty ways, so human and so charming, that even now they become our ideals."[60] Whereas Doyle praises the characters' charms, Myra Reynolds in *The Learned Lady in England, 1650–1750* (1920) praises their intellect. "Pamela and Clarissa Harlowe . . . have an education superior to that of most girls of their day, and they have educational ideas far ahead of their time," writes Reynolds. "They strive valiantly to direct the course of their lives according to the dictates of their own reason and conscience." Reynolds' only consideration of Fielding is her observation that Mrs. Western is satirized because she pretends to have learning, and that "for a modest woman of real learning and ability Fielding had great respect."[61] (There is no mention of the lengthy debate on women's education in *Amelia*.)

Admiration for female characters was, for the most part, divided along the lines of male Fieldingites and female Richardsonians. There are important exceptions, however. The most enthusiastic male critic to support Richardson's women—to the point of exaggeration—is Robert Palfrey Utter, who along with Gwendolyn Bridges Needham, published the eccentric and ingenious *Pamela's Daughters* in 1937. Utter and Needham see every literary heroine from the eighteenth to the twentieth centuries as being modeled in one way or another on Pamela. To select just one of Utter and Needham's many refreshingly original criteria of comparison for Richardson and Fielding, the characterization and sensibilities of Pamela and Sophia are revealed by how often and under what circumstances they faint. Pamela collapses in "the rarest of all causes for fainting," an overload of "self-esteem at the attack on her virtue." Sophia faints under opposite circumstances, "only when she is helpless to undo misfortune which has already befallen one she loves."[62]

Fielding's strongest support from a female critic reached a wide general audience when Pearl Mary Teresa Richards Craigie, writing under the pseudonym John Oliver Hobbes, published "Fielding for Girls" in the *New York Times* for 3 September 1904. Her words, which could have started riots in the mid-eighteenth century, were still controversial in the early years of the twentieth. In calm, simple sentences Craigie neatly overturns nearly every sexual taboo in the long Richardson/Fielding opposition: "Speaking for myself, I consider Fielding may be regarded as a nerve tonic nowadays, an antidote to the morbid and neurotic twaddle which, under various disguises romantic, sentimental, and historical is consumed by girl and women readers. If I had a daughter, I should certainly give her the works of Fielding."[63] In the same year Craigie writes elsewhere that "the epics of 'Tom Jones' and 'Amelia' ought to be given to every girl on her eighteenth birthday."[64] Craigie may or may not have offered a nerve tonic to young women, but she certainly succeeded in intoxicating several jubilant and vindicated male Fieldingites. J.M. Bulloch, for example, writes in *The Lamp* 29: "Certain it is that not for nearly a century could a reputable writer, especially a woman, have given such an admonition in the pages of a popular journal. . . . Yet Mrs. Craigie's literary advice is timely, even logical, to-day; for we are emerging from a long night of prudery which drew sharp demarcations between the man and the woman."[65] The twentieth-century decline in appreciations of Richardson may indeed indicate an emergence from a long night of prudery, but when readers compare Richardson to his rival, the demarcations between man and woman remain as sharp as they have ever been.

Type-Two Readers: The New Oppositions— Shallowness versus Depth

Debate over the power of Richardson's and Fielding's female characters is closely related to the binary of shallowness versus depth. From the mid-eighteenth through mid-nineteenth centuries, the novel was slow to shake off its associations with (what was seen to be) the trivial literary experiences of the romance. By the end of the nineteenth century, however, the novels of George Eliot, Thomas Hardy, Herman Melville, Henry James and others began to appear at the same time literature was becoming an academic discipline. The result was a radical change in the horizon of expectation for novels. Excellence became associated with profound thought and moral philosophy. Despite eighteenth-, nineteenth-, and late twentieth-century protestations of Richardson's profound explorations of the human heart in contrast to Fielding's coarse burlesque, early twentieth-century readers almost unanimously find Richardson the shallower of the two.

Most critics, such as Saintsbury, prefer Fielding's range and perception to Richardson's. Saintsbury writes that Fielding's technique rescues the English novel: "He relieved the novel of the tyranny and constraint of the Letter; he took it out of the rut of confinement of a single or a very limited class of subjects. . . . He gave it altogether a larger, wider, higher, deeper range. . . . He shook up its pillows, and bustled its business arrangements."[66] Robert Lovett and Helen Hughes are perhaps the most enthusiastic of all: "In social relations, education, and range of experience Fielding . . . was Richardson's superior. In his novels this superiority shows itself in a greater variety of human character, a more fully peopled world of outdoor as well as indoor life, and a wider sympathy and understanding."[67] Doyle, writing from the perspective of a fellow novelist rather than an academic critic, is the only reader to record a preference of Richardson over Fielding for depth of human understanding.[68] It is a strong testament to Fielding's overwhelmingly positive twentieth-century reception that in the age of James, Woolf, Joyce, Lawrence, and Faulkner, Richardson can be criticized for being "introspective."[69]

Type-Two Readers: The New Oppositions—
Narrative Technique

If it comes as something of a surprise to contemporary readers that Fielding is often favored for profundity and depth, then it may also be surprising that Richardson is often favored for plotting, cohesiveness, and technique. R.S. Crane's persuasive article, "The Plot of *Tom Jones*" (1950), has become so familiar to modern readers as one of the defining statements of the New Criticism that it is easy to make the mistaken assumption that all formalist, Structuralist and New Critics arrive at the same opinion about Fielding.[70] Actually, when twentieth-century critics (from different years and different critical perspectives) discuss form and technique, Richardson often holds up quite well and Fielding is appreciated for much more than just his plotting.

Most twentieth-century critics freely acknowledge the complexity and symbolic potential of Fielding's plotting as discussed in Crane's article, but complexity alone is less important to the New Critics than "organic unity." Long before formalism was an identifiable critical movement, Horne writes in 1908 that *Clarissa* bests *Tom Jones* as one of the few examples of the best type of plot, the "inevitable."[71] Holliday agrees, adding character to plot as part of the unified artistic effect, but prefers *Tom Jones* to *Clarissa*: "The incidents seem the logical results of the characters' natures; the natures of the characters are made evident by means of the incidents."[72] Horne, not only a devoted fan of Fielding but also a ferocious hater of Richardson, does not find organic unity in either author. When Richardson is ambiguous it is seen as simply bad writing, but Fielding's ambiguity is a strength and part of his contemporary relevance:

> Richardson in 'Pamela,' his earliest work, shows no recognition of the true closing point of his story but wanders on and on. . . . [Fielding] gave to his later work something of that air of incompleteness which a recent school of novelists has maintained to be essential for truth to life.[73]

Horne is not alone among twentieth-century readers who find Richardson's epistolary technique "wandering" away from modern tastes. The pace of Richardson's narrative did not please most academic critics who were perhaps more familiar with Conrad and Hemingway (and who had judgments to make about realistic reading assignments for their students). As J.B. Priestley warns his busy students in his brief textbook *The English Novel* (1927), the "actual stories [Richardson tells] are really very slight, particularly when compared with the time it takes to tell them. . . . We have to spend a week of our own time to spend, perhaps, a day of theirs."[74] Robert Naylor Whiteford coins a uniquely twentieth-century metaphor for the same uniquely twentieth-century critical viewpoint: "Fielding has knocked over the candle the flames of which had been fed by Richardson's never-ending pile of letters and presses the electric button of modern plot contrivance."[75] An equally modern metaphor for control and pacing, more critical of Fielding, comes from Utter and Needham: "Richardson would drive cautiously through the traffic of life in low gear. Fielding would keep the throttle open and condone such accidents as seem inevitable to high power and full speed."[76] Neither author, apparently, is a driver suited to modern urban conditions.

Type-Two Readers: The New Oppositions—Politics

Few aspects of twentieth-century criticism (and life itself) are more inherently dichotomized than politics. The political realm abounds with neatly opposed categories, almost always in pairs: conservative and liberal, capitalist and Marxist, Republican and Democrat, Tory and Whig, freedom and oppression. It is not surprising, therefore, that the neatly opposed categories of literary experience known as "Richardson" and "Fielding" should be subject to dichotomized political criticism.

As I have illustrated in chapter three, the French Revolution had little discernible effect on the reception of Richardson and Fielding.[77] It is not until the end of the Victorian period that literary criticism tends to turn from questions of biography and morality to questions of the novelist's role in, and portrayal of, the broader framework of society. Political criticism of Richardson and Fielding starts simply and gradually in the twentieth century, and it is not until the 1960s that Marxism becomes a fully developed and pervasive academic movement (and therefore beyond the range of this study).[78] In 1907, for example, W.R. Nicoll and Thomas Seccombe write simplistic oppositions: "[Fielding] is the Cavalier, Richardson the Roundhead; he is the gentleman, Richardson the tradesman; he represents church and country, Richardson chapel and borough."[79]

Ralph Fox represents a more complex and cynical view that takes root in the 1930s and is established by the 1950s. Fielding's novels are read as a reflection and an indictment of their times. In *The Novel and the People* (1937), Fox prefigures the concerns of much Marxist and postcolonial criticism:

> [Fielding] lived in a brutal world, the world of conquering capitalism, the period when the English squire was crushing the English peasant out of existence, when the English adventurer was stealing the wealth of the Indies by means as horrible as they were (in the abstract sense) immoral, and when that accumulation of stolen wealth was being made in the country which was to make possible the Industrial Revolution.[80]

Arnold Kettle's *An Introduction to the English Novel* (1951) labels both Richardson's and Fielding's characters as rebels against authority. Kettle uses the methods and vocabulary of revolutionary political economics to construct his argument about the development of the eighteenth-century novel. Richardson and Fielding are alike insofar as they have characters who rebel against the "mechanical materialism" of the eighteenth-century ruling class, and their strength lies in the "revolutionary assertion of the capacity of human nature to change itself and the world."[81]

Other critics are not as willing as Kettle to allow Fielding into the ranks of the revolutionary bourgeois. On the contrary, many Richardsonians were happy to take advantage of the antiaristocratic climate which was relatively new to the Anglo-American critical atmosphere and assign Fielding all the negative connotations of his privileged social class. Fieldingites, however, were just as happy to uphold eighteenth- and nineteenth-century critical traditions and dismiss Richardson's technique and morality along with his secondary social status. Even in works where critics are not discussing politics directly, it is often possible to find evidence of their political perspectives in how they handle the Richardson/Fielding opposition. Digeon, for example, writes that Richardson is "completely absorbed in the bourgeois existence which he describes." Fielding, on the other hand, approaches his material from a more professional class: "Fielding is detached, like a lawyer or a physician. . . ."[82] Doyle finds it amusing that Richardson's male heroes are more spiritual and noble than Fielding's ("Here I think that the plebeian printer has done very much better than the aristocrat"), as if Fielding's characters were assumed by default to have a higher spirituality and nobility because of their author's social class.[83]

Type-Two Readers:
Reconstructions of the Eighteenth Century

Twentieth-century impressions of eighteenth-century life did not always focus on politics, of course. The range of the responses to the eighteenth-century social horizon is united in only one respect: twentieth-century readers are happy that they are reading Richardson and Fielding in the twentieth century. It is difficult to imagine exactly whom Terry Eagleton has in mind when he writes in the preface to *The Rape of Clarissa* (1982), "I entirely lack what would appear to be one of the chief credentials for discussing the eighteenth century, namely a nostalgic urge to return to it."[84]

Eagleton certainly did not have in mind Knight, who writes of Richardson and Fielding in his textbook *The Novel in English* (1931), "To many of us these novels are garrulous, dull, and mawkish beyond endurance. . . . We think the device of telling the stories clumsy, the women brainless and spineless, the men cut from *papier-mâché*, the tone that of a provincial clergyman." Knight contrasts the taste for tight plotting, self-reliant women and spicy situations of the "age of speed" with the eighteenth-century taste for "leisurely eating, heavy sleeping, slow traveling, and ponderous writing."[85] Burton goes even further in privileging the twentieth century over the eighteenth, writing in naive praise of his own civilized generation just before the outbreak of World War I: "The truth is, the eighteenth century, whether in England or elsewhere, was on a lower plane . . . than our own time." Rather than citing the recovery of Fielding's literary reputation as evidence of a twentieth-century advance, however, Burton echoes the refined tastes of the mid-nineteenth century. "Fielding's novels in unexpurgated form are not for household reading to-day," Burton writes. "[T]he fact may not be a reflection upon him, but it is surely one to congratulate ourselves upon, since it testifies to social evolution."[86]

One element of eighteenth-century aesthetics that critics frequently congratulated themselves for rejecting is "sentiment." Modern readers do not seem to express great interest in recovering the alterity of "sentiment" and what it meant to Richardson's original audience. It is easy to claim that the New Criticism and its associated schools prioritize form over content, but the reality is that early twentieth-century critics were quick to claim personal distaste and lack of understanding as reason enough to reject sentimentality. Because the Richardson/Fielding dichotomy is so entrenched by 1894, the same critics who dismiss the sentiment in Richardson's novels are likely to underestimate the sentiment in Fielding's.

Examples are plentiful from across the period. "Judged from the modern point of view, Richardson is a tiresome, mawkish sentimentalist," writes John Drinkwater in *The Outline of Literature* (1923), associating "sentiment" with everything bad about the eighteenth-century novel. Fielding, not surprisingly, comes to the rescue: "If Richardson invented the English novel, Henry Fielding . . . gave it, for the first time, absolute literary distinction."[87] Even the devout Richardsonians Utter and Needham make the same associations, taking a cue from Jane Austen and dichotomizing sense and sensibility. "We call Richardson the father of the novel of sensibility," they write. "We call Fielding his opponent, and think of him as withering Richardson's sensibility with blasts of sense."[88] Kettle does not define what sentimentality meant to eighteenth-century readers, but he defines what it means to those in the twentieth: "[Richardson's] concern to extract from his reader on every occasion the price of a tear of sensibility is not likely to recommend him to an age which regards tears as either superficial or shameful. . . ."[89] Finally, one of the most learned and influential of the period's critics, Stephen, seems to understand and appreciate sentiment the least. Stephen writes in *English Literature and Society in the Eighteenth Century* (1904), "I will confess that the last time I read *Clarissa Harlowe* it affected me with a kind of disgust. . . . Richardson gave me the same shock from the elaborate detail in which he tells the story of Clarissa; rubbing our noses, if I may say so, in all her agony, and squeezing the last drop of bitterness out of every incident."[90]

Type–Two Readers: Morality

Stephen's words sound a familiar note from the eighteenth and nineteenth centuries. When Stephen speaks of his "disgust" at the "coarse nerves" of his ancestors, he is continuing the debate on Richardson's and Fielding's comparative morality. Literary critics who find discussions of morality in literature irrelevant, patriarchal, condescending, and intrusive still make exceptions when they come to contrast Richardson and Fielding. The dichotomized tendency of twentieth-century criticism is such that if one novelist provides healthy moral examples, then the other novelist perforce provides *unhealthy* moral examples. Early modern critics are virtually unanimous in finding Richardson to be the most unhealthy of the two, resulting in a complete reversal from mainstream eighteenth-century criticism.

The aspects of Richardson's morality that most offend twentieth-century tastes are his calculation, inflexibility, and "Puritanism." The rediscovery of *Shamela* and its positive attribution to Fielding in 1916 coincided with a fresh look at exactly what Fielding objected to in Richardson's novels.[91] Readers often found Richardson's characters to be scheming and self-interested behind a mask of sanctimonious meekness. "Richardson's conception of virtue is formal and calculating; Fielding's is based on the conception of a natural goodness which expresses itself imperfectly but spontaneously in the active life of the world," writes McKillop.[92]

Elsewhere McKillop makes use of a very common twentieth-century approach to Richardson and Fielding, one perhaps based on the same principles underlying the New Criticism. The critic simply links the two authors together and then differentiates them in the principle that they share. In this case the linking element is the experimental practicality of their moral themes. "Both Richardson and Fielding begin with ethical and social ideas and propose to try them out in the stress of actual life, to see whether they cover the situations that arise," writes McKillop in his biography of Richardson. "In Fielding the principle must become elastic if it is to fit the facts. . . . In Richardson the principle remains rigid, and does not easily accommodate itself to the individual case."[93] Bowen, too, finds Richardson's morality inflexible and impractical when contrasted with Fielding's. "Fielding's conscience—or call it morality—was a thing tempered out of his own furious living," claims Bowen, whereas "Richardson's conscience remained a theory—though a theory brought to a fine point."[94] Holbrook Jackson in *The*

Great English Novelists (1908) also finds Richardson's morality to "remain a theory." Jackson speculates that Richardson's novels are now less popular than Fielding's because "no fiction can live whose figures are merely the puppets of some preconceived idea or precept. . . . [Fielding] preferred honest and frank frailty with its immense possibilities of goodness, rather than stereotyped and pompous rectitude."[95]

Just as many twentieth-century critics have transformed the eighteenth-century word "sentimental" into an insult, so have they colored the seventeenth-century word "Puritan." It is interesting to speculate on why the word appears with such regularity in twentieth-century Richardson and Fielding criticism when it is only used twice in the nineteenth century and not at all in eighteenth.[96] Perhaps Nathaniel Hawthorne's novels brought Puritanism back into the literary horizon, perhaps Americans became more critical of their national character after the Civil War, perhaps the surge of British patriotism in the two World Wars brought back animosity toward the party that once executed a king, or perhaps the violent effects of American prohibition left a legacy of scorn for members of any minority that promote themselves as moral spokespersons for their age. In any case, British and American readers alike have dissociated the word "Puritan" from any actual religious sect and used it as a catchphrase for everything that is unyielding, judgmental, and cruel about Richardson's morality. As a result, twentieth-century critics often underplay the high moral tone of Fielding's novels in favor of his congeniality and tolerant good humor.

Ernest Baker, for example, speaks of Richardson and Fielding in terms of "war" being declared between "the forces of Puritanism and respectability and the free-lances of wit, and art, and intellect," paralleling the opposition with that of "freedom and humour" and "intolerance and restraint."[97] Pritchett also speaks of warfare when discussing the Puritanical side of Richardson's novels. Pritchett does not even allow Richardson the advantages of free will or emotion, since Richardson is "the victim of that powerful cult of the will, duty and conscience by which Puritanism turned life and its human relations into an incessant war. There is no love in Puritanism; there is a struggle for power." Pritchett goes so far as to blame Puritanism for the crises in *Clarissa*: "By setting such a price upon herself, Clarissa represents that extreme of puritanism which desires to be raped."[98] Finally and most famously, D.H. Lawrence connects Puritanism with an unhealthy prurience in Richardson's novels. He does not call Richardson a Puritan in *Pornography and*

Obscenity (1929), but Richardson's novels come to mind when Puritanism is mentioned. "Boccaccio at his hottest seems to me less pornographical than *Pamela* or *Clarissa Harlowe*," writes Lawrence. "There's nothing wrong with sexual feelings in themselves, so long as they are straightforward and not sneaking or sly."[99]

Type-Two Readers: Psychoanalytic Criticism

D.H. Lawrence's comment that there is "nothing wrong with sexual feelings" speaks volumes for the change in the horizon of expectation that Freud bequeathed to literary criticism in general and the Richardson/Fielding opposition in particular. If the most frequently used word in eighteenth-century criticism is "morality" and the most frequently used word in nineteenth-century criticism is "character," then the most frequently used word in early twentieth-century criticism is "analysis." Modern readers may not understand or care for sentimentality or Puritanism, but they fully understand and relish Freudian interpretations of the author, the characters, and their fellow readers.

Psychoanalytic criticism may not always produce sympathetic readings of Richardson and Fielding, but it at least brings them attention during an unsympathetic era in which they could have been almost totally neglected. The increased attention is particularly important for Richardson's reception history. Richardson's novels seemed a profitable target for psychoanalytic critics, especially in the 1920s and 1930s. Mario Praz' *The Romantic Agony* (1933), for example, paints Clarissa as an archetypal suffering virgin and exemplar of western literature's history of tragic sadomasochism. In 1928 Brian Downs devoted an entire book, *Richardson*, to an analysis of Richardson's stream of consciousness and "divided mind." Oddly, among those who make direct comparisons of Richardson and Fielding, no one uses Freud's specific terminology, and only Allen and Watt mention Freud by name.

"I doubt whether it is possible for the critic who comes to *Clarissa* after reading Freud to deny that the novel must have been written by a man who was, even though unconsciously, a sadist in the technical sense," writes Allen. His next words are moderately famous in later twentieth-century Richardson criticism:

[T]he loving, lingering, horrified, gloating descriptions of Clarissa's long-drawn-out sexual humiliation at the hands of Lovelace, the rape that is constantly threatened and constantly deferred until, when it oc-

curs, it has an additional horror simply because of its long postpone-
ment, provide an element of quite inescapable pornography. . . ."[100]

Allen's string of adjectives seems exaggerated today, but when Allen
wrote in 1954 he was building on received opinion in Richardson
scholarship. Dorothy Van Ghent, for example, describes Clarissa
"lifting her eyes in gratitude to heaven for a simple bowl of gruel
or glass of water" and claims that Richardson's version of saintly
femininity offers a "ripe temptation to violence." Fielding's novel,
by contrast, offers the relief of the open lawn in May. Coleridge's
descriptive contrast seems to inspire Van Ghent to a derivative idea
and an unfortunate metaphor. Whereas Clarissa is so "deeply
rooted in subliminal matter" that "strange, only half-transparent
growths still attach to it, like the rubbery growths of the sea bottom," Tom Jones is "all out in mental sunlight."[101]
Richardson's original audience would no doubt be appalled at
readings like Van Ghent's that praise Richardson's genius and defend his literary status precisely because of his dark sexual psychology. Freudian criticism provides both the highest and the lowest
points of Richardson's twentieth-century reception while leaving
Fielding criticism essentially where it finds it. Critics in turn praise
and damn Richardson for his explorations of the subconscious
mind, but they all agree that he has no peer among other eighteenth-century novelists in the attempt. In a 1948 article about
Richardson titled "The Greatest English Novelist," A.E. Carter
writes that Richardson's strongest suit and the source of his admirable prolixity is "his power as a psychologist. In this respect he has
no rivals amongst English novelists and very few abroad."[102] Williams makes even greater claims for Richardson as the "inaugura-
tor of the psychological novel" and finds his "objective, cold, hard,
and unsympathetic" investigations true to the "logical and scientific spirit of his age. . . . This is only to say that he belonged to his
time, and knew nothing of that over-strained subjective temperament which is common with us."[103] Burton believes Richardson
"exhibited such a knowledge of the subtler phases of the nooks and
crannies of woman's heart, as to be hailed as past-master down to
the present day by a whole school of analysts and psychologues. . .
."[104] Pelham Edgar also finds Richardson's psychological explorations the key to his modern relevance: "Richardson rather than
Fielding must rank as the ancestor of those who choose to explore
the complexities of our tortured mortality."[105]
Not surprisingly, critics often contrast the analytic strengths of
Richardson's novels with their absence in Fielding's novels. Al-

though Fielding is generally seen as the deeper of the two in terms of his broad social canvas and range of human sympathy, several critics draw sharp dichotomies between Richardson's serious psychological analyses and Fielding's carefree, two-dimensional characterizations. Burton writes that Fielding's fiction is "buoyant, objective, giving far more play to action and incident. . . . Unquestionably, the psychology is simpler, cruder, more elementary than that of Richardson."[106] Edgar points out in 1933 that contemporary novelists all consider themselves qualified psychologists, "interested mainly in the morbid anatomy of the soul, and threading his way through its obscurest labyrinths," and for that reason Richardson is their favorite of the eighteenth-century novelists. "The occasions when we occupy a character's mind in Fielding are astonishingly rare."[107]

Nevertheless, my survey shows that modern readers still overwhelmingly prefer Fielding. It is at least true that the stated preferences of these critics tend to be based on matters of technique and formal control rather than psychological insight.

Type-Two Readers: Frederic T. Blanchard

The scholarly appropriation of Richardson and Fielding has brought about not only new kinds of commentary on each author, but also the first overviews of how the dichotomy has affected the novelists' literary reputations. The most comprehensive statement on the Richardson/Fielding opposition has been, up to the present work, Blanchard's *Fielding the Novelist: A Study in Historical Criticism* (1926). The topic of the book is a survey of Fielding's reception from 1742 to 1923, but Blanchard structures much of his account around the rises and falls of Richardson and Fielding. Blanchard treats the rivalry as a kind of narrative where one author "gains" on his rival as if they are in a race for the prize of literary respectability. Much as Fielding portrays his hero in *Tom Jones*, Blanchard portrays Fielding as a man whose natural literary goodness is temporarily obscured by those who have been misled by his jealous, malignant and scheming rival, only to have his enemy reveal his own treachery and resign the coveted hand of that Coy Mrs. Fame to the one whom she has truly loved all along.

Blanchard sees Richardson and Fielding as essentially and eternally opposed. "Rarely in their outlook upon life have two writers been so diametrically opposed as were Richardson and Fielding,"

Blanchard writes. "Richardson threw the accent upon conduct; Fielding, upon character."[108] Richardson and Fielding orbit one another in a series of critical oppositions: taste of the times versus life of the times; conservative versus radical; conduct versus character; idealism versus realism; judgment versus tolerance; and many others. Blanchard cannot understand how anyone could sincerely prefer Richardson to Fielding, and he treats those periods in history where Richardson is dominant as disgraceful and passing moments in a critical Dark Ages. Blanchard gleefully records the turning point in Richardson's reputation as the 1804 publication of his *Correspondence*, but Blanchard tends to overstate the degree to which Richardson's fall translates into an immediate and parallel rise for Fielding. Those who have based their work on Blanchard's formidable research tend to make the same mistake. Heinz Ronte's 1935 dissertation makes heavy use of Blanchard and labels all Richardsonians as anti-Fieldingites and vice versa. Ronte dichotomizes Richardson and Fielding to the point that they represent two universal forces, "Bihel and Mythos," corresponding roughly to the Christian and the Classical.[109]

Type-Two Readers: F.R. Leavis

Leavis' *The Great Tradition* (1948) undid in a single stroke much of Blanchard's massive project to secure Fielding's reputation. Leavis was exactly the type of critic that English Departments seemed to need in that particular phase of their early development: an opinionated, authoritative, and unapologetic leader prepared to bypass delicate negotiations about literary taste and make definitive pronouncements about what did and did not belong in the literary canon. Unflattering parallels to certain European leaders from the same World War II period were made only by later generations who felt the long-term impact of his influence.[110]

Blanchard recorded literary history, but he did not make it. Blanchard should have learned from his own accounts of Johnson, Coleridge, and Thackeray that single epigrammatic statements about Richardson or Fielding tend to have more lasting impact on the dichotomy than the most carefully researched books (the remarkable exception of Ian Watt will be discussed below). Despite all of Blanchard's efforts to secure Fielding a permanent place in the canon, Leavis used his critical authority to give his generation permission to skip Fielding entirely. Reserving the criteria of greatness for those authors who "change the possibilities for the art" and show an "awareness of the possibilities of life," Leavis writes:

> Fielding deserves the place of importance given him in the literary histories, but he hasn't the kind of classical distinction we are also invited to credit him with. He is important not because he leads to Mr. J.B. Priestley but because he leads to Jane Austen, to appreciate whose distinction is to feel that life isn't long enough to permit of one's giving much time to Fielding or any to Mr. Priestley.[111]

Life *is* long enough, however, to read the works of Richardson. "Fielding's attitudes, and his concern with human nature, are simple, and not such as to produce an effect of anything but monotony," writes Leavis. "We all know that if we want a more inward interest it is to Richardson we must go. . . . Richardson's strength in the analysis of emotional and moral states is in any case a matter of common acceptance; and *Clarissa* is an impressive work."[112] Leavis prefers Richardson to Fielding, but Leavis excludes both from the Great Tradition. Adding a twist to the familiar critical ploy of privileging Richardson or Fielding insofar as one author "makes possible" the other, Leavis values both Richardson and Fielding only insofar as they make possible the novels of Jane Austen.[113]

Type-Two Readers: Ian Watt

Watt, even more so than Leavis, elevated personal bias to the level of scholarly pronouncement. Readers seemed to make allowances for Leavis' cantankerous eccentricities of character, but they took Watt seriously on the basis of his work alone. Whereas other critics have made an impact on Richardson and Fielding's reputations with passing comments and epigrammatic statements, Watt makes his impact in *The Rise of the Novel* (1957) with a carefully developed and brilliantly consistent argument. Not since Johnson's remarks almost two hundred years earlier has a critic shown evidence of making such a deep impact. Not only is Watt's book frequently assigned in the same college courses that assign Richardson and Fielding, but Watt's book is *still* the starting point for any serious contemporary critic's understanding of the eighteenth-century novel. The most recent major studies of the early British novel—Michael McKeon's *The Origins of the English Novel* (1987), Paul Hunter's *Before Novels* (1990), Margaret Doody's *The True Story of the Novel* (1996), and Homer Obed Brown's *Institu-*

tions of the English Novel (1997)—all begin by explaining their relationship to *The Rise of the Novel*.

Watt subtitles his book "Studies in Defoe, Richardson and Fielding," but Fielding is marginalized for most of the book. The phrase "Defoe and Richardson" usually appears when Watt provides a literary example for some aspect of eighteenth-century culture. Even the section on male chastity focuses on *Sir Charles Grandison* and does not mention *Joseph Andrews*. As with many early academic textbooks, the discussion of Fielding follows that of Richardson, with *Shamela* as the transition, to the effect that Fielding's account is steeped in comparisons to Richardson and not the other way around. In the case of *The Rise of the Novel*, however, the structure works to Fielding's distinct disadvantage. Watt consistently measures Fielding in relation to the higher Richardsonian norm. For example, "Fielding allotted characterization a much less important place in his total literary structure, and [this] precluded him even from attempting the effects which were suited to Richardson's very different aim."[114] Watt does not seem to consider that from another and equally valid point of view Richardson's characterization precludes him from the effects that were suited to Fielding's very different aim.

Watt not only strategically ignores Fielding, he also places him at a disadvantage at every turn. Watt's definition of the "true" novel, every element of which supposedly reflects the emerging middle-class reader, privileges Richardson: the original rather than the classical imagination, realistic rather than humoristic characters, detail of setting, freedom from aristocratic patronage, close contact with the reading public, unified rather than episodic narratives, deep personal relationships rather than mere story-telling, the role of money as a controlling element, and most importantly, the dominance of character over plot.

Watt presents his Richardsonian criteria for the novel as if they are self-apparent and imminently logical. Watt writes, for example,

Since it was *Pamela* that supplies the initial impetus for the writing of *Joseph Andrews*, Fielding cannot be considered as having made quite so direct a contribution as Richardson to the rise of the novel. . . . [Fielding's roots are] not so much in social change as in the neo-classical literary tradition.[115]

Watt does not address the possibility that being neoclassical or less "direct" may not necessarily make a novel any less significant, less aesthetically valid, and less influential than any other novel. There are many other critics cited in this chapter who argue precisely the opposite of Watt—that Fielding could achieve much more than Richardson since Richardson was there first to pave the way. Sainstbury, an equally influential critic in his own earlier generation, writes of *Joseph Andrews*: "In short, Fielding here used his reluctant and indignant forerunner as a springboard, whence to attain heights which that forerunner could never have reached . . . ."[116]

Formal realism is so important because Watt's strongest critical motivations are *poiesis* rather than *aesthesis*, or are based on the reader's passive appreciation of the appearance of truth rather than on an active participation in a text that is self-consciously and deliberately fictional. Watt criticizes Fielding whenever the narrative technique "breaks the illusion" for the reader. "[I]t is not surprising that [*Tom Jones*] has been condemned by most modern critics," Watt writes, citing Ford Maddox Ford's opinion that Fielding does not care if the reader believes in the characters.[117] On the contrary, "most" modern critics have not rejected Fielding, as this chapter amply demonstrates, and by no means is Ford a representative example of "most" critics.[118] A much better example of a critic who represents a consensus opinion on Fielding's characterization would have been R.S. Crane, but Crane's enthusiastic appreciation of Fielding's form would have done serious damage to Watt's argument.

Watt's preference for the illusion of reality may also make him seem dated to readers in the Postmodern age: "[Fielding] is, indeed, almost as attentive to his audience as to his characters, and his narrative, far from being an intimate drama which we peep at through a keyhole, is a series of reminiscences told by a genial raconteur in some wayside inn. . . ."[119] Watt's attitudes seem somewhat antiquated now, especially in contrast to the work of McKeon, Hunter, and others who delight in multiplying and problematizing the sources of the English novel. "*Tom Jones* is only part novel, and there is much else—picaresque tale, comic drama, occasional essay," writes Watt, thereby dismissing Fielding's eligibility for a permanent place in the canon.[120]

What realism Fielding does achieve is limited to the "realism of assessment," which Watt contrasts with Richardson's "realism of presentation," a new spin on the old idealism/realism dichotomy (only reversed from its traditional assignment of superior realism to Fielding). Both realism of assessment and realism of presentation are said to be united in *Tristram Shandy* and to an even greater extent in the novels of Jane Austen. There is a Richardsonian double standard operating at this point in the argument: Watt criticizes Fielding for being derivative and neoclassical (as if the plot and characters of *Clarissa* were not partially derived from the romance and Restoration drama), yet Watt lionizes Austen precisely because she used both Richardson and Fielding as sources for her fiction. Fielding makes less of a contribution to the novel because *Pamela* supplied the original impetus for *Joseph Andrews*, yet with Austen it is "largely to her successful resolution" of the Richardson/Fielding opposition that she owes "her eminence in the tradition of the English novel."[121]

The damage Watt did to Fielding's reputation was proportionate to the good he did to Richardson's. Never before in Richardson and Fielding's reception history has a single reader caused such a radical shift of opinion. Richardson and Fielding both had few active readers in 1957, but among that small readership Fielding's position had never been so relatively high and Richardson's had never been so relatively low. Since *The Rise of the Novel*, however, Fielding has retained his readership but is yet to fully recover his former critical respect. Watt caused his one-man Richardson revival not only by giving Richardson an unusual amount of serious critical attention, but also by recalling and reversing many of the standard Richardson/Fielding oppositions.

Readers often claim, for example, that Fielding painted the world as it is and Richardson painted it as it should be. Watt debunks the myth with the simplest and most essential critical technique, one amazingly neglected by most Richardson/Fielding critics from all periods: reproducing long, carefully chosen examples from the texts. Watt's contrast of Sophia's meeting with Blifil to Clarissa's meeting with Solmes is particularly unflattering to Fielding, as is the contrast of Squire Western's reaction at Sophia's disobedience to Mr. Harlowe's reaction at Clarissa's. "[O]ur own emotional involvement in the inner world of Clarissa makes it possible for a father's silent look to have a resonance that is quite lacking in the physical and rhetorical hyperbole by which Fielding demonstrates the fury of Squire Western," writes Watt.[122] Watt's eloquent illustrations of Richardson's formal realism and psychological insight also serve as a defense of Richardson's prolixity, one of the major stumbling blocks in Richardson's twentieth-century reception.[123] Just as Blanchard sees Fielding ultimately defeating his rival in the race toward the finish line of literary fame, Watt claims that the future, despite the uphill struggle, belongs to Richardson:

Fielding had indeed much of the countryman's robustness, and the disparity between the two novelists and their works may therefore stand as a representative example of a fundamental parting of the ways in the history of the English civilization, a parting in which it is the urban Richardson who reflects the way that was to triumph.[124]

The influential nature of *The Rise of the Novel* has made Watt's prediction, to a large extent, self-fulfilling.

Type-Three Readers: General Readers

Richardson and Fielding no doubt had early-twentieth-century readers who were not reading for literary inspiration or to complete an assignment from an English teacher.[125] None of them, however, has left a permanent public record of their opinion. It seems fair to assume, however, that there are even fewer nonacademic general readers who have read *both* Richardson and Fielding.

One possible exception is that of William Hale White (a.k.a. Mark Rutherford), and it is still a dubious call to designate him a "general reader." White is certainly an academic: his remarkable career includes various turns at the ministry, biography, mathematics, philosophy, fiction, the essay, and literary biography. The latter three endeavors are what make it difficult to claim he is not a literary critic in some capacity, although it is safe to say that literary criticism was not his primary vocation. White enjoys Richardson's prolixity and slow tempo: "I cannot say that I find it wearisome. This is the complaint most people make, but to me the genius of Richardson is sufficient to carry me on without any sense of fatigue." Richardson's repetition of images and retelling of the same lurid incidents from different perspectives "makes the story more immoral by far than anything Fielding ever wrote, although there are not perhaps half a dozen gross phrases in Richardson's three thousand pages."[126]

For the most part, we must rely on the word of type-two readers as to why there are no type-three readers for Richardson and Fielding. Since Richardson has the fewest readers, he elicits the most speculation. As Richardson's loyal biographer, McKillop, writes in 1936, "[I]t is hard to account for the air of amused pity with which people nowadays regard the little printer."[127] Richardson not only had to endure having so few general readers, but also the scorn of Fieldingite critics who relished pointing that fact out. (If Richardson indeed had so few modern readers, then one wonders exactly whom the Fieldingite critics were trying to provoke.)

Edward Wagenknecht puts things bluntly in 1943 when he writes of *Sir Charles Grandison*, "[T]here must be few people alive today who would read it through except for money."[128] The most frequently-cited reason for Richardson's neglect is the length of his novels. Even Carter, one the periods strongest Richardson supporters, imagines a casual reader browsing in the library and mistaking Richardson's novels for a shelf of encyclopedias: "[T]he substantial tomes of Richardson are a terrifying apparition. . . . The common reader puts the book back with a shudder."[129] Dobson seems positively resentful of the amount of primary research needed for his biography of Richardson. Dobson writes of Richardson's "extraordinary diffuseness and inordinate prolixity," which "must be allowed to be graver disadvantages than ever to-day, when, with the headlong hurry of life, the language of literature seems to tend less towards expansion and leisurely expression than towards the culture of the short-cut and the snap-shot."[130] Dobson is not the only critic who juxtaposes Richardson's length with the demands of "modern life." As an anonymous critic writes in the *Academy* (1901), Richardson is "not for the wireless age."[131] Utter finds another technological metaphor: "If Scott is beyond the stretch of the railroad novel reader who measures his fiction at sixty miles an hour between Buffalo and Albany, what has such a reader to do with *Pamela* and *Clarissa Harlowe* in prim little rows of four and eight calf-bound volumes?"[132]

Another frequently cited reason for Richardson's unpopularity among general readers is his foreignness to twentieth-century morality. "To-day, we find that virtue, and that human heart as Richardson envisaged it, somewhat mechanically posed, and meanly explored," writes Church.[133] Most surprisingly, C.A. Whittuck does not include *Sir Charles Grandison* in *The "Good Man" of the XVIIIth Century: A Monograph on XVIIIth Century Didactic Literature* (1901), writing that Richardson is "didactic enough" for inclusion, "but not *human* enough."[134] Other modern objections to Richardson's morality are discussed in the sections on Puritanism and psychoanalytic criticism, above.

Only an "elect few" read *Clarissa*, writes Williams in *Two Centuries of the English Novel* (1911).[135] Of Fielding, however, Williams gives us the twentieth-century equivalent of Johnson's statement that Richardson is the "greatest genius that had shed its lustre on this path of literature" when he writes of *Tom Jones* that there is "a larger and more imposing consensus of opinion that it is the greatest novel ever written than any other piece of prose-fiction penned by the hand of man."[136] The "consensus" is, of course, that of literary critics and not of general readers. Although Fielding's critical reputation soars throughout most of the early twentieth century, even his strongest advocates admit that Fielding, too, does not find a large following among general readers. An author named "Ranger" in *The Bookman* (February 1906) writes that "there is little doubt that with most readers of modern fiction, the perusal of Fielding is a custom honoured only in the breach. . . . [T]he leaves of 'Tom Jones' in the modern circulating library are more likely to be uncut than sullied."[137] Or, as Orwell puts it in 1944, "People pay lip service to Fielding and the rest of them, of course, but they don't read them, as you can discover by making a few inquiries among your friends. How many people have ever read *Tom Jones*, for instance?"[138]

Perhaps because Fielding receives more thoughtful and serious attention in the early twentieth century, critics are vocal about the possible reasons behind Fielding's popular neglect. Priestley treats the issue at length in "Henry Fielding: Then and Now," a valuable estimate of the horizon of expectations for general readers in 1954. Priestley sounds as if he would like to retranslate La Place's original French translation of *Tom Jones*: "I will admit there is a good deal that . . . a reader will want to skip . . . the mock heroic stuff, the reflections on human nature, the essay material, can be tedious. Again, much of the horse-play, the slapstick, is no longer to our taste." On the balance, however, Priestly finds a place for Fielding's eighteenth-century morality in the still-fallen world of the twentieth. "Fielding is about as obscenely corrupting as a brisk walk," Priestly writes. "Has he anything to say to us now? Not, of course, if the England of 1954 is so very different from the England of 1754, if sheer goodness of heart can now be taken for granted, if cant, humbug, meanness, hypocrisy, have vanished for ever."[139]

Conclusion

A full account of the Richardson/Fielding opposition from the late 1950s to the present is beyond the scope of this book. Academic literary criticism, which begins to increase with the growth of English departments in the 1890s, continues to multiply exponentially. The volume of commentary on Richardson and Fielding from the last twenty years alone is, in my unscientific estimation, approximately equal to the amount of commentary from the entire nineteenth century. Any attempt at a summary of this work would, in this space, seriously distort the diversity, complexity and theoretical underpinnings of this innovative body of scholarship. What is possible, however, is a snapshot of Richardson's and Fielding's reception in the present day.

One simple way to measure what it has meant to be "Richardsonian" or "Fieldingesque" over the course of the century is to trace the evolution of those words in the Oxford English Dictionary. "Richardsonian" appears in every edition of the O.E.D. since the first in 1914, when the adjective was apparently used as a compliment: of the three examples given, one is neutral and two are positive (from Dickens and Stevenson). By 1972, however, the word has become a stinging pejorative. No less than seven new examples are given, four of which are negative and three are neutral. It is difficult to say whether it is better to be ignored or insulted. The O.E.D. ignores the adjective "Fieldingesque" until it begins issuing supplements in 1972. Of the three examples given (all from the twentieth century), one carries a negative tone (from Aldous Huxley) and two are neutral.

Despite lackluster receptions in the dictionary, Richardson and Fielding's sales remain steady, and their relative positions remain consistent. Listing sales figures is not a perfectly accurate way to evaluate total readership, of course, but it nevertheless reveals which books are most likely getting attention in the college classroom. Penguin is currently the only publisher to have the major novels of both Richardson and Fielding in stock (no one is publishing *Sir Charles Grandison* at the moment), each produced with identical format and editorial policy, so their sales provide the most accurate direct comparisons. From 1996 to August 1998, *Pamela* ends up with the full coach and six at 11,400 copies. Her upstart foster brother *Joseph Andrews* comes in next at 7200, followed by *Tom Jones* (6900), *Clarissa* (3110), *A Journal of a Voyage to Lisbon* (1197), and *Jonathan Wild* (1178). *Amelia* still has her troubles, coming in last at 700 copies sold. All told, the combined sales of *Pamela* and *Clarissa* outstrip *Joseph Andrews* and *Tom Jones* by a narrow margin.

As shortly back as 1992 (when we can include *Sir Charles Grandison*), however, things were very different. According to sales figures from the major publishers with works by Richardson or Fielding in print (Penguin, Signet, Meridian and Oxford University Press), Fielding's sales were a daunting 287 percent greater than Richardson's. The combined sales of *Pamela*, *Clarissa*, and *Sir Charles Grandison* did not even equal the sales of *Tom Jones*, even though *Clarissa* saw a 17 percent jump in sales due to the BBC's popular 1992 television adaptation. Richardson and Fielding may not be attracting new readers in impressive numbers, but their reception history is currently as volatile as it has ever been.

Fielding also has a measureable, although not quite comfortable, edge over Richardson in the rivalry for critical attention. According to the Modern Language Association index from 1963 to 1998 (a representative, if not wholly accurate, gauge), Fielding's name appears 26 percent more than Richardson's (977 compared to 776). However, of all their novels, *Clarissa* attracts the most attention (310 entries), followed at a distance by *Tom Jones* (255), *Pamela* (194), *Joseph Andrews* (123), *Sir Charles Grandison* (enjoying something of a revival at 70 entries), *Amelia* (69), Fielding's dramas (63), and *Jonathan Wild* (43). (The contrast between the sales figures and the academic reference figures perhaps signals the priority of length over significance as English teachers block out their crowded syllabi.) Of the topics covered, a significant majority of academic work in the last twenty years is informed by feminist theory (especially for Richardson's works) and varieties of political/historical criticism (especially for Fielding's). It is still quite common to find the two authors mentioned together, even when the rivalry is not directly relevant to the topic under discussion.

Epistolary formats and self-reflective narrators can be found in much contemporary fiction, although a direct influence from (and creative commentary on) Richardson or Fielding is scarce at the moment. For general audiences, the best thing that has happened to Richardson and Fielding in the late twentieth century is cinema and television. Tony Richardson's adaptation of *Tom Jones* won an Academy Award for "best picture" in 1963, followed by a less successful version of *Joseph Andrews* in 1977. The less said about *The Bawdy Adventures of Tom Jones* (1976) the better. *Clarissa* was broadcast on the BBC and American public television in 1992, to considerable popular stir (and renewed comparisons to Fielding) in Great Britain. Overall ratings of *Clarissa*, however, were lower than the much-hyped BBC/Arts & Entertainment Network miniseries of *Tom Jones* in 1997. This was no doubt due, in part, to the parental advisories warning yet another generation of impressionable youth away from the nudity and "adult content" of Fielding's scandalous story.

Conclusion

*As we have seen, the processes of critical action and reaction,
whereby one generation's dogma becomes another generation's
taboo, and one generation's guru becomes another generation's
straw man, have long been in operation. But the fact that these
processes currently operate at an unprecedented speed poses unprecedented problems for modern critics. This is why it seems
important, if we are to be its beneficiaries, and not just its un-
witting instruments or victims, to take the dialectical process
itself into account.*

—Harriett Hawkins, *The Devil's Party:*
Critical Counter-Interpretations of
Shakespearean Drama

Dichotomies and Distortions

As I HOPE TO HAVE AMPLY DEMONSTRATED BY THIS POINT, THE RECEP-
tion history of either Richardson or Fielding is closely intertwined
with the reception history of his rival. While the critical criteria,
motivations, and perspectives vary according to the horizon of expectations in which they are situated, the dichotomy between the
two authors has remained a constant. The variety of criticism docu-
mented here contrasts sharply with the narrow range of authors it
chooses or excludes. The range of different critical paradigms
which arises from an opposition of only two authors demonstrates,
therefore, how unstable the opposition must be in the first place.
In other words, commentary on Richardson and Fielding keeps
veering away from Richardson and Fielding.

The institutionalized opposition has become a fountainhead for
criticism, often more so than the novels themselves. The result has
been an ongoing distortion of both Richardson and Fielding as individual authors, each with a rich, complex, and diverse body of
work.[1] As Duncan Eaves and Ben Kimpel observe, "There is no
more logical reason for not admiring both men as human beings
and as writers than for not admiring, for instance, both Milton and
James Joyce. . . ."[2]

There is, of course, nothing inherently *wrong* with pairing Richardson and Fielding together. An insightful contrast of the two novelists can reveal a great deal about many different aspects of eighteenth-century literature. The problem with the Richardson/ Fielding opposition is not that it is *invalid*, but that 250 years of literary tradition has conditioned us to believe that it is *inevitable*. Any critical formula naturally excludes as much or more than it highlights, and the Richardson/Fielding opposition is no exception. Because it is virtually second-nature for critics to foreground one author against the overt or implied background of the other, certain novels have become more canonical than others. Richardson's critical fame now stems primarily from *Clarissa*, but *Pamela* is still his most-read novel partly because it provides a pedagogical transition to Fielding. This odd phenomenon also holds true for Fielding. Fielding's critical attention focuses primarily on *Tom Jones*, but *Joseph Andrews* still sells more copies partly because it satirizes Richardson. "Shamela," a relatively minor work in Fielding's bibliography, has more readers than all his dramas and essays combined. The rivalry brings recurring critical attention to *Pamela*, "Shamela," and *Joseph Andrews*, but the modern emphasis on the novelists' rivalry is at the price of an almost total neglect of *Sir Charles Grandison*, *Amelia* and aspects of the other works that show a positive rather than negative mutual influence.[3] The battle is apparently more exciting than the peace.[4]

Questions and Answers

Contemporary literary theory may or may not offer a way out of dichotomized critical thinking. Modern theory often searches out the gray areas between traditional oppositions. Critics currently privilege concepts such as the androgyny between the "feminine" and "masculine," the postcolonial between the empire and wilderness, the political unconscious between the id and ego, the whole individual between the mind and body, the slippery text between the signifier and signified, and the marginalized between the winners and losers of history. On the other hand, the effort to free criticism from dichotomies is often one half of a larger dichotomy that is all the more pernicious for being less visible. One either supports the dichotomies or their deconstruction.

Critics often build the dichotomy of "dichotomies versus compromise" into their most progressive literary theories. Feminist criticism, for all its variety and complexity, still relies upon the "feminine"/"masculine" dichotomy by definition. Michel Foucault tends to see language, literary history, and almost all human behavior as part of an ongoing struggle for power and domination, just as one author's reputation can only rise at the expense of another's. The linguistic theory of Jacques Derrida claims that the very nature of language is oppositional. Both structuralism and poststructuralism hold that any utterance has meaning only within the implied context of what it is not, just as readers often see Richardson's works as "not Fielding's" and vice versa.[5]

The critical approach that initially appears to offer the greatest challenges to dichotomized thinking is the carnivalization and multiplicity of voices in Mikhail Bakhtin's theory of Dialogism. Bakhtin's writing is, however, steeped in the language of dichotomies and taut oppositions. Bakhtin writes in "Discourse in the Novel" that meaning in an utterance exists between the two competing forces of "centripetal" language that coalesces truth and "centrifugal" language that decentralizes it. Once meaning is located within the opposition of centripetal and centrifugal language, that opposition then becomes one half of a still larger opposition between the *individual* utterance and heteroglossia. Dialogism's pattern of escalating dichotomies brings us to the opposite conclusion of Deconstruction, allowing us to locate the precise meanings of texts rather than losing meaning in a process of infinite deferral:

> The process of centralization and decentralization, of unification and disunification, intersect in the utterance; the utterance not only answers the requirements of its own language as an individualized embodiment of a speech act, but it answers the requirements of heteroglossia as well; it is in fact an active participant in such speech diversity. . . . It is possible to give a concrete and detailed analysis of any utterance, once having exposed it as a contradiction-ridden, tension-filled unity of two embattled tendencies in the life of language.[6]

Even heteroglossia, the very principle of mixed voices and interlocking social forces, is in a one-to-one dialogue with its "other": heteroglossia is "aimed sharply and polemically against the official languages of its given time."[7]

Heteroglossia, despite its opposition with all that is *not* heteroglossia, is strikingly similar to what Jauss refers to as the "horizon of expectations" which defines the parameters of reader response. As Bakhtin writes, heteroglossia consists of "thousands of living dialogic threads, woven by socio-ideological consciousness around the given object of an utterance; it cannot fail to become an active participant in social dialogue."[8] Similarly, Jauss writes that the ho-

rizon of expectations arises out of and in turn contributes to the
socio-ideological consciousness of the day: the horizon is a "historical marker and, at the same time, the necessary condition for the
possibility of experiential knowledge—constitut[ing] all structures
of meaning related to human action and primary modes of comprehending the world."⁹ There is a possible opposition between
heteroglossia and the horizon of expectations, however. Whereas
Bakhtin describes heteroglossia as impossible to resolve and something a unitary language system must suppress, Jauss argues that
the precise identification of the horizon is central to literary understanding and is therefore the true substance of literary history.¹⁰ It
is in the tension between these two halves of a critical dichotomy
that I believe we can find a new approach to criticism of Richardson and Fielding. If heteroglossia represents a fertile and impossi-
bly commingled plurality of voices and if the horizon of
expectations represents identifiable chains of interlocking responses in chronological sequence, then the middle ground must
lie with studies that find order in how readers perceive the disorder
in their environment.

As I have shown, people often respond to uncertainty in the form
of two-part oppositions. Most questions can, at some level, be re-
duced to a simple "yes" or "no." The bewildering number of op-
tions available to us are at times only manageable in the form of
such simplistic equations. We can safely assume that dichotomized
thinking is an inevitable and even healthy psychological response
to unstructured experience. I propose, therefore, that perceptual
distortions of experience are proportional to the how wide we set
the parameters to our "yes"/"no" oppositions. Jauss's theory of
"questions and answers" suggests that the readers' reception of
works hinge on how they perceive the "answers" that any given
work offers to the "questions" of previous works; I am suggesting
that how broadly we choose to *bracket* those questions has an equal
influence on literary history.

For example, one of many oppositions created to summarize the
debate on a dizzying array of cultural, philosophical, moral, sexual,
economic, historical, and aesthetic issues is "Richardson versus
Fielding." As single authors became the two sides of an established
opposition, two massive and diverse collections of texts written by
each individual rose and fell along with their authors, thereby distorting the receptions and reputations of individual works. The
more general the opposition the easier it is to construct literary histories, since it is simpler to canonize an author than to select from
a long and inconsistent bibliography of texts. ("The death of the

author" in our poststructuralist age has had no appreciable effect on this familiar practice of literary histories.) Smaller-scale oppositions increase the complexity of literary histories as they increase their specificity. For example, Richardson versus Fielding becomes *Clarissa* versus *Tom Jones*, or, as the focus narrows, Lovelace versus Blifil, Lovelace versus Belford, or Belford's character before and after Clarissa's rape. Literary history becomes, as it narrows, inseparable from reader-response criticism. Specific records of reader responses are (or should be) the basis of literary history, but too often critics start with the largest possible dichotomies and work their way down. Reception theory offers a framework for starting at the bottom and working one's way up.

In conclusion, therefore, I suggest that we can partially compensate for the distortions caused by the Richardson/Fielding opposition by redirecting the remarkable critical energy which it still inspires toward a much more specific study of how tensions and oppositions work within the novels themselves. For example, Watt observes of *Pamela* that the "latent ambiguities" of the Puritan sexual code not only helped Richardson produce the first "true novel," but also "conspired to create something that was new and prophetic in quite another sense: a work that could be praised from the pulpit and yet attacked as pornography, a work that gratified the reading public with the combined attractions of a sermon and a strip tease."[11] Surely this type of criticism is more likely to draw readers to Richardson's novels than bitter and irrelevant comparisons to Fielding. To select another example, readers have often found Richardson the "feminine" author and Fielding the "masculine" author. Many of the same standards that make *Clarissa* "feminine" and *Tom Jones* "masculine," however, also make *Amelia* "feminine" and *Sir Charles Grandison* "masculine." Locating the "feminine"/"masculine" opposition on the broadest possible level of the author's identity is not at all useful or accurate. Better still is to avoid the troublesome anthropomorphism of entire texts and locate which *parts* of which novels are "feminine" or "masculine," under what conditions, in what terms, and why. Both Richardson and Fielding will still profit from this tighter focus of dichotomized critical thinking, and if one author still outstrips the other it will at least be a race on more level ground.

Literary critics of all types are in the rare and powerful position of having their personal impressions of entertainment become cultural history. It is increasingly important to remember that novelists may have rivalries, but novels do not. If we choose to contrast

Richardson and Fielding, then we should also study the contrasts *themselves* as a kind of a cultural "text" that shapes our expectations and conclusions. Only then are we likely to be aware of exactly what we inherit and bequeath whenever we pick up a novel by Richardson, Fielding, or by extension, anyone else.

Appendix

Chronological Summary

Much of the information in this book is arranged by type of reader or by theme, true to Jauss's suggestion that reception studies should break with the strict chronology of standard "horizontal" literary histories. Nevertheless, an undeniable part of the horizon that governs readers' expectations of Richardson and Fielding is an awareness of which author is "dominant" at any given moment. Readers from all three centuries tend to write on Richardson and Fielding as self-conscious insiders or outsiders, writing from either the group mentality of the literary fashion or from the fringes promoting their favorite author as ripe for rediscovery. By way of summary, therefore, I will rearrange the key moments in the Richardson/Fielding opposition into chronological order to illustrate how the perceived rise and fall of reputations influences reception.

I will also summarize each century's reception history according to the three types of readers as defined by Jauss: creative writers (type one), professional critics (type two) and general readers (type three). The three types of readers fit into four modes (or motives) of aesthetic appreciation. As defined in chapter one, these modes are *aesthesis* (passive appreciation), *poeisis* (active participation), *catharsis* (reading for improvement), and *theoria* (reading for understanding).

Patterns of Reception: The Eighteenth Century

There is some truth to the received opinion that Richardson was the most popular novelist of the eighteenth century and that he owes his success largely to a group of unsophisticated general readers. When the eighteenth-century readership is limited to the subset of those who make direct comparisons between Richardson and

Fielding, however, then the opposite is true: Fielding carries the day, albeit narrowly.

In the decade in which Richardson and Fielding's novels first appear, during the height of *Pamela* fever, Fielding still receives slightly more of the comparative support. Richardson has a devoted ally in Lady Bradshaigh, but the defection of Elizabeth Carter from Richardson's circle in 1743 and 1749 tips the balances to Fielding. Richardson soon makes a powerful comeback, however. The anonymous authors of *Critical Remarks on Sir Charles Grandison, Clarissa and Pamela* (1754) and a review in *The Magazine of Magazines* (1757) are the only voices in favor of Fielding throughout the 1750s. General readers such as May Delany, Anne Donnellan, and Thomas Edwards are most vocal, generally reading Richardson for *catharsis* and faulting Fielding's *aesthesis*. Critics of the same period use the same criteria to the opposite effect: they prefer Fielding's *aesthesis* to Richardson's. Creative writers make more commentary on Richardson and Fielding during the 1750s than in any other decade of the century, all focusing on *aesthesis* and all surprisingly neutral in their evaluations. It would seem Richardson and Fielding's general readers are more concerned with ethics, not considering Fielding as a moralist one way or another, while the critics and creative writers focus on technique and characterization. Readers continue to prefer Richardson throughout the 1760s, and his support is split evenly between critics (notably Lady Mary Wortly Montagu and Samuel Johnson) and general readers (notably James Fordyce). Fielding has only one supporter in the entire decade, the critic in the *New and General Magazine* of 1762, using the same *aesthesis* criteria Johnson used in 1768.

Fielding meets and narrowly exceeds Richardson's popularity in the 1770s, largely due to John Ogilvie, Charles Jenner, and other literary critics who contrast his *aesthesis* favorably to Richardson's. Johnson even prefers the morals (*catharsis*) of Amelia to those of Clarissa in 1776. Richardson nevertheless retains has support among the critics as his base of general readers starts to erode. More readers (especially Nicolas Barthe and the author of *Letters Concerning the Present State of England*) begin to admit a controversial neutrality of opinion in the late 1770s. The reception begins to signal the transition of Richardson and Fielding's works from current bestsellers to canonical touchstones used to evaluate newer works.

As Richardson and Fielding's works grow older, the commentary on both authors only continues to increase. There is more comparative criticism of Richardson and Fielding in the 1780s than in any other decade of the century, including the 1750s when the novels were new. The 1780s are also, remarkably, the only decade in which Richardson and Fielding have the same number of supporters. Richardson has readers from all three categories who read with all four types of motives, whereas the readers who prefer Fielding are mostly professional critics. The decade is full of diverse readers with diverse opinions, but no single critic emerges with any lasting influence on the reception of either author.

One would think that the sentimental, Gothic, and romantic tastes in literature would create a broader appreciation for Richardson's introspective and imperiled heroines at the close of the century, but there is not a single reader who records a preference for Richardson over Fielding. Only the *Monthly Review* of 1799 is neutral. Fielding's supporters are almost all professional critics (excepting "le Citoyen Davaux" and James Boswell), and their key concerns are *aesthesis* and *poeisis*. *Poeisis* is relatively rare in eighteenth-century criticism up to this point, but perhaps sentimental and early romantic literature brought more attention to emotional involvement and the readers' roles in Richardson and Fielding's narratives.

Overlooking the century as a whole, it becomes clear that Richardson's support comes as much from professional critics as from general readers. For all of Richardson's influence on other novelists, only Albinia Gwynn supports him against Fielding. There is almost as much praise for Richardson's artistic technique as for his morality. Among those who disparage Richardson, however, artistic technique is the main source of complaint. Fielding's support comes almost exclusively from the critics. *Aesthesis* commands the most attention from Fielding's readers, positive and negative. Those who object to Fielding tend to do so because of his narrative technique and characterization, *not*, ultimately, for his dubious sexual ethics.

Type-one readers across the century tend to be neutral in their comparative evaluations of Richardson and Fielding. Eighteenth-century novelists differ from novelists of other periods by being colleagues of Richardson and Fielding rather than descendants. *The Dunciad* (or, of course, *Shamela*) is evidence enough that creative writers in the Augustan period are happy to attack one another, so perhaps the neutrality of Richardson and Fielding's fellow novelists stems more from artistic and capitalistic concerns. Authors may have been in a unique position to appreciate the artistic validity of each novelist's different methods. Alternately, since coveted readers presumably felt strongly about Richardson and Fielding, perhaps creative writers simply wanted to associate their names with those of their famous predecessors. Richardson and Fielding (along with Laurence Sterne) were the most innovative novelists of their day, and the mere mention of their names had a certain commercial appeal.

Critics of the period favor Fielding, and *aesthesis* is their most common basis of comparison. Whereas critics tend to appreciate the more passive and intellectual qualities of a disciplined form and realistic characterization, general readers favor Richardson and take more interest in the pragmatic effects of the novels on impressionable young ladies and men. Despite all the strong words about morality and despite the subsequent generation's patronizing characterizations of eighteenth-century readers, *aesthesis* is marginally more important to Richardson and Fielding's body of readers than *catharsis*.

Patterns of Reception: The Nineteenth Century

Richardson's decline in the nineteenth century started slowly and accelerated rapidly. Most readers heralded Richardson's fall as Fielding's rise, as if there could not be room in the literary canon for both authors. Critics began to call upon imagination as well as research to recreate the culture that informed Richardson and Fielding's novels as the eighteenth century became increasingly distant, unfamiliar, and repugnant.

Anna Barbauld's edition of Richardson's *Correspondence* in 1804 marks the beginning of Richardson's long descent. Fielding attracts more of the comparative support than Richardson in the earliest years of the decade, mostly from critics (excepting Samuel Taylor Coleridge) with a wide range of aesthetic motivations. Richardson's readers are almost all critics as well, and *catharsis* carries over from the eighteenth century as the primary mode of Richardson appreciation.

Throughout the 1810s the Richardson/Fielding debate became especially sharp and bitter. Even Richardsonians were beginning to acknowledge that Fielding was rapidly outstripping their favorite. Actually, the 1810s are the last years (to 1957, at least) in which Richardson enjoys a majority of praise among those readers who compare him directly to Fielding. Richardson appeared to be on the way to something of a minor comeback by 1814, but with the appearance of Walter Scott's *Waverley*, discussion of all other novels slowed to a crawl. Richardson and Fielding were compared to Scott (negatively) more often than to one another. Richardson had a wide and supportive readership balanced between creative writers and critics. *Catharsis* is still the dominant motive. Appreciation of Richardson takes a variety of forms, but criticism of Fielding emphasizes almost exclusively his bad morality. Fielding had scant support in the decade, although William Hazlitt was particularly proud that he was able to persuade Charles Lamb in 1810 that Fielding was a better novelist than Richardson.

The 1820s are an inverse of the 1810s. Richardson does not have a single advocate throughout the decade. T. N. Talfourd alone is neutral in 1820, contrasting Richardson's *catharsis* favorably with Fielding's *aesthesis*. Aesthesis continues to be what Fielding's readers find strongest in his works and weakest in Richardson's. Librarians were still occasionally banning and burning Fielding's novels in the early 1830s,[1] but critics began using Fielding and Richardson as touchstones for canonical quality in reviews of the new novels by Charles Dickens and, later, William Thackeray. The popularity of Scott's novels lasted through the 1830s and still seemed to eclipse interest in older works, especially those that did not conform to the current fashion for historical romance. A key moment in the debate is Coleridge's famous comment in 1834 that reading Fielding after Richardson is like leaving a sick room heated by stoves for an open lawn in May.

By midcentury the great early critics of Richardson and Fielding—Coleridge, Lamb, Hazlitt and Scott—were all dead. A new generation of critics was emerging, reflecting a more genteel Victorian mentality. The popularity of Dickens and Thackeray in the 1840s created a situation similar to the 1810s after the publication of *Waverley*: there was a major drop-off in commentary on either novelist, especially for Richardson. Critics ignore Richardson once again, and Fielding has a small number of critics who compare his *aesthesis* favorably to Richardson's. The Victorians compare every century to their own, and conclude that the eighteenth century is without imagination, manners, and the inquisitive spirit. An unusual split occurs between biographical and critical accounts of Fielding—as a man he can do no good, and as a novelist he can do no wrong.

The years following Thackeray's opinionated lectures in 1851 see an increased interest in Fielding. Fielding has twice the number of critics as creative writers on his side. A majority of Fielding's readers compare him to Richardson in terms of *aesthesis*, although comparisons of laughter and tears begin to make *poeisis* increasingly prevalent in nineteenth-century criticism. Richardson has the backing of only two critics, David Masson and a tentative writer from the *Westminster Review*.

The 1860s are relatively uneventful for both Richardson and Fielding with one major exception. Margaret Oliphant's 1869 article in *Blackwood's* is the first of many feminist appreciations of Richardson (and critiques of Fielding), and almost one hundred years must pass before there are others. Richardson's critical good fortune does not last because he has no supporters against Fielding for over twenty years. Fielding has several substantial victories, however, most notably a glowing entry (at Richardson's expense) in the 1878 *Encyclopedia Britannica*. Fielding also won the endorsement of the fellow novelists George Meredith and Thomas Hardy, who were writing on *poeisis* and *aesthesis* respectively, as well as several critics who appreciate both *aesthesis* and *catharsis*. Fielding also began his escape from his malicious biographers. Austin Dobson, George Saintsbury, Edmund Gosse, and William Henley all published flattering biographies and/or collected works of Fielding in the 1880s and 1890s, all of which sold quickly. Fielding's greatest year in the nineteenth century was unquestionably 1883. The *Spectator* review of Leslie Stephen's edition of Richardson's works launches a merciless attack on Richardson, his novels, and his aesthetics. The timing could not have been worse for Richardsonians, as 1883 was also the year of a gala ceremony at Taunton to unveil the first public bust of Fielding. Finally, Fielding finds a hyperbolic advocate in Samuel Butler (balancing Richardson's advocate in Denis Diderot, who had placed Richardson's novels on the same shelf with the Bible): *The Psalms*, *Job*, and the *Prophets* cannot "hold their own" against *Tom Jones*.[2]

The majority of Richardson and Fielding's readers in the nineteenth century are professional literary reviewers, essayists, and historians. It is significant, however, that the most *influential* statements on the opposition come from creative writers. Despite a number of extremely unflattering biographies of Fielding from the high Victorians in the nineteenth century, the remarks of Coleridge, Scott, Hazlitt, Thackeray, and Hardy are the deciding factors in giving the nineteenth century to Fielding.

Patterns of Reception: The Early Twentieth Century

"Most recent reevaluations of Fielding's work indicate that the old Richardson-Fielding contrast has now come full circle—from the belief that Richardson was sentimental and moral and Fielding was realistic and immoral to its exact opposite," writes Ronald Paulson in 1962.[3] Fielding leads Richardson from 1894–1957 not only because he has more readers, but because he has new and different *kinds* of readers. Both authors' reputations have profited from the relatively recent explosion of literary criticism, history, biography, and theory, all written by the new class of professional literary academics. The intellectual tone of the Richardson/Fielding debate may be higher, but twentieth-century criticism on both authors is as divisive as it had ever been. Rarely does a modern critic indulge in the type of personal attacks so familiar from the eighteenth and nineteenth centuries, but individual agendas are still very much in play.

At the turn of the century, "English Studies" programs were establishing themselves at colleges and universities throughout England and America. Fielding has only one neutral reader who is willing to share the praise of *aesthesis* with Richardson, and the rest are a small number of Fieldingites for whom *catharsis* is still the basis of comparison. Clara Thomson's *Samuel Richardson: A Biographical and Critical Study* (1900) and Dobson's *Samuel Richardson* (1902) begin the new century on a more optimistic note for Richardson, although even his biographers defect to Fielding's camp when they make direct comparisons. Whereas Richardson's few supporters defend his *aesthesis* over Fielding's, Fielding has more support than in any other decade of the century. Along with the increase in academic readers comes an increase in academic motives for reading. *Aesthesis* is still the dominant mode of appreciation as realism, form, and characterization become increasingly important, but *theoria* (reading for information about the author, political implications, the author's relation to his period in history, etcetera) begins to make its presence felt. Richardson marks perhaps the lowest point of his early twentieth-century decline on 20 November 1901 when his bust was revealed in London. The occasion did not receive anything close to the fanfare of 1883 when Fielding's bust was revealed, and in his opening speech J. Passmore Edwards tells the small audience that Richardson's works are no longer important. In contrast to Richardson's fizzled revival, a reporter covering the festivities surrounding Fielding's bicentennial in 1907 writes that the "gigantic crop of Fielding appreciation raised by the anniversary has been distinctly overpowering. . . ."[4]

Beginning in the 1910s bibliographies of criticism show whole years going by with no references to Richardson at all, and most of his works go out of print. The period's most significant critical work on the Richardson/Fielding dichotomy is Wilbur Cross's three-volume *The History of Henry Fielding* (1918). Cross is eager to take the slander and name-calling that previous biographers had aimed at Fielding and redirects much of it toward Richardson. All the contributors to the debate are critics, and Richardson has about one-third the support of Fielding. Readers become increasingly diverse in their range of motives and critical dichotomies, moreso than at any other time in the Richardson/Fielding debate and with no particular pattern. Saintsbury's work is typical of one trend, however: Richardson and Fielding are discussed at length in *The English Novel* (1913), one of many introductory literary histories to follow throughout the century, and Saintsbury introduces the two authors by comparing them directly from a variety of critical perspectives. Richardson is always discussed first, with *Shamela* as the transition to Fielding.

Richardson gains increased attention in the early years of the century as psychoanalytic criticism finds its way into literary studies. Freudian criticism is not always flattering, of course. D.H. Lawrence finds Richardson's hothouse prurience to be lower than the lowest pornography in "Pornography and Obscenity" (1929), marking a full reversal from the years when Richardson's novels were recommended from eighteenth-century English pulpits. Virtually all of Richardson's backers, twice as many in the 1930s than in the 1920s, are concerned with the *aesthesis* of characterization and psychological realism. Fielding's numerous backers, however, compare the two almost exclusively with the political terms of *theoria* rather than the psychological terms of *aesthesis*.

Claud Rawson claims that it is not until the 1940s that the floodgates of academic publishing open to release some of the best—and the worst—literary criticism of the period. Criticism of both Richardson and Fielding is plentiful, both promoting and discrediting each author. Not only is there more criticism, but it is also at its most divisive. Never before has the Richardson/Fielding opposition been so evenly split: of the fifteen direct comparisons made during the 1940s, five support Richardson, five support Fielding, and five are neutral. Readers tend to contrast Fielding's positive *catharsis*, atypically, with Richardson's negative *aesthesis*. *Poeisis*, in the form of attention to Fielding's narrative addresses to the reader, also becomes important as formalism develops late in the decade. All but one of Richardson's critics, including the powerful F.R. Leavis, compare Richardson's *aesthesis* favorably to Fielding's.

R.S. Crane temporarily rescues Fielding from Leavis' banishment in 1954. His article "The Plot of *Tom Jones*" became a classic piece of the New Criticism, and, coupled with Priestley's impassioned bid for a new generation of readers in "Henry Fielding: Then and Now" (1954), Fielding seemed destined to leave the 1950s with at least the same reputation he brought into it. Fielding's admirers write mostly on *aesthesis*, but also *catharsis* and *theoria*, and they double the number of Richardson's admirers. There are as many neutral critics (writing primarily on *theoria*) as there are Fieldingite critics, so Fielding's high position is already precarious. Academic textbooks were still treating Richardson and Fielding as major historical figures, contrasting them in politics (Arnold Kettle's *An Introduction to the English Novel*, 1951), personality (Richard Church's *The Growth of the English Novel*, 1951), technique (Walter Allen's *The English Novel*, 1954), and sensibility (Alan McKillop's *The Early Masters of English Fiction*, 1956). All of the above demonstrate some degree of a Fielding bias. Richardson's supporters are few and write exclusively on the *aesthesis* of realism and form, but they are enormously influential. The most important of these supporters, Ian Watt, argues in *The Rise of the Novel* (1957) that Richardson is much more significant than Fielding in the development of the English novel because his forward-looking realism reflects eighteenth-century economic and social conditions more accurately than Fielding's backward-looking and improbable neoclassicism.

Notes

Chapter One: Reception Theory

1. Paulson and Lockwood, *The Critical Heritage*, xxi.
2. Frye, *Anatomy of Criticism*, 18.
3. Blanchard, *Fielding the Novelist*, 97.
4. Ibid., 97, 111, 565.
5. Wellek, "Theory of Literary History," 184.
6. Segers, "Interview with Hans Robert Jauss," 84.
7. Jauss, *Toward an Aesthetic of Reception*, 32.
8. Ibid., 20. Jauss is unclear about literary interpretation being the sum total of interpretations that have come before it. At some points Jauss emphasizes the ways in which any single reception of a text is informed by every other previous reception of that text; at other points Jauss emphasizes nonsequentiality as a reality of an individual's aesthetic experience, offering it as an advance on the narrowly chronological literary histories of the past. The weakness in the first point of view is that the historical sequence of reception is not the same thing as the historical *evolution* of reception, since all interpretations of a literary work coexist rather than update and invalidate one another.

   Jauss best addresses the problem with his distinction between "actual" (i.e., original audience reaction) and "virtual" (i.e., collective judgment over time) significance. The virtual significance is sometimes a rehabilitated version of the actual: "The distance between the actual first perception of a work and its virtual significance . . . can be so great that it requires a long process of reception to gather in that which was unexpected and unusable within the first horizon" (35).

   This paradigm accounts for how a neglected work comes into favor after its first appearance, but it does not account for works which were initially popular, went out of favor for a time, then reappeared (such as *Clarissa*). Is something from the original reception found to be "unusable" by the second audience, or is the work neglected because of earlier receptions, making the neglect itself a kind of reception? Does the third audience, the one that brings the work back into favor, recover elements from the actual significance of the first audience, the second, or a synthesis of both?

9. Ibid., 52.
10. Wlad Godzich, in Jauss, *Aesthetic Experience*, x–xi.
11. Wünsch, "Status and Significance of Reception Studies." Marianne Wünsch is typical of critics whose initial approbation of reception theory becomes more skeptical when faced with grandiose claims of revolution. Great promises create great expectations: reception theorists have "significantly failed to fulfill their programmatic aim of revitalizing literary studies and literary history by introducing new problems and methods," Wünsch writes. "The responsibility for this failure lies not with reception studies themselves but rather with the over-inflated hopes

which were invested in an area of enquiry which plays an admittedly significant but nevertheless subordinate role in literary studies as a whole" (324).

12. Holub, "American Reception of Reception Theory." Robert C. Holub argues that reception theory has had a comparatively weak reception in America for two reasons. First, the academic climate in English departments during the sixties was centered on political reform rather than specific methodological adjustments. Second, Americans resolutely cling to formalism (via structuralism or deconstruction), blocking a full exposure to the background of German literary theory. Reception theory has not been greatly influential in American English departments because it postulates "a non-textual referent in either history, the reader, or the society," conflicting with what Holub calls the American "obsession with the text" which has lasted since the 1960s (85–87).

Holub's own blind spot, however, concerns what would happen if his position were to be taken to its logical extreme. If everyone were a reception critic, there would soon be no more receptions to write about. The paradox has not been lost on unsympathetic critics of reception theory such as Wünsch:

> Given, on the one hand, that the study of reception cannot replace interpretation, and on the other, that the available documents of the past reception of texts generally only offer a partial, unrepresentative view of the reception process as a whole, it would seem that the project of substituting reception history for literary history is doomed to fail. The history of literature has no option but to base itself on the study of literary texts, to interpret them and construct models to order and structure them. Reception studies can only play a subordinate, secondary role in literary history. ("Status and Significance," 327)

13. Richter, "Reception of the Gothic Novel," 119.

14. Jauss, *Toward an Aesthetic of Reception*, 18.

15. As I am not making extensive use of Iser's theories in this book, I am not including a detailed summary and analysis of his work. Iser's position is explained, contrasted with Jauss's, and placed into the wider context of reception theory in Holub, *Reception Theory*, Schlaeger, "Recent German Contributions to Literary Theory," and Orr, "Reception-Aesthetics as a Tool," all cited in the bibliography.

16. Holub, "American Reception of Reception Theory," 88.

17. Schlaeger, "Recent German Contributions to Literary Theory," 63.

18. Holub, "American Reception of Reception Theory," 90.

19. Notable studies of how readers construct meanings from Richardson and Fielding's works include Indyk, "Interpretive Relevance and Richardson's *Pamela*," Howard, "Intrusive Audience in Fielding's *Amelia*," Castle, *Clarissa's Ciphers*, Preston, "Plot as Irony" and *The Created Self*, Warner's *Reading Clarissa*, Iser, "Role of the Reader in Fielding's *Joseph Andrews* and *Tom Jones*," and Keymer, *Richardson's "Clarissa,"* all cited in the bibliography.

20. Reception theory is so little-known among Americans that the word "reception" is not even a subject heading for the Library of Congress. Jauss's *Toward an Aesthetic of Reception* is listed under the subject heading "Reader-response criticism," and Holub's *Reception Theory* (to date the only book-length survey of reception theory originally written in English) is listed as "Reader-response criticism Germany (West)."

21. Iser, *The Implied Reader*, 34.

22. Jauss, *Toward an Aesthetic of Reception*, 26.

23. Ibid., 26–27.

24. Jauss, *Aesthetic Experience*, xxix–xxx.

25. Schlaeger, "Recent German Contributions to Literary Theory," 66. This is

not wholly fair to Jauss, who does outline a method in immense detail for identifying "the processes underlying the constitution of meaning" and its "dialogic structure" in *Question and Answer*. Schlaeger may not have been familiar with the book before he wrote his remark, as both were published 1982. Jauss's "question and answer" method, discussed below, is nevertheless highly individualistic and subjective compared to Iser's rigorous approach of locating the specific textual structures which guide interpretation.

26. Jauss, *Toward an Aesthetic of Reception*, 21.

27. Ibid., 64.

28. Jauss, *Aesthetic Experience*, xxx–xxxi.

29. Jauss, *Toward an Aesthetic of Reception*, 12. For example, Jauss explains that Marxist criticism diminishes the complex historicity of literature by using the traditional canon of great authors to create quick and simple insights into the material conditions of the social process.

30. Ibid., 40.

31. Ibid., 41.

32. Ibid., 45.

33. Armstrong, *Desire and Domestic Fiction*, 29.

34. Jauss, *Toward an Aesthetic of Reception*, 32.

35. Jauss, *Question and Answer*, 104. Jauss provides a more detailed example of author-to-author reception from Goethe's *Werther*, reading it as a response to Rousseau's *La Nouvelle Héloïse* (178).

36. Excellent "mutual influence" essays include Digeon, "Autour de Fielding," Anderson, "Answers to the Author of *Clarissa*," and Saintsbury, *The English Novel*, all cited in the bibliography. Most introductory studies of *Joseph Andrews* and *Amelia* analyze Fielding's debt to Richardson: among the best are Battestin Introduction to *Joseph Andrews*, Jenkins, "Richardson's *Pamela* and Fielding's 'Vile Forgeries'," Sabor, "*Amelia* and *Sir Charles Grandison*," and Eaves, "Amelia and Clarissa," all cited in the bibliography. Critics often mention the influence of *Tom Jones* on *Sir Charles Grandison*, but surprisingly there are no essay-length considerations of the issue.

37. Jauss, *Toward an Aesthetic of Reception*, 148.

38. Jauss, *Question and Answer*, 224.

39. Jauss, "Paradigmawechsel in der Literaturwissenschaft," 55.

40. Many of Iser's theoretical principles are applicable here, but because the focus of this study is on the simultaneous reception of *two* authors, Jauss's paradigm is still the most efficient.

41. Jauss, *Toward an Aesthetic of Reception*, 25–26.

42. Jauss, *Question and Answer*, 197.

43. Richter, "Reception of the Gothic Novel," 119–21.

44. Godzich, in Jauss, *Aesthetic Experience*, xii.

45. Richter, "Reception of the Gothic Novel," 118.

46. Audiences "catching up" with the horizons of innovative literary works may account for much of the rise and fall of attention given to Richardson and Fielding over the years. As I will theorize in the third chapter, Richardson in particular fell victim to his own earlier success: in general terms, the moral conservatism he advocated so strongly became ingrained in Victorian high society to the point where Victorians found little else interesting do with his works than search for points of sexual prurience.

47. Eagleton, *Literary Theory*, 84–85. Perhaps one reason why it seems that Jauss and Iser ignore the question is because they assume it as a given. Of course

their interpretation, like anyone else's, is nothing more than exactly that: an interpretation. Who would suggest or expect otherwise?

48. Ibid., 83.
49. Jauss, *Question and Answer*, 198.
50. Jauss, *Toward an Aesthetic of Reception*, 23.
51. Ibid., 24.
52. Jauss, *Question and Answer*, 149–50.
53. Zavala, "Textual Pluralities," 263.
54. Richter, "Reception of the Gothic Novel in the 1790s," 128–29.
55. Jauss, *Aesthetic Experience*, xxxvi.
56. Ibid., 34–35.
57. Ibid., 34.
58. Ibid., 35.
59. Richter, "Reception of the Gothic Novel in the 1790s," 129.
60. Jauss, *Toward an Aesthetic of Reception*, 19.
61. Ibid., 19.
62. Ibid., 19.
63. Holub, *Reception Theory*, 134.
64. Carter, *A Series of Letters*, 1:16.
65. Jauss, *Aesthetic Experience*, 35.
66. Richter, "Reception of the Gothic Novel in the 1790s," 119. I cannot find anything in Jauss's work to support the notion that shifts of audience motivation cause literary change. To the contrary, Jauss would be more likely to believe that literary change causes shifts in audience motivation. Richter's misreading of Jauss is nevertheless useful and thought-provoking, and I am using it as a basis for my deliberate "misreading" to claim that the modes can conflict as well as cooperate.
67. *Critical Remarks on Sir Charles Grandison, Clarissa and Pamela*, 18–19.
68. I use the term "turning point" in the reception critic Claude de Grève's sense:

Instead of the concept of 'date,' it seems more suitable here to use the concept of 'turning point,' the 'turning point' corresponding to a historical event as well as to the renewal of an author's success, or to the appearance of a new interpretation or new criteria for evaluation, or corresponding simply to a jubilee year that gives everybody the opportunity to summarize phenomena and open up new perspectives. ('Comparative Reception': A New Approach to 'Rezeptionästhetik',", 238)

69. Schücking, *Sociology of Literary Taste*, 64.

Chapter Two: The Eighteenth Century: *Shamela* to Richardson's *Correspondence*, 1741–1804

1. *Laureate*, 94.
2. Battestin, *Henry Fielding*, 77.
3. *The Champion* No. 69 (22 April 1740), No. 72 (29 April 1740), No. 75 (6 May 1740), and No. 80 (17 May 1740).
4. Battestin *Henry Fielding*, 304, states that Fielding initially had "no notion at all" who wrote *Pamela* at the time he composed *Shamela*. Fielding does make several pointed references to the author of *Pamela*, however, which suggest what may be his best guess. For example, Parson Oliver says of the "composer" of *Pam-

ela, "Who that is, though you so earnestly require of me, I shall leave you to guess from the *Ciceronian* Eloquence, with which the Work abounds; and that excellent Knack of making every Character amiable, which he lays his hands on" (Fielding, "Shamela," 324). The full title of the work, *An Apology for the Life of Mrs. Shamela Andrews,* along with Parson Williams' words to Shamela, bring to mind Cibber's recently published autobiography *An Apology for the Life of Mr. Colley Cibber.* As Austin Dobson writes, "These are certainly not obvious references to Richardson. On the contrary, they seem rather to point obscurely to Cibber . . ." (*Fielding,* 45). (Dobson's opinion is seconded by McKillop, "Personal Relations" 424; Digeon, *Novels of Fielding,* 47, 49; Johnson, Introduction to *Shamela,* iii; and Banerji, *Henry Fielding,* 108–9). Fielding also signs *Shamela* as "Mr. Conny Keyber," a name he had applied to Cibber ten years earlier in "The Author's Farce."

By the time Fielding writes *Joseph Andrews* he certainly knows that Richardson wrote *Pamela.* The first chapter of *Joseph Andrews* speaks of Cibber and the author of *Pamela* as two different people. Fielding may mention Cibber early in *Joseph Andrews* to clear him of any false blame, as there is little other reason for Fielding to have mentioned Cibber in this context.

For an argument that Fielding originally believed the Reverend Thomas Birch wrote *Pamela,* see Woods, "Fielding and the Authorship of *Shamela.*"

5. This overview of Richardson's and Fielding's personal relationship makes no attempt to be exhaustive and is offered only as background for the context of their readership. I am not considering Richardson and Fielding's reception of one another individually as part of their *combined* reception, except insofar as it influences other readers (most notably those after 1804 reacting to the publication of Richardson's *Correspondence*; see chapter three). See McKillop, "Personal Relations between Fielding and Richardson"; MacAndrew, "Debate Between Richardson and Fielding"; and the biographies by McKillop, Eaves and Kimpel, Cross, and Battestin.

6. Cheyne, *Letters of Dr. George Cheyne to Samuel Richardson,* 85.

7. The fanatical Richardsonian Thomas Edwards writes to Daniel Wray on 16 June 1755: "Fielding's malevolence against our friend was the more unpardonable as the Good Man had once by his interposition saved his bones and at the very last by his correspondence at Lisbon had procured him accommodations which he could not otherwise have had" (McKillop, *Samuel Richardson,* 177). Biographers have not been able to verify the story, although it has provided fodder for imagining ways in which critics could use it to reinforce the vindictive nature of the rivalry: "How eagerly would James Boswell have run this story down, and what a highly colored paragraph could Thackeray have made of it for his *English Humourists!*" (McKillop, "Personal Relations," 432). If true, Fielding would have been uncharacteristically ungracious in his reply, as Richardon is mercilessly mocked in the preface to *The Journal of a Voyage to Lisbon.*

8. Miles, in "Richardson's Response to Fielding's Felon," suggests that *Clarissa* contains the barest reference to *Jonathan Wild* when Clarissa asserts that a "great" and a "good" man are the same thing: Richardson "could not allow Fielding's premise to go unchallenged without jeopardizing the glory of his heroine. Raising any kind of objection would only serve as an acknowledgment that he had read Fielding's *Jonathan Wild.* Richardson, caught in a dilemma, extricated himself ingeniously" (374).

9. Digeon, *Novels of Fielding,* 132. Battestin, *Henry Fielding,* 455, finds several places in *Tom Jones* where Sophia is implicitly compared to Clarissa, however: 15:3, 16:5, and 18:9.

10. Fielding, *Tom Jones*, 468–69.

11. Paulson and Lockwood, *Henry Fielding*, 11. Texts that deal with the mutual influence of Richardson and Fielding during the compositions of *Sir Charles Grandison* and *Amelia* include Sabor, "Amelia and Sir Charles Grandison," and Sitter, *Literary Loneliness*. Both critics document the characteristic traits which Richardson and Fielding switch with one another in their final novels. As Sabor writes, "There is not merely a convergence but almost an exchange of roles" (5). Along the way, Sabor draws clearly defined oppositions between traits that are Fieldingesque (outdoor adventures, action-oriented plotting, external narration) and Richardsonian (domestic scenes, complex psychology of characters, limited perspective in narration). Sitter is more flexible in his oppositions: "Richardson and Fielding did not need to learn everything of the modes of their last novels from each other, since their own earlier work contains hints of them. But it seems unlikely that they both would have pursued their least promising tendencies without the spur—and blinders—of emulation" (191). For an impassioned but unconvincing argument that *Tom Jones* was written in direct response to *Clarissa*, see Digeon, *Novels of Fielding* (130–61).

There is room for more work to be done along these lines, especially comparisons of Richardson and Fielding's novels which do not follow one another in immediate chronologly. For example, Fielding's narrative digressions on "mixed characters" in *Jonathan Wild* may be in part a continued response to *Pamela*, and *Grandison* may be in turn as much a response to *Jonathan Wild* as to *Tom Jones*. Critics have given more attention to *Grandison*'s relationship to *Tom Jones* than to *Amelia*'s relationship to *Clarissa*, perhaps because the debt is less obvious, making the symmetry of the "convergence" more difficult to sustain.

The danger in such a comparative approach is making close readings of Richardson and Fielding's works a witch hunt for evidence of the rival's superior presence. Elizabeth Brophy's oversimplification is a case in point: "[A]fter *Pamela* made fiction respectable other talents were attracted to the form. It is certainly arguable that Fielding would never have become a novelist if Richardson had never written" (115).

12. Richardson, *Sir Charles Grandison*, 3:464–66.

13. Fielding, *Journal of a Voyage to Lisbon*, 124. There is no direct evidence that Fielding ever read *Sir Charles Grandison*, but as is clear from Richardson's probable nonreading of *Tom Jones*, that does not necessarily prevent any critical commentary. If Fielding's comment about the reform of morals refers to *Grandison*, according to Blanchard, "it was a singularly mild statement from a writer who had witnessed the failure of his Amelia and the triumph of the egregious Sir Charles" (*Fielding the Novelist*, 123).

14. Fielding, *Journal of a Voyage to Lisbon*, 129.

15. Fielding, *Correspondence*, 71. It is not known if Richardson ever responded, but he did share this letter with his admirers (Battestin, *Henry Fielding*, 444).

16. Richardson, *Correspondence of Samuel Richardson*, 3:33–34.

17. Hazlitt, *Complete Works of William Hazlitt*, 17:129.

18. Paulson and Lockwood, *Henry Fielding*, 19.

19. The special cases of Lady Mary Wortley Montagu and Sarah Fielding—admirers of Richardson but relatives of Fielding—will be discussed below.

20. Bradshaigh to Richardson, 16 December 1749, *Correspondence of Samuel Richardson*, 4:295–96.

21. Aaron Hill to Richardson, 11 August 1749, in Dobson, *Fielding*, 133.

22. For appraisals of Richardson's radical *political* philosophy, see Eagleton,

Rape of Clarissa, as well as other twentieth-century works discussed in chapter four and in the conclusion. Richardson's most radical political statements are nevertheless always informed by his consistently conservative Christian moral philosophy.

23. Boswell, *Boswell's Life of Johnson*, 2:495.

24. "Morals of Fielding," 421.

25. Porter, *English Society in the Eighteenth Century*, 266.

26. Bartolomeo, "Johnson, Richardson, and the Audience for Fiction," 517.

27. See Iser, *The Implied Reader*.

28. Fielding, *History of Tom Jones*, 467.

29. Cross, *History of Henry Fielding*, 1:354–55.

30. See McKeon, *The Origins of the English Novel 1600–1740*.

31. Jenner, *Placid Man*, 72–73.

32. Perhaps the distance between aristocratic readers and bourgeois characters in *Pamela* accounts for the assumptions of a diverse audience, whereas the readership of *Tom Jones* tends to be demographically close to the characters represented.

33. Whitehead, *Plays and Poems*, 2:313, 315.

34. Griffith, *Genuine Letters Between Henry and Francis*, 1:153.

35. Charles Jenner, *Placid Man*, 71–72.

36. Barthe, *La Jolie Femme*, 455.

37. It is admittedly a minor influence. It could also be argued that novels *preceded* essays in literary criticism, or at least developed simultaneously, or that the influence was mutual. The "book review" as we know it has its origins in earlier criticism of the drama, however, most notably in Dryden, "Essay on Dramatic Poetry," 1668. See Bartolomeo, *A New Species of Criticism*.

38. Gwynn, *The Rencontre*, 136–37.

39. Smythies, *Stage Coach*, 1:71–72.

40. The ultimate cause for this blending of horizons may lie in a complex chain reaction of receptions, but the immediate cause may be much more practical and prosaic. Allusions to Richardson and Fielding had, "as every hack-writer well knew, a market value," writes Blanchard (*Fielding the Novelist*, 104).

41. Graves, *Spiritual Quixote*, 1:vi.

42. Cooper, *Exemplary Mother*, 1:14.

43. *History of Charlotte Summers*, in Cross, *History of Henry Fielding*, 2:135.

In a masterpiece of equivocation, Dorothy Bradshaigh writes to Richardson (25 March 1750) about the allusion made to him in *Charlotte Summers*. Richardson took all the credit for the complimentary reference, and Lady Bradshaigh gently corrects him: "I doubt I do not remember what he says; but I think it is, that we are taught the art of *laughing* and *crying*, from your *melancholy* disposition, and Mr. Fielding's *gay* one; and I think passes a compliment upon each, though perhaps he might design to sneer. There are different kinds of laughter: you make me laugh with pleasure; but I often laugh, and am angry at the same time with the facetious Mr. Fielding" (Richardson, *Correspondence* 6:7–8).

As Cross writes of this letter, "So it was that a compliment intended rather for Fielding than for Richardson was turned by flattery into a sneer" (*History of Henry Fielding*, 2:145).

44. The lack of poetic commentary on Richardson and Fielding suggests that the opposition's relevance as a phenomenon of popular culture may have been fairly limited to those readers and critics who drew sharp lines between the "romance" and more distinguished types of literature. With the major exception of

Shakespeare, Richardson and Fielding are almost never compared to poets of any period.

The first book to discuss literary rivalries after Richardson and Fielding's day is Disraeli, *Quarrels of Authors*, and the focus is almost exclusively on poets and philosophers.

45. Burns, *Poetry of Robert Burns*, 4:11.

46. Cumberland, *Henry*, 1:97–98.

47. Blanchard, *Fielding the Novelist*, 246.

48. Keymer, *Richardson's "Clarissa" and the Eighteenth-Century Reader*, xx.

49. The sad irony is that the fire was started during the Gordon Riots by an angry mob—the exact kind of mob that Henry and John Fielding worked so hard to control by dispensing justice from that very house. William Henry Fielding, Henry's grandson, wrote in 1820 that "some Novels and other works, ready for the press, were in the House of *Sir John Fielding* when it was destroyed . . . and they thus fell a sacrifice to the flames" (quoted in Battestin, *Henry Fielding*, 617).

Battestin and Clive T. Probyn have recently suggested that the corpus of Fielding's correspondence is so small because Fielding was never a prolific correspondent. "Fielding, quite simply, hated writing letters," (Fielding, *Correspondence*, xvi). Battestin and Probyn cite a letter from Fielding to James Harris dated 8 September 1741 (which Rosemary Bechler finds in her review "marvellously un-Richardsonian" ["Detested Exercise," 21]), in which Fielding reminds Harris that a letter is a "Token of a violent Affection" and "an Exercise which, notwithstanding I have in my time printed a few Pages, I so much detest, that I believe it is not in the Power of three Persons to expose my epistolary Correspondence" (Fielding, *Correspondence*, xvi). Fielding has great foresight in this regard, as Richardson's "exposure" with the 1804 publication of his *Correspondence* contributed to Richardson's falling reputation throughout the next century.

50. See Battestin, Introduction to *Joseph Andrews*, xxxiv; and Cross, *History of Henry Fielding*, 1:357.

51. Paulson and Lockwood, *Henry Fielding*, 6. Paulson and Lockwood's point is nevertheless valid about the relative scarcity of journals. The situation was to improve with time, according to McKillop, since "in the long run both authors profited" as the new modes of sentimentalism which came from Lawrence Sterne and Jean Jacques Rousseau in the 1760s led to "more frequent and more elaborate" criticism (McKillop, *Samuel Richardson*, 231). There is an interesting parallel to the explosion of literary criticism after the 1960s wherein "both authors have profited" once again.

52. Paulson and Lockwood, *Henry Fielding*, 6.

53. Williams, Preface, ix–x.

54. Blanchard, *Fielding the Novelist*, 39.

55. Hunter, *Before Novels*, 196.

56. Blair, *Dr. Blair's Lectures on Rhetoric*, 198–99.

57. Hunter, *Before Novels*, 19.

58. Reeve, *Progress of Romance*, 1:139–41.

59. Welleck, *A History of Modern Criticism*, 1:122.

60. Moore, "Commencement and Progress of Romance," 171.

61. Hunter, *Before Novels*, 21.

62. Paulson and Lockwood, *Henry Fielding*, 20.

63. Review of *The History of Amanda*, 182.

64. *The Adventures of a Valet*, in Paulson and Lockwood, *Critical Heritage*, 337.

65. Gibbon, *Mémoires littéraires de la Grande Bretagne*, 1:76.

66. Johnson quoted in Burney, *The Early Diary*, 1:90.

67. Review of *Cecilia*, 453.

68. Reeve, *Progress of Romance*, 2:133.

69. Anna Williams, in Blanchard, *Fielding the Novelist*, 112.

70. J.W. Von Archenholz, in Smith, *Samuel Richardson*, 77.

71. Canning, "On Novel Writing," 303.

72. Mathias, *The Pursuits of Literature*, 59–60.

73. The *New and General Biographical Dictionary* of 1762 does integrate Richardson and Fielding into the Shaftesbury/Hobbes debate, but the question being answered has more to do with philosophy than literary canonization. In any case, the comparison is indirect (Chalmers, 10:142–23).

74. *Letters Concerning the Present State of England*, 357–58; 393–94.

75. "Despite the tinge of hysteria, Diderot's outburst is the most important criticism of Richardson in the eighteenth century," claims McKillop (*Samuel Richardson*, 275).

76. Ibid.

77. Béclard, *Sébastien Mercier*, 425.

78. McKillop, *Samuel Richardson*, 261. Among the other comparisons of Richardson and Rousseau are *The Critical Review* 12 (Sept. 1761), 203–11; *The Monthly Review* 25 (1761), 260; *Anecdotes of Polite Literature* (1764, 2:2 78–79); and "A Critical Examination of the Respective Merits of Voltaire, Rousseau, Richardson, Smollett, and Fielding," *Universal Museum*, n.s. 2 (August 1766), 391–93.

79. Pratt, "On Novel-Writing," 124–25.

80. Denis Diderot in Eaves and Kimpel, *Samuel Richardson*, 605.

81. The reason why I am not following this track in detail is because it was the jealous and easily insulted Smollett himself who decided that Fielding was a rival, not so much other novelists, the critics, or the general readership. Comparisons between Fielding and Smollett can still be found, of course, but not with anything near the frequency or historical impact of the comparisons with Richardson. Comparative reception studies of Fielding/Smollett and Richardson/Rousseau would likely yield some interesting results, however, and are areas that need future research.

82. Fielding, *The Covent Garden Journal*, 65–66.

83. Blanchard, *Fielding the Novelist*, 97.

84. Ibid., 242.

85. Lang, *Adventures Among Books*, 175–76.

86. Anderson, *Poets of Great Britain*, 10:946. In conclusion, it is interesting to speculate on the comparisons that were *not* frequently made to Richardson and Fielding. Paulson and Lockwood's book of selected criticism, *Henry Fielding: The Critical Heritage*, has a useful index to the authors compared to Fielding throughout the century. (The editors make no claim to represent accurate proportions.) Richardson leads with sixteen references (I have found over fifty); Cervantes follows with fifteen; Gay with eight; Molière and Smollett with six; Hogarth, Scarron, and Swift with five; Le Sage and Marivaux with four; Aristophanes, Congreve, Lucian, and Wycherley with three; and two each for Addison, Buckingham, Cibber, Crébillon, Dryden, Jonson, and Vanbrugh. There is no companion volume in the same series for Richardson.

Surprisingly, there are no surviving eighteenth-century comparisons between Richardson and Mackenzie. (Mackenzie does allude to Richardson, however, in the preface to *The Man of Feeling*.) The only comparison of Fielding and Sterne is from Cumberland's *Henry*: "Amongst our countrymen, the great masters of contrast in our own day are Fielding and Sterne: Square and Thwackum, Western and his sister, the father and the uncle of Tristram Shandy, are admirable instances" (8:6).

87. Jauss, *Question and Answer*, 224.

88. Cumberland, "From *The Observer*," 332–33.

89. Barthe, "Excerpt from *La Jolie Femme*," 455.

90. Cumberland, *Henry*, 334.

91. Fielding and Richardson are both aware of the realism/idealism dichotomy throughout their rivalry. The *Tom Jones*, *Grandison*, and *Journal of a Voyage to Lisbon* exchange on "mixed characters" is discussed above, pp. 000.

92. Beattie, *Dissertations Moral and Critical*, 572.

93. Ogilvie, *Philosophical and Critical Observations*, 1:342–43.

94. Thomas Edwards to Rev. Lawry, 12 February 1752, in Paulson and Lockwood, *Critical Heritage*, 320.

95. Bisset, "History of Literature and Science for the Year 1799," 57.

96. Ibid., 56.

97. Reeve, *The Progress of Romance*, 1:139–41; *Olla Podrida* 15 (1787); *Olla Podrida* 16 (1787); Barthe, "Excerpt from *La Jolie Femme*," 455.

98. Johann Gottfried von Herder, *Über die Wirkung'* in Smith, *Samuel Richardson*, 73.

99. Blanchard, *Fielding the Novelist*, 124–25.

100. Paulson and Lockwood, *Henry Fielding*, 6.

101. A close analysis of the argument and meaning of Fielding's preface can be found in Goldberg, "Comic Prose Epic or Comic Romance," and in Battestin, Introduction to *Joseph Andrews*.

102. Cross, *History of Henry Fielding*, 1:357–58.

103. Beattie, *Dissertations Moral and Critical*, 567–73.

104. Samuel Johnson to Hannah More in Roberts, *Correspondence of Mrs. Hannah More*, 1:101.

105. Samuel Johnson to James Boswell, in Boswell, *Boswell's Life of Johnson*, 2:48–49. Critics who have responded in way or another to this particular statement include Boswell, Hazlitt, Walter Scott, John Forster, and George Saintsbury.

106. Robert Moore disagrees that Johnson cannot stay focused on Fielding without digressing on Richardson: "The condition of his censure of Fielding is nearly always in its comparison with Richardson . . . for the occasions on which Johnson belittles Fielding are usually those where Richardson is the real center; when speaking of Fielding alone, his attitude is different" ("Dr. Johnson on Fielding and Richardson," 171).

107. Samuel Johnson to James Boswell, in Boswell, *Boswell's Life of Johnson*, 2:174–75.

108. Ibid, 2:49.

109. Ian Donaldson finds the image of the clock, a symbol of precise and intelligent human artistry, used by John Locke in *An Essay Concerning Human Understanding* (Book III, c. vi, 3); Fielding in *Tom Jones* (V iv) and *Jonathan Wild* (opening paragraph); Thomas Hobbes in the introduction to *Leviathan*; Jonathan Swift in *Tale of a Tub* ("Digression on Madness"); and most famously in the first chapter of Sterne's *Tristram Shandy* ("The Clockwork Novel").

110. Samuel Richardson to Sarah Fielding, 7 December 1756, in Fielding, *Correspondence*, 132.

111. Boswell, *Boswell's Life of Johnson*, 2:49.

112. Cross, *History of Henry Fielding*, 2:130.

113. Watt, *Rise of the Novel*, 329.

114. Moore, "Dr. Johnson on Fielding and Richardson," 163–64. Hunt's "Johnson on Fielding and Richardson" is another detailed expression of bafflement over Johnson's preferences.

115. Johnson, "Prefaces, Biographical and Critical," 671.

116. Johnson, "Preface to *The Plays of William Shakespeare*," 439.

117. Samuel Johnson to Mrs. Thrale, in Piozzi, *Anecdotes*, 221–22.

118. Johnson, Introduction to "*Rambler 97*," 153.

119. Eaves and Kimpel, *Samuel Richardson*, 337. Watt, in *Rise of the Novel*, argues that Johnson's respect for Richardson's novels does not always correlate to respect for Richardson the man, citing Johnson's "lethal jibe" that Richardson "could not be content to sail quietly down the stream of reputation without longing to taste the froth from every stroke of the oar" (296–97). Watt also points out that Johnson's critical favor "was not usually at the mercy of such considerations" as friendship and personal obligations (296).

120. Vaughan, *English Literary Criticism*, lxiii.

121. In "The New Realistic Novel" from *The Rambler* (1750) Johnson does not mention Fielding by name, but probably has *Tom Jones* and *Roderick Random* in mind when he warns against novels aimed at "the young, the ignorant, and the idle, to whom they serve as lectures of conduct." Novels that "so mingle good and bad qualities in their principle personages" are the most dangerous:

> There have been men indeed splendidly wicked, whose endowments throw a brightness on their crimes, and whom scarce any villainy made perfectly detestable, because they never could be wholly divested of their excellencies; but such have been in all ages the great corrupters of the world, and their resemblance ought no more to be preserved than the art of murdering without pain. (176–77)

122. Samuel Johnson to James Boswell, in Boswell, *Boswell's Journal*, 350.

123. For figures on editions and reprints of the novels, see the bibliography in McKillop, *Samuel Richardson*, 321–33, references in Eaves and Kimpel's *Samuel Richardson*, the bibliography in Battestin, *Henry Fielding*, 689–705, the prefaces to the Wesleyan editions of Fielding's novels, and Dickson, "Fielding and Richardson on the Continent," 7–8.

124. Piozzi, *Letters to and from the Late Samuel Johnson*, 2:30–31. The novelist Henry James Pye writes of this comment in 1797 that Thrale "exceeded every stretch of hyperbolic partiality, in preferring Richardson to Fielding as a painter of manners" (*Sketches on Various Subjects*, 196).

125. Thrale, in Rogers, "Richardson and the Bluestockings," 160.

126. Edwards, Eaves and Kimpel, *Samuel Richardson*, 327.

127. Seward, *Letters*, 1:293.

128. Even though this section of the chapter is devoted to general readers, I have saved examples from creative writers and critics to use in this section to help illustrate the range and importance of didacticism in the eighteenth-century reception of Richardson and Fielding. Of the three types of readers, however, general readers give it the highest priority.

129. *Critical Remarks on Sir Charles Grandison, Clarissa and Pamela*, 7.

130. Hunter, *Before Novels*, 82–84.

131. For a fuller treatment and defense of didacticism in the early novel, see Hunter, *Before Novels*, 225–302.

132. Blanchard, *Fielding the Novelist*, 109.

133. Addison, *Admonitions from the Dead in Epistles to the Living*, 217–19.

134. Wilberforce, *Prevailing Religious System of Professed Christians*, 271.

135. Hunter, *Before Novels*, 246–47.

136. Attempts to dovetail the art of Fielding's structure with his moral intentions can still be found in the twentieth century. See especially Battestin, *The Moral Basis of Fielding's Art*, and Preston, "Plot as Irony." For an opposing point of view in Richardson's favor, see Kermode, "Richardson and Fielding."

137. Astreae and Minerva Hill, in Paulson and Lockwood, *Critical Heritage*, 173–74.

138. Reeve, *The Progress of Romance*, 2:139.

139. Canning, "On Novel Writing," 303–5.

140. Carter, *Series of Letters*, 1:315.

141. Hunter, *Before Novels*, 242.

142. Canning, "On Novel Writing," 304.

143. Fielding, *Tom Jones*, 37.

144. For arguments about how Richardson and Fielding assume active, role-playing readers of their texts, see Keymer, *Richardson's "Clarissa" and the Eighteenth-Century Reader*, and Iser, "The Role of the Reader in Fielding's *Joseph Andrews* and *Tom Jones*."

145. Jauss, *Toward an Aesthetics of Reception*, 41.

146. Reeve, *The Progress of Romance*, 2:139.

147. Canning, "On Novel Writing," 306.

148. Carter, *Series of Letters*, 1:315.

149. Cumberland, "From *The Observer*," 333.

150. Keymer, *Richardson's "Clarissa" and the Eighteenth-Century Reader*, xviii.

151. Cumberland, "From *The Observer*," 334–35.

152. Goldsmith, *Works*, 3:311–12. Richardson and many of his devoted contemporaries would no doubt have been unamused by Choderlos de Laclos' *Les Liasons Dangereuses* (1782), which uses many of Richardson's techniques and character types to an effect accurately described by Goldsmith's quote.

153. Fordyce, *Sermons to Young Women*, 1:71–72.

154. Carter, *Series of Letters*, 1:23–24.

155. Ibid., 1:16.

156. Blanchard, *Fielding the Novelist*, 73.

157. Carter, *Series of Letters*, 1:206.

158. Astreae and Minerva Hill, in Paulson and Lockwood, *Critical Heritage*, 173–74.

159. Turner, "Novel Panic," 70–71.

160. Blanchard, *Fielding the Novelist*, 2. According to the *Encyclopedia Brittanica* of 1878, an unnnamed "industrious antiquary" has "cast doubt upon this anecdote, pointing out that Ranelagh Gardens were not open to the public till eighteen months after *Pamela* had begun to run through many editions. Vauxhall, however, was open if Ranelagh was not, and the incident may have been observed there" (543).

161. Erasmus Reich, in Richardson, *Correspondence*, 1: clxvii–clxx.

162. Warton, *Essay on the Genius and Writings of Pope*, 2.

163. Denis Diderot, in Wellek, *History of Modern Criticism*, 1:60.

164. McKillop, *Samuel Richardson*, 261.

165. Mathias, *Pursuits of Literature*, 60.

166. Gwynn, *Rencontre*, 136–37.

167. Barthe, "Excerpt from *La Jolie Femme*," 455.

168. Advertisement for *Tom Jones*, *General Advertiser*, 28 February 1749, 4.

169. Carew, *Apology for the Life of Bampfylde-Moore Carew*, 2.

170. Lady Bradshaigh, letter of 16 December 1749, in Richardson, *Correspondence*, 4:295–96.

171. Porter, *Thaddeus of Warsaw*, vii.

172. Luxborough, *Letters to Shenstone*, 369.

173. Lady Bradshaigh, letter of 29 October 1749, in Richardson, *Correspondence*, 4:280–81.

174. Jauss, *Toward an Aesthetic of Reception*, 39.

175. Montagu, *Letters and Works*, 2:285.

176. Blanchard, *Fielding the Novelist*, 165.

177. Samuel Richardson, in Paulson and Lockwood, *Henry Fielding*, 336.

178. For fuller accounts of German reaction to Richardson and Fielding see Wood, *Einfluss Fieldings auf die deutsche Literatur*; Price, "On the Reception of Richardson in Germany;" and Fabian, "English Books and Their Eighteenth-Century German Readers."

179. McKillop, *Samuel Richardson*, 260–61.

180. Friedreich Resewitz, in McKillop, *Samuel Richardson*, 262.

181. Clarke, *Fielding und der deutsche Sturm und Drang*, 15–18.

182. Cross, *History of Henry Fielding*, 3:192. See Liljegren, *English Sources of Goethe's Gretchen-Tragedy* for an account of the 200-plus novels and plays that bear some type of Richardsonian influence.

183. Cross, *History of Henry Fielding*, 3:192.

184. See Smith, *Samuel Richardson*, 97.

185. For a more complete treatment of Richardson and Fielding's individual receptions in eighteenth-century France, see McKillop, *Samuel Richardson*, 250–83, and Cross, *History of Henry Fielding*, 3:177–94.

186. Calderwood, quoted in Paulson and Lockwood, *Critical Heritage*, 20.

187. Davaux, Preface to *Tom Jones*, 1:i.

188. Paulson and Lockwood, *Henry Fielding*, 21.

189. J.B. Defreval, letter to Samuel Richardson, 17 April 1751, in Richardson, *Correspondence*, 5:277. It is not true that the French clergy placed a ban on La Place's translation of *Tom Jones* or that it was refused import into the country by the French government. This rumor, happily repeated by Richardson and Charles Bellers, was an exaggeration of the fact that an *arrêt du conseil* was issued on 24 February 1750 against the original bookseller who had published the translation without a license (Battestin, *Henry Fielding*, 530). Defreval writes in the same letter to Richardson, "I am sorry to say it, but you do my countrymen more honour than they truly deserve, in surmising that they had virtue enough to refuse a licence to Tom Jones. . . ." (*Correspondence*, 5:276)

Curiously, the only author who was actually banned anywhere in Europe was Richardson. His is one of the very few English names which appears on the official Vatican *Index* of banned books during the eighteenth century. The reasons why are open to speculation—no doubt Richardson thought himself especially generous in his treatment of Catholicism during the courtship of Grandison and Clementina.

190. Harpe, *Lycée ou Cours de Littérature*, 16:271–74.

191. Other French writers and critics with input on the Richardson/Fielding opposition include Abbé Desfontaine (preface to his French translation of *Joseph Andrews*, 1744, in Paulson and Lockwood, *Henry Fielding*, 127) who praises *Pamela*

but generally prefers Fielding's masculine style to the watery French romances of the day; and Friedreich Melchior Grimm (in Wellek, *History of Modern Criticism*, 1:71), a Richardsonian who had a preference for "emotional realism" but whose opinion of Fielding improved over the years. For a brief overview of Richardson's French reception, see Streeter, "The Vogue of Richardson's Novels in France."

For Richardson and/or Fielding's eighteenth-century reception in countries other than Germany and France, see Slattery, "Samuel Richardson in the Netherlands," Orians, "Censure of Fiction in American Romances and Magazines 1789–1810"; Watters, "The Vogue and Influence of Samuel Richardson in America"; Coe, "Richardson in Spain"; Lanzisera, "I romanzi de Samuele Richardson in Italia."

For the reception in Holland, see Christel van Boheemen-Saaf, "Fielding and Richardson in Holland: 1740–1800":

> Though with the vogue for sentiment the popularity of Fielding—he is mentioned less often—may have diminished toward the end of the century, and even taking into account the fact that Fielding did not spawn an imitation industry like Richardson, we may conclude that Richardson and Fielding were not seen as rivals or in opposition, as they were in England; and it is difficult to judge whether Richardson was better known, or ranked higher in popular and professional evaluation, especially with regard to the period 1740–80. (305)

192. Grant, *Letters from the Mountains*, 2:46.
193. Denis Diderot, in McKillop, *Early Masters of English Fiction*, 102.
194. Bisset, "History of Literature and Science for the Year 1799," 56.
195. Sade, "Reflections on the Novel," 106.
196. Ibid, 107.
197. Bisset, "History of Literature and Science for the Year 1799," 57.
198. "Review of *The Italian*, by Ann Radcliffe," 282–84.
199. "Henry Fielding" in *Encyclopedia Britannica* (1797), 7:229.
200. "Samuel Richardson" in *Encyclopedia Britannica* (1797), 16:233.
201. *Encyclopedia Brittanica*, 9th ed., 1879. The first sentence of Richardson's entry sets the tone: "As the inventor or the accidental discoverer of a new literary form, the modern novel of domestic life and manners, is entitled to a more prominent place in history than his powers, whether of thought or style, would justify" (20:543). The epistolary style of *Pamela* is viewed as "voluminous moralizing" which was "more in harmony with the general taste than it is now" (20:543). The contributor's highest praise is the neutral observation that Richardson "had the art of interesting his own generation" (20:544).

The first sentence of Fielding's entry quotes Gibbon's famous assertion that Fielding will outlive the ruling houses of Austria. Not only does this edition mention Fielding's dramas, but lists them with dates and substantial commentary. Perhaps the most telling difference from the 1797 edition is the segment on Fielding's poverty and illness. Rather than blaming Fielding's condition on his debauchery, the critic writes: "No man ever wrote in more desperate and pitiable circumstances. Yet there is no perceptible diminution in the splendid force of his humour. He shook off his troubles like a giant, and gave no sign of the pain at his heart, save in the fiercer energy of his blows" (9:145). The contributor looks back over Fielding's eighteenth- and nineteenth-century reception and notes that it is a curious and disappointing phenomenon that this "true soldier in the war of humanity" should be read more for the sake of "indelicate passages which he wrote in pursuance of fidelity to nature" than for "the generous sentiment and wise philosophy with which his work as a whole is penetrated" (9:146). Both entries are signed W. Minto.

Chapter Three: The Nineteenth Century: Richardson's *Correspondence* to *The Saturday Review*, 1804–1893

1. Barbauld, preface to Richardson, *Correspondence*, 1:lxxx.
2. Forsyth, *Novels and Novelists of the Eighteenth Century*, 7.
3. Blanchard, *Fielding the Novelist*, 279.
4. Watson, *Life of Henry Fielding*, 169–70.
5. *The British Critic*, in Blanchard, *Fielding the Novelist*, 291.
6. Review of *The Works of Samuel Richardson*, 1284.
7. Roscoe, Preface, xxv.
8. Barbauld, in Richardson, *Correspondence*, 1:lxxix.
9. Stephen, "Preface," 1:xxiv.
10. Southey, *Selections from the Letters of Robert Southey*, 1:304.
11. Oliphant, "Historical Sketches of the Reign of George II," 261–62.
12. Eaves and Kimpel, *Samuel Richardson*, 296.
13. Dobson, *Fielding*, 175.
14. There are other significant nineteenth-century writers who comment on either Richardson or Fielding, but not both or not at the same time. William Wordsworth recalls a boyhood fondness for Fielding's works (*Memoires* 1:9–10). Thomas De Quincey lectured Wordsworth about his "extreme delight" with a novelist "so disgusting" as Fielding (*Literary Reminiscences*, 2:252). Wordsworth elsewhere mentions a "reluctance" to read the distressful parts of *Clarissa* (*Memoires*, 1:48). Keats mentions Fielding along with Hogarth as two artists who now seem dated (*Poetry and Prose*, 115), and Percy Shelley read Fielding but did not find him interesting (Droop, *Die Belesenheit Percy Bysshe Shelley's nach den direkten Zeugnissen und den bisherigen Forschugen*, 61).

Jane Austen's satire and ironic narrative voice were probably influenced by Fielding, but she left no direct references to him apart from a passing comment on the fashion for *Tom Jones* in *Northanger Abbey*. Richardson's Hariett Byron is mentioned in a number of Austen's letters, mostly in reference to clothes and manners (Austen, *Letters to Her Sister Cassandra*). Austen also collaborated with her young niece, Anna Austen, on a dramatic adaptation of *Sir Charles Grandison* to entertain the family (see Speirs, "*Sir Charles Grandison*"). For other, more general influences of Richardson on Austen, see Harris, "The Influence of Richardson on *Pride and Prejudice*"; Honan, "Richardson's Influence on Jane Austen"; and Harris, "As If They Had Been Living Friends."

George Barnett Smith, a critic who knew Charles Dickens personally, writes in 1876 that Fielding's "power over Dickens was unquestionably immense" (*Poets and Novelists*, 304). Dickens had kind words for Fielding on a number of occasions, and named one of his children Henry Fielding Dickens. Richardson, however, was "no great favorite" of Dickens' (Charles Dickens to Rev. Edward Tagart, 28 January 1847, in Dickens, *Letters*, 5:20).

Alfred, Lord Tennyson spoke highly of Richardson's "great *still* books" (Tennyson, *Alfred Lord Tennyson*, 2:372). Matthew Arnold does not mention either author, and Robert Browning reportedly gave up on English fiction entirely after discovering Balzac.

15. Brophy, *Samuel Richardson*, 116.
16. Byron, *Letters and Journals of Lord Byron*, 3:87–88.
17. The impassioned Romantic views of Richardson and Fielding by the Marquis de Sade are discussed in chapter two.
18. Coleridge, *Shakespearean Criticism*, 101.
19. Hazlitt, *Complete Works*, 16:15–17; 6:118.
20. Coleridge, "With Fielding's Amelia," ll. 5–8.
21. Hazlitt, *Complete Works*, 12:274.
22. Coleridge, *Anima Poetae*, 166–67.
23. Coleridge, *Shakespearean Criticism*, 217.
24. Coleridge, *Complete Works*, 4:226.
25. Ibid., 4:380.
26. Blanchard, *Fielding the Novelist*, 321.
27. Coleridge, "Table Talk," 437.
28. Shaw, *Outlines of English Literature*, 263–64.
29. T.N. Talfourd, in Blanchard, *Fielding the Novelist*, 343.
30. Hunt, "Johnson on Fielding and Richardson," 412.
31. Review of *The Works of Samuel Richardson*, 1285.
32. Masson, *British Novelists and their Styles*, 139.
33. Review of *The Newcomes*, 108.
34. *Bentley's Miscellany*, in Blanchard, *Fielding the Novelist*, 431.
35. Review of *Ballantyne's Novelist's Library*, 408.
36. Scott, *Lives of the Novelists*, 226.
37. Blanchard, *Fielding the Novelist*, 365–66.
38. Scott, *Lives of the Novelists*, 255.
39. Ibid., 250.
40. Ibid., 21.
41. Review of *Ballantyne's Novelist's Library*, 414.
42. Edgeworth, *Life and Letters*, 239–40.
43. Mackenzie, *Sir Walter Scott*, 204.
44. Thackeray, *English Humourists of the Eighteenth Century*, 216.
45. Ibid., 213.
46. Ibid., 220.
47. Cross, *History of Henry Fielding*, 3:225.
48. Thackeray, *English Humourists of the Eighteenth Century*, 218–19.
49. Ibid., 217–18.
50. Edgeworth, *Ormond*, 56–57.
51. Eliot, *Letters*, 1:240.
52. Ibid., 2:65.
53. Ibid., 6:320.
54. Eliot, *Middlemarch*, 138–39.
55. Stevenson, *Works*, 12:194–95.
56. Stevenson's opinions on Richardson and Fielding may seem ill-conceived because he admits that he has not read all of *Joseph Andrews* or *Sir Charles Grandison*. He skips through the parts of *Joseph Andrews* which do not feature Parson Adams. Stevenson has a sentiment on the length of *Sir Charles Grandison* which is no doubt shared by many well-intentioned students of literature:

[T]here are many impediments in this brief life of man; I have more than once, indeed, reconnoitred the first volume with a flying party, but always decided not to break ground before the place till my siege guns came up; and it's an odd thing—I have been all these years in the field, and that powerful artillery is still miles in the rear. The day it overtakes me, Baron Gibbon's fortress shall be beat about his ears, and my flag be planted on the formidable ramparts of the second part of Faust. (*Works*, 12:317–18.)

57. Stevenson, *Letters*, 1:141.

58. Stevenson, *Works*, 12:316–17.

59. Ibid., 12: 318–19.

60. Hardy, "The Profitable Reading of Fiction," 69.

61. Ibid., 69–70.

62. Brophy, *Samuel Richardson*, 115.

63. William Hazlitt, in Lucas, *Life of Charles Lamb*, 1:519.

64. Walter Scott is the only critic of the period who finds the Richardson/Fielding opposition an embarrassment rather than a spectator sport: "Of all pictures of literary life, that which exhibits two men of transcendent, though different, talents, engaged in the depreciation of each other, is most humbling to human nature, most unpleasing to a candid and enlightened reader" (*Lives of the Novelists*, 217). Even Scott, however, relishes repeating the lurid rumors of Fielding's life.

65. North, "Soliloquy on the Annuals," 1: 74; Ruskin, *Works*, 1:418; Stephen, "Richardson's Novels," 49; Masson, *British Novelists and their Styles*, 111; Dobson, *Fielding*, 71.

66. Lowell, "Fielding," 74.

67. Review of *The Works of Richardson*, 1285.

68. "Growth of the English Novel," 46.

69. Mill, *Autobiography*, 117.

70. Millar, introduction to "Samuel Richardson," 4:58.

71. Artists belong in the third category of readers because literary criticism is not their vocation, but I am discussing them here because the larger issue of art as an interpretive metaphor belongs primarily to the critics. The case can also be made that John Ruskin is as much a man of letters as he is a painter.

72. Ruskin, *Works*, 35:308; 1:418.

73. Frith, *Autobiography and Reminiscences*, 307.

74. Haydon, *Benjamin Robert Haydon: Correspondence and Table-Talk*, 2:325–326.

75. James Northcote, in William Hazlitt, *Conversations of James Northcote*, 287.

76. Ibid., 294–296.

77. Dunlop, History of Prose Fiction, 2:571–75; Mackintosh, *Memoirs*, 2:238; Scott, in Birrell, "Samuel Richardson," 26.

78. Stephen, *The History of English Thought in the Eighteenth Century*, 2:380.

79. "Progress of Fiction as an Art," 196.

80. Scott, *Lives of the Novelists*, 250.

81. Chambers, *Cyclopedia of English Literature*, 254.

82. "Growth of the English Novel," 46, 48.

83. Jusserand, *Le Roman Anglais*, 56.

84. Samuel Johnson, in Boswell, *Boswell's Life of Johnson*, 2:49.

85. Coleridge, "Table Talk," 437.

86. Leslie Stephen, in Blanchard, *Fielding the Novelist*, 495.

87. Taine, *History of English Literature*, 168.

88. Oliphant, "Historical Sketches of the Reign of George II," 265.

89. Shaw, *Outlines of English Literature*, 260.

90. Birrell, "Samuel Richardson," 17.

91. Blanchard, *Fielding the Novelist*, 482–83.

92. Cross, *History of Henry Fielding*, 3:246.
93. Stephen, in Cross, *History of Henry Fielding*, 3:246.
94. Collier, *History of English Literature*, iii, 311.
95. Curtis, "Easy Chair," 414.
96. Smith, *Poets and Novelists*, 1–18.
97. Mudford, *British Novelists*, 5, 9.
98. Traill, "Richardson and Fielding," 201.
99. Ibid., 202.
100. Ibid., 212.
101. Ibid., 204–205.
102. Ibid., 206.
103. Ibid., 207.
104. Leigh Hunt, "A Novel Party," 91.
105. Ibid., 92.
106. Ibid., 94.
107. Ibid., 94.
108. Ibid., 95.
109. Ibid., 97.
110. Ibid., 100.
111. Ibid., 96.
112. William Hazlett, in Wellek, *History of Modern Criticism*, 2:206.
113. Stephen, *History of English Thought in the Eighteenth Century*, 2:380.
114. Collier, *History of English Literature*, 313–314.
115. Lowell, "Fielding," 69.
116. Gosse, *Henry Fielding*, xxx–xxxi.
117. Ibid., xxxi–xxxii.
118. Stephen, "Richardson's Novels," 53.
119. Tuckerman, *History of English Prose Fiction*, 203.
120. Masson, *British Novelists and their Styles*, 115. Only Coleridge believes that his century is *less* lethargic than the eighteenth century: Richardson, Fielding, and Sterne were popular in a "less stimulated & therefore less languid Reading-World" (*Selected Letters*, 217).
121. Tuckerman, *History of English Prose Fiction*, 211.
122. "Progress of Fiction as an Art," 186.
123. Alexander Macmillan, in Graves, *Life and Letters of Alexander Macmillan*, 249.
124. Forsyth, *Novels and Novelists of the Eighteenth Century*, 7.
125. Ibid., 216–17.
126. Ibid., 258.
127. Ibid., 277.
128. Dickens, *Oliver Twist*, xxvii.
129. Stephen, "Richardson's Novels," 49.
130. Ibid., 52.
131. Smith, "Review of *Cælebs*," 156.
132. Jeffrey, *Contributions to the Edinburgh Review*, 44.
133. Blanchard, *Fielding the Novelist*, 391.
134. Mangin, *Essay on Light Reading*, 42, 48.
135. William Brown, in Cross, *History of Henry Fielding*, 3:175.
136. Hugh Blair, in Blanchard, *Fielding the Novelist*, 234.
137. "Progress of Fiction as an Art," 186.
138. Tuckerman, *History of English Prose Fiction*, 211.

139. Southey, *Selections from the Letters of Robert Southey*, 2:297.

140. Roscoe, *Poems and Essays*, 2:301–02.

141. "Growth of the English Novel," 44.

142. Masson, *British Novelists and their Styles*, 128.

143. Dunlop, *History of Prose Fiction*, 2:569.

144. Barbauld, in Samuel Richardson's *Correspondence*, 1:lxxix–lxxx.

145. Coleridge, *Complete Works*, 4:226.

146. Meredith, "Essay on the Idea of Comedy," 42.

147. Masson, *British Novelists and their Styles*, 128–30.

148. Tuckerman, *History of English Prose Fiction*, 203–204.

149. Dobson, *Fielding*, 178.

150. Mudford, *The British Novelists*, i.

151. Review of *The Newcomes*, 112.

152. Northcote, in Hazlitt, *Conversations of James Northcote*, 2:325–26.

153. Dickens, *Oliver Twist*, xxvii.

154. Coleridge, *Shakespearean Criticism*, 217.

155. Macaulay, "Copyright. I," 739–40.

156. Stephen, *History of English Thought in the Eighteenth Century*, 2:380.

157. Masson, *British Novelists and their Styles*, 141–42.

158. West, *Letters to a Young Lady*, 2:453–54.

159. "Growth of the English Novel," 47.

160. Cross, *Development of the English Novel*, 57–58.

161. Gosse alone is a possible exception: "Even in the hands of [Richardson] . . . the novel remained prolix in form, primitive in evolution. When all is said and done, the prose fiction of the world first stood up, erect and splendid, when 'Tom Jones' was published in 1749" (*Henry Fielding*, v–vi).

162. Brophy, *Samuel Richardson*, 117.

163. Stephen, "Richardson's Novels," 50.

164. Review of *The Works of Samuel Richardson*, 1284.

165. "Growth of the English Novel," 63.

166. Thackeray, *English Humourists of the Eighteenth Century*, 227.

167. Lowell, "Fielding," 76–77.

168. Jeffrey, *Contributions to the Edinburgh Review*, 44.

169. Edmund Gosse, *Henry Fielding*, xxii–xxiii.

170. Masson, *British Novelists and their Styles*, 111. A minor dichotomy used for Richardson and Fielding during the age of Earl Gray is tea versus liquor. The oppositional beverages usually fall within the larger framework of the "feminine"/"masculine" dichotomy, as in Masson's excerpt.

"If *Tom Jones* has about it an occasional suspicion of beer and pipes at the bar, *Sir Charles Grandison* recalls an indefinite consumption of tea and small talk," writes Stephen in "Richardson's Novels" (52). Thackeray's Fielding

> had been nursed on sack-posset, and not on dishes of tea. *His* muse had sung the loudest in tavern choruses, had seen the daylight streaming in over thousands of emptied bowls, and reeled home to chambers on the shoulders of the watchman. Richardson's goddess was attended by old maids and dowagers, and fed on muffins and bohea. (*English Humourists of the Eighteenth Century*, 217–18)

Stevenson in "Some Gentlemen in Fiction" imagines Fielding to be "a favourite in the tap-room" while Richardson is "a tea-bibber in parlours" (*Works*, 12:316–17). Finally, Traill has Fielding sympathize with Richardson in the afterlife that they are both denied their earthly pleasures: "Tea and tittle-tattle must be almost as bad to go without as a bottle of Burgundy and a rousing catch" ("Richardson and Fielding," 200).

171. Birrell, "Samuel Richardson," 21.

172. Oliphant, "Historical Sketches of the Reign of George II," 265.

173. "Growth of the English Novel," 48.

174. Ibid., 48. Thomas Shaw is the only critic to comment specifically on Richardson's male characters, and they too are located within Richardson's feminine temperament: they are men "as seen by women" (*Outlines of English Literature*, 260).

175. Hunt, "A Novel Party," 100.

176. Thomson, "Old Friends," 17.

177. Haydon, *Correspondence and Table-Talk*, 2:325–26.

178. Fordyce, *Sermons to Young Women*, 1:71–72. Other dichotomies critics occasionally use for Richardson and Fielding include the sentimental versus common sense (Gosse, *Henry Fielding*, xxx–xxxi; Stephen, *English Thought in the Eighteenth Century*, in Cross, *History of Henry Fielding*, 3:239); passive versus active temperament (Gosse, xxii–xxiii and xxx–xxxi; *Bentley's Miscellany* in Blanchard, *Fielding the Novelist*, 160; Taine, *History of English Literature*, 174); and prolixity versus reserve (Stevenson, "Some Gentlemen in Fiction," in *Works*, 12:317–18; Stephen, "Review of *The Works of Samuel Richardson*", 1285; and Barbauld, in Richardson, *Correspondence*, 1:cxxvi). Of the latter dichotomy, Barbauld finds Fielding more unnecessarily prolixic than Richardson:

> There is not, in any of Richardson's works, one of those detached episodes, thrown in like make-weights, to increase the bulk of the volume, which are so common in other works: such is the story of *The Man of the Hill*, in Tom Jones. If [Richardson's] works are laboured into length, at least his prolixity is all bestowed upon the subject, and increases the effect of the story. (Barbauld, in Richardson, *Correspondence*, 1:cxxvi.)

179. Oliphant is a type-one reader whom I am discussing in this section in order to connect her statements on Richardson and Fielding with the "feminine"/"masculine" dichotomy used by other critics.

180. Colby, *Equivocal Virtue*, xiv.

181. Ibid., 1.

182. Oliphant, "Historical Sketches of the Reign of George II," 267–68.

183. Ibid., 268.

184. Ibid., 257. For the sake of contrast, the more typical critique of Lovelace's characterization is the class-based assumption made by Thomas Gray. According to the reminiscences of Norton Nicholls, "In the delineation of the character of Lovelace alone [Gray] thought the author had failed, not having lived among persons of that rank, it was impossible for him to give the portrait from the life of a profligate man of fashion" (Gray, *Letters*, 2:287).

185. Ibid., 253–54.

186. Ibid., 254–55.

187. Ibid., 257.

188. Oliphant, *Autobiography and Letters*, 160.

189. Ibid., 221.

190. Jay, *Mrs Oliphant*, 76.

191. Colby, *Equivocal Virtue*, 114.

192. Virginia Woolf recognizes this about Oliphant and finds her in this respect to be representative all Victorian women writers. Woolf writes in *Three Guineas*:

[Souse] yourself in the innumerable faded articles, reviews, sketches of one kind and another which she contributed to literary papers. When you have done, examine the state of your own mind, and ask yourself whether that reading has led you to respect disinterested culture and intellectual liberty. Has it not on the contrary smeared your mind and dejected your imagination, and led you to deplore the fact that Mrs. Oliphant sold her brain, her very admirable brain, prostituted her culture and enslaved her intellectual liberty in order that she might earn her living and educate her children? (91–92)

193. Oliphant, "Historical Sketches of the Reign of George II," 254–55.
194. Clarke, "Mrs. Oliphant," 127.
195. Rubik, *Novels of Mrs. Oliphant*, 12.
196. Margaret Oliphant, in *Mrs Oliphant*, 81–82.
197. Oliphant, "Historical Sketches of the Reign of George II," 264–65.
198. Ibid., 261.
199. Ibid., 268.
200. Oliphant, *Autobiography and Letters*, 222.
201. Blanchard, *Fielding the Novelist*, 522.
202. The *Quarterly Review* takes Oliphant's line of argument about Richardson, remarking in amazement that a novel such as *Clarissa* could have come from such a dull and simple man and claiming Richardson portrays women better than women themselves. Oliphant and the *Quarterly Review* both find Fielding to have "no conception of the inner mind of women," in contrast to Richardson whose "idea of the inmost nature of women was a primitive ingredient, an essential element of his mental constitution" ("The Growth of the English Novel," 48). Both writers also make the observation that Tom Jones would have been unworthy to worship Clarissa (48). The *Quarterly Review* probably draws upon Oliphant's distinctive critical language, as well. Oliphant refers to Jones's "frank animalism," and the *Quarterly Review* refers to his "full-blooded animalism" (44). Oliphant writes of Clarissa that the reader "can see the chill that comes upon the opening flower, can see the soft virginal husks closing up over the arrested bud; and then the drooping and the fading" ("Historical Sketches of the Reign of George II," 264), and the *Quarterly Review* writes that Clarissa is a "tender maidenly girl, whose heart had barely begun to unfold with the spring-like warmth of an unacknowledged fancy, before it was numbed, withered, and frozen to death" ("Growth of the English Novel," 45).
203. Blanchard, *Fielding the Novelist*, 306.
204. Ibid., 306.
205. Birrell claims that admiration of Richardson was the initial impetus for Hazlitt's massive biography of Napoleon: "The great Napoleon was a true Richardsonian," writes Birrell.

Only once did he ever seem to take any interest in an Englishman. It was whilst he was first consul and when he was introduced to an officer called Lovelace: 'Why,' he exclaimed with emotion, 'that is the name of the man in *Clarissa*!' When our own great critic, Hazlitt, heard of this incident he fell in love with Napoleon on the spot, and subsequently wrote his life in numerous volumes. ("Samuel Richardson," 32)

206. Hazlitt, *Complete Works*, 16:11. "Standard Novels and Romances" originally appeared in *The Edinburgh Review* vol. 29 (February 1815), but is better known as "On the English Novelists," lecture 6 of *Lectures on the English Comic Writers* (1819).
207. Ibid., 16:17.

208. Ibid., 16:15–16.
209. Ibid., 12:221–22.
210. Ibid., 12:226–27.
211. Lady Bradshaigh to Richardson, 10 October 1748, in Richardson, *Correspondence*, 4:181.
212. Tuckerman, *History of English Prose Fiction*, 203.
213. Stephen, "Richardson's Novels," 48.
214. Ibid., 48–49.
215. Scott, *Lives of the Novelists*, 256.
216. Review of *Ballantyne's Novelist's Library*, 408.
217. Elwin, in Blanchard, *Fielding the Novelist*, 426–27.
218. Fitzgerald, *Letters*, 3:77.
219. Traill, "Richardson and Fielding," 215.
220. William Hazlitt, in Blanchard, *Fielding the Novelist*, 366.
221. Borrow, *Bible in Spain*, 1:8.
222. Stuart, *Letters*, 2:289.
223. Thackeray, *The Newcomes*, 1:38.
224. Birrell, "Samuel Richardson," 9–10.
225. Altick, *English Common Reader*, 253.
226. Ibid., 217.
227. Ibid., 217–18.
228. Chambers, *Youth's Companion and Counselor*, 94–95.
229. Wellek, *History of Modern Criticism*, 2:79.
230. Schlegel, *Lectures on the History of Literature, Ancient and Modern*, 261.
231. Schlosser, *History of the Eighteenth Century*, 4:3–5.
232. Eliot, *Letters*, 6:320.
233. Balzac to Madame Hanska, 1 April 1838, in *Oeuvres*, 1:471.
234. Hippolyte Taine, *History of English Literature*, 171.
235. Ibid., 171–72.
236. Ibid., 169.
237. Ibid., 169–76.
238. Staël-Holstein, *Influence of Literature upon Society*, 1:293.
239. Jusserand, *Le Roman Anglais*, 58.
240. Coe, "Richardson in Spain," 62.
241. "Memorial Literario," in Coe, "Richardson in Spain," 59–60.
242. Lanier, *English Novel*, 181.
243. Ibid., 184.
244. Ibid., 187.
245. Hill, *Writers and Readers*, 91.
246. "Morals of Fielding," 421.
247. Birrell, "Samuel Richardson," 17–18.

Chapter Four: The Twentieth Century: Raleigh's *The English Novel* to Watt's *The Rise of the Novel*, 1894–1957

1. McKillop, *Early Masters of English Fiction*, 145.
2. Bowen, *English Novelists*, 13.
3. Hudson, *A Quiet Corner in a Library*, 223; 212–13.
4. Shaw, *Plays*, 1: xvii, xviii.

5. Doyle, *Through the Magic Door*, 138.

6. Ibid., 145.

7. Ibid., 139.

8. Ibid., 140–41.

9. Ibid., 148.

10. Ibid., 141–42.

11. Ibid., 143–44.

12. Pritchett, *The Living Novel*, 20.

13. Ibid., 18.

14. Ibid., 24–25.

15. Ibid., 28.

16. Chapone, *Works*, 1:175.

17. The first English departments were formed at University College and King's College, London, in 1828 and 1835. It was not until A.J. Scott began teaching at University College in 1848, however, that English was taught as something more than the study of linguistics, grammar, and classical rhetoric. A complex network of motives, many of them stemming from the economic and demographic effects of the Industrial Revolution, accelerated the spread of English Departments in the 1870s (a moment in intellectual history captured in Matthew Arnold's *Culture and Anarchy*). See Palmer, *Rise of English Studies*; Court, *Institutionalizing English Literature*; and Eagleton, *Literary Theory*.

18. Williams, *Two Centuries of the English Novel*, 48.

19. Paulson and Lockwood, *Critical Essays*, 1.

20. Dobson, *Samuel Richardson*, 197.

21. W.L. Renwick offers a telling example of how Fielding is commodified by practical-minded teachers and conscientious undergraduates in 1947. Renwick refers to Fielding's phrase "Comic Epic in Prose": "Every examination candidate has picked up the phrase, worn smooth in the brook of lectures that goes on for ever, carries it in the same pouch with *the age of prose and reason—in the depths, on the heights—unified sensibility—the return to nature* — to sling it in due season at the thrice-battered heads of his examiners" (40).

22. Rawson, Introduction, 367–68.

23. Ibid., 370.

24. Cross, *History of Henry Fielding*, 2:127.

25. Dickson, "Fielding and Richardson on the Continent," 7.

26. The first dissertation on Richardson is Louis A. Strauss, *The Ethical Character of the English Novel from Lilly to Richardson* from Michigan University in 1900. The first dissertation on Fielding is Gerard Edward Jensen, *The Covent-Garden Journal, by Sir Alexander Drawcansir, Knt. Censor of Great Britain (Henry Fielding), Edited with Introduction and Notes* from Yale University in 1913.

27. Rawson, Introduction, 152.

28. The titles of these introductory textbooks alone give an accurate impression of their generality, frequent unoriginality, and competition. Between 1894 and 1957 we have Ernest Baker's *The History of the English Novel*, Elizabeth Bowen's *English Novelists*, Richard Burton's *Masters of the English Novel*, Richard Church's *The Growth of the English Novel*, Pelham Edgar's *The Art of the Novel*, Charles F. Horne's *The Technique of the Novel*, Arnold Kettle's *An Introduction to the English Novel*, Grant C. Knight's *The Novel in English*, Alan D. McKillop's *The Early Masters of English Fiction*, and no less than five books titled *The English Novel* (Walter Allen, Ford Maddox Ford, J.B. Priestley, George Saintsbury and Ian Watt).

29. Otis and Needleman, *Survey History of English Literature*, 388–89.

30. Ibid., 389–90.

31. Church, *Growth of the English Novel*, 65.

32. McCullough, *Representative English Novelists*, 45.

33. Noting that women's names that end in -a or -ia were popularized in the Brunswick dynasty, are typical of romance, and most commonly take the form of "Sophia" and "Amelia," Watt concludes that Fielding's "acquiescence in the romance tradition was formal and unenthusiastic. The names that Richardson chose for his first two heroines, on the other hand . . . were rare and distinctively romantic" ("Naming of Characters," 327). Watt reads Richardson and Fielding's naming into the internal/external and specific/general dichotomies which recur throughout the twentieth century:

[Richardson's] vicarious participation in the private and often unconscious complexities of personal life is reflected in the names he uses, names which suggest the unique individuality of his main characters, and round which cluster all kinds of complex and yet obscurely relevant associations. Fielding, on the other hand, avoids suggesting, even in their names, that his characters are unique human beings. . . . Fielding's use of names is therefore in agreement with the assertions of his critical writing: that his interest as a novelist lies in those aspects of character which are representative of all mankind. (338)

34. In the latest research on the subject, Battestin claims 6 August 1754 is the date Fielding arrives in Portugal, and it is Edward Goldwyre who set Charlotte Cradock's nose (*Henry Fielding*, 97–98).

35. See Stoler and Fulton, *Henry Fielding*.

36. McKillop, *Samuel Richardson*, 107.

37. Thomson, *Samuel Richardson*, 36, 259.

38. Williams, *Two Centuries of the English Novel*, 75.

39. Edmund Gosse and Frederic Harrison, in Blanchard, *Fielding the Novelist*, 547.

40. Cross, *History of Henry Fielding*, 1:303, 2:142–43.

41. Williams, *Two Centuries of the English Novel*, 53.

42. Holliday, *English Fiction from the Fifth to the Twentieth Century*, 233.

43. Blanchard, *Fielding the Novelist*, 136.

44. Burton, *Masters of the English Novel*, 53.

45. Horne, *Technique of the Novel*, 216.

46. A plausible argument could be made, however, that Fielding's omniscient, commenting narrative voice makes his novels more subjective than those of Richardson, who claims to be nothing more than the passive and objective editor of a collection of letters. See Keymer, *Richardson's "Clarissa" and the Eighteenth-Century Reader* for an argument that it is Richardson's narrative objectivity that channels the reader's subjectivity into a sympathetic identification with the heroine.

47. Dobson, "Richardson at Home," 82–83.

48. Burton, *Masters of the English Novel*, 71.

49. Cross, *History of Henry Fielding*, 2:159.

50. Shepperson, *Novel in Motley*, 30.

51. Mack, Introduction, ix.

52. Holliday, *English Fiction from the Fifth to the Twentieth Century*, 230.

53. Church, *Growth of the English Novel*, 69.

54. Ibid., 73.

55. Moore, "Dr. Johnson on Fielding and Richardson," 172.

56. Green, *Minuet*, 386.

57. Digeon, *Novels of Fielding*, 146–147.

58. Henley, "Essay on the Life," 16:xxxiv.

59. Knight, *The Novel in English*, 38.

60. Doyle, *Through the Magic Door*, 139.

61. Reynolds, *The Learned Lady in England*, 337–338, 343.

62. Utter and Needham, *Pamela's Daughters*, 162. In a complex and wide-ranging argument that cannot be fully retraced here, Utter and Needham link fainting to the wider eighteenth-century political context. Passing out is most frequent between the Cromwellian and French revolutions, according to the authors, and is therefore a kind of "aristocracy complex" and a result of a Gothic "dream of feudalism by way of escape from an inevitably rising tide of democracy" (163).

63. Hobbes, "Fielding for Girls."

64. Hobbes, *Letters from a Silent Study*, 51.

65. J. M. Bulloch, *The Lamp* 29, in Blanchard, *Fielding the Novelist*, 520.

66. Saintsbury, *English Novel*, 112–13.

67. Lovett and Hughes, *History of the Novel in England*, 63.

68. Doyle, *Through the Magic Door*, 141–42.

69. Church, *Growth of the English Novel*, 54.

70. Other influential noncomparative accounts of Fielding's plotting and narration include Thornbury, *Henry Fielding's Theory of the Comic Prose Epic* and Booth, "The Self-Conscious Narrator in Comic Fiction before *Tristram Shandy*." R.S. Crane's "The Plot of *Tom Jones*" originally appeared in *The Journal of General Education* 4 (1950), was revised as "The Concept of Plot and the Plot of *Tom Jones*" in *Critics and Criticism Ancient and Modern*, and has been reprinted many times in critical anthologies.

71. Horne, *Technique of the Novel*, 273.

72. Holliday, *English Fiction from the Fifth to the Twentieth Century*, 233.

73. Horne, *Technique of the Novel*, 195.

74. Priestley, *The English Novel*, 22–23.

75. Whiteford, *Motives in English Fiction*, 103.

76. Utter and Needham, *Pamela's Daughters*, 115.

77. The only direct statement linking Richardson or Fielding to the French Revolution is from Byron, writing of *Jonathan Wild* in 1821 that Fielding's inverted portrait of what is "great" in politicians is such that "had he lived *now*, he would have been denounced in 'The Courier' as the grand Mouthpiece and Factionary of the revolutionists" (*Letters and Journals*, 5:465).

78. The two major political readings of Richardson and Fielding are Eagleton, *The Rape of Clarissa: Writing, Sexuality and Class Struggle in Samuel Richardson* and Cleary, *Henry Fielding: A Political Writer*. See also McCrea, *Henry Fielding and the Politics of Mid-Eighteenth-Century England*. For a Marxist comparison of Richardson and Fielding, see Karl, *A Reader's Guide to the Development of the English Novel in the Eighteenth Century*.

Fielding was one of Karl Marx's favorite authors. "I should add that Marx read and reread Walter Scott," recalls Marx's daughter, Eleanor, in 1858. "[H]e admired him and knew him almost as well and he knew Fielding . . . " (Marx, "Eleanor Marx on Her Father," 50).

79. Nicoll and Seccombe, *History of English Literature*, 2:653.

80. Fox, *The Novel and the People*, 53.

81. Kettle, *Introduction to the English Novel*, 1:79.

82. Digeon, *Novels of Fielding*, 228.

83. Doyle, *Through the Magic Door*, 141.
84. Eagleton, *Rape of Clarissa*, ix.
85. Knight, *Novel in English*, 37.
86. Burton, *Masters of the English Novel*, 53.
87. Drinkwater, in Blanchard, *Fielding the Novelist*, 549.
88. Utter and Needham, *Pamela's Daughters*, 113.
89. Kettle, *Introduction to the English Novel*, 1:63.
90. Stephen, *English Literature and Society in the Eighteenth Century*, 150.
91. See Castro, "Did Fielding Write *Shamela*?" and Jensen, "*Apology for the Life of Mrs. Shamela Andrews*, 1741."
92. McKillop, *English Literature from Dryden to Burns*, 269.
93. McKillop, *Samuel Richardson*, 127.
94. Bowen, *English Novelists*, 17.
95. Jackson, *Great English Novelists*, 83.
96. Curtis and Taine are the two nineteenth-century critics who apply the word "Puritan" to Richardson, and both of them do so indirectly. Curtis writes in "Easy Chair," "[Fielding's] cheerful, robust, sensible mind stood between the supercilious Cavalier and the sanctimonious Puritan. Beyond doubt he called Richardson 'Sammy,' and dashed off his parody of Pamela with infinite gusto" (414). Taine's comparison of Richardson and Fielding in *History of English Literature* is very similar: "Such a man was sure to dislike Richardson. He who loves expansive and liberal nature, drives from him like foes the solemnity, sadness, and pruderies of the Puritans" (171).
97. Baker, *History of the English Novel*, 56.
98. Pritchett, *Living Novel*, 25, 28.
99. Lawrence, *Pornography and Obscenity*, 174.
100. Allen, *English Novel*, 49.
101. Van Ghent, *English Novel, Form and Function*, 49, 65.
102. Carter, "Greatest English Novelist," 392.
103. Williams, *Two Centuries of the English Novel*, 51.
104. Burton, *Masters of the English Novel*, 43.
105. Edgar, *Art of the Novel*, 58–59.
106. Burton, *Masters of the English Novel*, 50–51.
107. Edgar, *Art of the Novel*, 33–35.
108. Blanchard, *Fielding the Novelist*, 136.
109. For comments on my own work's relationship to Blanchard's, see chapter one.
110. For a balanced account of F.R. Leavis' life, thought, and academic influence, see Samson, *F.R. Leavis*.
111. Leavis, *Great Tradition*, 2–3.
112. Ibid., 4.
113. Ibid., 4–5.
114. Watt, *Rise of the Novel*, 305.
115. Ibid., 272.
116. Saintsbury, *English Novel*, 102.
117. Watt, *Rise of the Novel*, 325.
118. Ford raves about Richardson in *The English Novel* (1929), finding him one of the few original geniuses in English along with Shakespeare, Trollope and Austen. Ford writes of Fielding, "[T]here are few books that I more cordially dislike than *Tom Jones*. . . . I dislike Tom Jones, the character, because he is a lewd, stupid, and treacherous phenomenon; I dislike Fielding, his chronicler, because he

is a bad sort of hypocrite" (98). Ford goes on to say that Blifil should have been Fielding's hero.

119. Watt, *Rise of the Novel*, 325.

120. Ibid., 327.

121. Ibid., 337.

122. Ibid., 305.

123. Ibid., 271.

124. Ibid., 209.

125. I am not claiming that students who read Richardson and Fielding for class assignments are not "general readers"—an enormous majority of English students go on to careers other than literary criticism. Students do not fit the particular definition of "general readers" that I have been using throughout this text, however, because they are reading Richardson and Fielding *in the role of* literary critics. Only when the *motives* of reading are different is there is any discernible difference between one group of readers and another. Students who read for *theoria* most probably did not choose the texts for themselves, and the range of acceptable reactions they are permitted to record is limited by the outside factors of academic requirements.

126. White, *Letters to Three Friends*, 95.

127. McKillop, *Samuel Richardson*, 107.

128. Wagenknecht, *Cavalcade of the English Novel*, 51.

129. Carter, "Greatest English Novelist," 390.

130. Dobson, *Samuel Richardson*, 196.

131. "Richardson Revival," 485.

132. Utter, "On the Alleged Tediousness of Defoe and Richardson," 185.

133. Church, *The Growth of the English Novel*, 72–73.

134. Whittuck, *The "Good Man" of the XVIIIth Century*, 71.

135. Williams, *Two Centuries of the English Novel*, 50.

136. Ibid., 53.

137. Ranger, "Henry Fielding," 202.

138. George Orwell, in Rawson, *Henry Fielding*, 384.

139. Priestly, "Henry Fielding: Then and Now," 610.

Conclusion

1. The dichotomy has also affected the criticism of Sarah Fielding's novels. Critics have only relatively recently seen her novels as something more than a watered-down fusion of traits culled from Richardson and Fielding. As discussion of her novels becomes increasingly free of the rivalry in which she took pains not to participate, her novels find increasingly more readers.

2. Eaves and Kimpel, *Samuel Richardson*, 2.

3. Works discussing the positive mutual influence of Richardson and Fielding in good faith include Sitter, "The Final Novels of Fielding and Richardson," in *Literary Loneliness in Eighteenth-Century England*; Eaves, "*Amelia* and *Clarissa*," and Spacks, "Of Plots and Power: Richardson and Fielding," in *Desire and Truth*.

4. There is a long tradition of critics reinforcing and perpetuating literary rivalries for no other reason than for the pleasure they offer as narratives. When open competition between professional colleagues is not appropriate, tensions and misplaced enthusiasms sometimes take the form of exaggerated battles between

pairs of long-dead authors. Myrick Land's flippant book, *The Fine Art of Literary Mayhem* (1962), makes no apologies for enjoying the game. Careful to distinguish the difference between "high-spirited name calling" and a genuine feud, Land sadistically defines feuding as a "genuine, deep, and usually prolonged alienation between men of letters" (7). Land is happy to report that "these real feuds still flourish, even though it has become the custom for literary historians to lament that they are neither as frequent nor as lively as they used to be" (7). Isaac Disraeli takes a very different perspective on established literary rivalries in his much earlier work, *Quarrels of Authors* (1814):

> Should these Volumes disappoint the hopes of those, who would consider the Quarrels of Authors as objects for their mirth or their contempt, this must not be regretted. Whenever passages of this description occur, they are not designed to wound the Literary Character, but to chasten it; by exposing the secret arts of calumny, the malignity of witty ridicule, and the evil prepossessions of unjust hatreds. (1:iii)

5. Derrida writes in "Différance":

> It is because of *différance* that the movement of signification is possible only if each so-called 'present' element, each element appearing on the scene of presence, is related to something other than itself, thereby keeping within itself the mark of the past element, and already letting itself be vitiated by the mark of its relation to the future element, this trace being related no less to what is called the future than to what is called the past, and constituting what is called the present by means of this very relation to what it is not. . . . (126–27)

6. Bakhtin, "Discourse in the Novel," 272.
7. Ibid., 273.
8. Ibid., 276.
9. Jauss, *Question and Answer*, 197.
10. Bakhtin writes:

> A unitary language is not something given [*dan*] but is always in essence posited [*zadan*]— and at every moment of its linguistic life it is opposed to the realities of heteroglossia. But at the same time it makes its real presence felt as a force for overcoming this heteroglossia, imposing specific limits to it, guaranteeing a certain maximum of mutual understanding and crystallizing into a real, although still relative, unity—the unity of the reigning conversational (everyday) and literary language, 'correct' language. ("Discourse in the Novel," 270)

11. Ian Watt, *The Rise of the Novel*, 195–96.

Appendix

1. See Cross, *History of Henry Fielding* (3:175), for dramatic examples of anti-Fielding sentiments throughout the nineteenth century.
2. Butler, *Note-Books*, 202.
3. Paulson, Introduction, 3–4.
4. "Drift of London Literary Talk," 305.

Bibliography

Addison, Joseph. *Admonitions from the Dead in Epistles to the Living*. London, 1754.

Allen, Walter. *The English Novel: from "The Pilgrim's Progress" to "Sons and Lovers."* Harmondsworth, Middlesex: Pelican, 1954.

Altick, Richard. *The English Common Reader; A Social History of the Mass Reading Public, 1800–1900*. Chicago: University of Chicago Press, 1957.

Anderson, Howard. "Answers to the Author of *Clarissa*: Theme and Narrative Technique in *Tom Jones* and *Tristram Shandy*." *Philological Quarterly* 51 (1972): 859–73.

Anderson, Robert. *A Complete Edition of the Poets of Great Britain*. 13 vols. London, 1794.

Armstrong, Nancy. *Desire and Domestic Fiction: A Political History of the Novel*. New York: Oxford University Press, 1987.

Austen, Jane. *Letters to Her Sister Cassandra and Others*. Edited by R. W. Chapman. Oxford: Oxford University Press, 1932.

Baker, Ernest. *The History of the English Novel: Intellectual Realism from Richardson to Sterne*. London: H. F. & G. Witherby, 1930.

Bakhtin, Mikhail Mikhailovich. "Discourse in the Novel." In *The Dialogic Imagination*, edited by Michael Holquist, translated by Caryl Emerson and Holquist, 259–422. Austin: University of Texas Press, 1981.

Balzac, Honoré de. *Oeuvres*. Edited by Marcel Bouteron and Henri Longnon. Paris: Calmann-Lévy, 1899.

Banerji, H.K. *Henry Fielding*. Oxford: Oxford University Press, 1929.

Barthe, Nicolas T. "Excerpt from *La Jolie Femme: ou La Femme du Jour*." *The Gentleman's Magazine* 40 (October 1770): 455–56.

Bartolomeo, Joseph F. "Johnson, Richardson, and the Audience for Fiction." *Notes and Queries* 33:231, no. 4 (December 1986): 517.

———. *A New Species of Criticism: Eighteenth-Century Discourse on the Novel*. Newark: University of Delaware Press, 1994.

Battestin, Martin C. Introduction to *Joseph Andrews* and *Shamela*, by Henry Fielding. World's Classics. Oxford: Oxford University Press, 1980.

———. *The Moral Basis of Fielding's Art: A Study of Joseph Andrews*. Middletown, Conn.: Wesleyan University Press, 1959.

———, *Henry Fielding: A Life*. London: Routledge, 1989.

Beattie, James. *Dissertations Moral and Critical*. 1783. Reprint, New York: Garland, 1971.

Bechler, Rosemary. "Detested Exercise." Review of *The Correspondence of Henry and Sarah Fielding*, edited by Martin C. Battestin and Clive T. Probyn. *Times Literary Supplement* (London) 4714, 6 August 1993, 21.

236

Béclard, Léon. *Sébastien Mercier; sa Vie, son Oeuvre, son Temps . . . Avant la Révolution, 1740–1789.* Paris: Champion, 1903.

Birrell, Augustine. "Samuel Richardson." In *Res Judicatæ: Papers and Essays,* 1–34. London, 1892.

Bisset, Robert. "History of Literature and Science for the Year 1799." In *The Historical, Biographical, Literary. and Scientific Magazine: The History of Literature and Science, for the Year 1799,* 1:55–56. London: 1799.

Blair, Hugh. *Dr. Blair's Lectures on Rhetoric, Abridged, with Questions.* New York, 1835.

Blanchard, Frederic T. *Fielding the Novelist: A Study in Historical Criticism.* New Haven: Yale University Press, 1926.

Bloom, Harold. *The Anxiety of Influence: A Theory of Poetry.* New York: Oxford University Press, 1973.

Boheemen-Saaf, Christel van. "Fielding and Richardson in Holland: 1740–1800." *Dutch Quarterly Review of Anglo-American Letters* 14, no. 4 (1984): 293–307.

Booth, Wayne. "The Self-Conscious Narrator in Comic Fiction before *Tristram Shandy.*" *PMLA* 67 (1952): 163–85.

Borrow, George. *The Bible in Spain.* 4th ed. London, 1843.

Boswell, James. *Boswell's Journal of a Tour to the Hebrides with Samuel Johnson.* Edited by Frederick A. Pottle. New York: McGraw Hill, 1961.

―――. *Boswell's Life of Johnson.* Edited by G.B. Hill and L.F. Powell. 6 vols. Oxford: Clarendon, 1934.

Bowen, Elizabeth. *English Novelists.* London: Collins, 1946.

Brooke, Henry. *Fool of Quality; or, the History of Henry Earl of Moreland.* 5 vols. London, 1766.

Brophy, Elizabeth Bergen. *Samuel Richardson.* Boston: Twayne, 1987.

Burney, Francis. *The Early Diary of Francis Burney, 1768–1778.* Edited by Annie Raine Ellis. 2 vols. London: G. Bell, 1904.

Burns, Robert. *The Poetry of Robert Burns.* Edited by William Ernest Henly and Thomas F. Henderson. 4 vols. Edinburgh, 1897.

Burton, Richard. *Masters of the English Novel: A Study of Principles and Personalities.* New York: Holt, 1909.

Butler, Samuel. *The Note-Books of Samuel Butler.* Edited by Henry Festing Jones. London: Fifield, 1912.

Byron, George Gordon, Lord. *Letters and Journals of Lord Byron.* Edited by Thomas Moore. 3rd ed. 2 vols. London, 1833.

Canning, George. "On Novel Writing." *The Microcosm* 26 (14 May 1787): 295–307.

Carew, Bampfylde-Moore. *An Apology for the Life of Bampfylde-Moore Carew.* 2nd ed. London, 1751.

Carter, A. E. "The Greatest English Novelist." *University of Toronto Quarterly* 17, no. 2 (January 1948): 390–97.

Carter, Elizabeth. *A Series of Letters Between Mrs. Elizabeth Carter and Miss Catherine Talbot.* 2 vols. London, 1808.

Castle, Terry. *Clarissa's Ciphers: Meaning and Disruption in Richardson's "Clarissa."* Ithaca: Cornell University Press, 1982.

Castro, Paul de. "Did Fielding Write *Shamela?*" *Notes and Queries* (8 January 1916): 24–26.

Chalmers, Alexander, ed. *A New and General Biographical Dictionary.* 32 vols. London, 1812–17.

Chambers, Robert. *Chambers's Cyclopedia of English Literature.* Edited by Reverend Robert Caruthers. 3rd ed. 8 vols. New York, 1879.

Chambers, William. *The Youth's Companion and Counselor.* London, 1820.

Chapone, Hester. *The Works of Mrs. Chapone.* 4 vols. London, 1807.

Cheyne, George. *Letters of Dr. George Cheyne to Samuel Richardson, 1733–43.* Edited by C.F. Mullett. University of Missouri Studies 18. Columbia: University of Missouri Press, 1943.

Church, Richard. *The Growth of the English Novel.* Home Study Books. London: Methuen, 1951.

Clarke, C. H. *Fielding und der deutsche Sturm und Drang.* Freiburg, 1897.

Clarke, John Stock. "Mrs. Oliphant: A Case for Reconsideration." *English* 27 (1979): 123–33.

Cleary, Thomas R. *Henry Fielding: A Political Writer.* Waterloo, Ontario: Wilfrid Laurier University Press, 1984.

Coe, Ada. "Richardson in Spain." *Hispanic Review* 3 (1935): 56–63.

Colby, Vineta, and Robert A. Colby. *The Equivocal Virtue; Mrs. Oliphant and the Victorian Literary Market Place.* Hamden, Conn.: Archon Books, 1966.

Coleridge, Samuel Taylor. *Anima Poetae.* London, 1895.

———. *The Complete Works of Samuel Taylor Coleridge.* Edited by William Greenough Thayer Shedd. 7 vols. New York, 1864.

———. *Selected Letters.* Edited by H. J. Jackson. Oxford: Clarendon, 1987.

———. *Shakespearean Criticism.* Edited by Thomas Middleton Raysor. 2 vols. London: Everyman's Library, 1960.

———. "Table Talk." In *Coleridge's Miscellaneous Criticism,* edited by Thomas M. Raysor, 401–39. London: Constable and Company, 1936.

———. "With Fielding's Amelia." In *The Poetical and Dramatic Works of Samuel Taylor Coleridge,* 1:31. London, 1877.

Collier, William Francis. *A History of English Literature: In a Series of Biographical Sketches.* London, 1881.

Cooper, Maria Susanna. *The Exemplary Mother, or, Letters Between Mrs. Villars and Her Family.* 2 vols. London, 1769.

Court, Franklin E. *Institutionalizing English Literature: The Culture and Politics of Literary Study, 1750–1900.* Stanford, Calif. Stanford University Press, 1992.

Crane, R.S. "The Plot of *Tom Jones.*" *The Journal of General Education* 4 (1950). Revised as "The Concept of Plot and the Plot of *Tom Jones*" in *Critics and Criticism Ancient and Modern,* edited by R. R. Crane. Chicago: University of Chicago Press, 1952.

Critical Remarks on Sir Charles Grandison, Clarissa and Pamela. The Augustan Reprint Society 4, no. 3. Reprint, Los Angeles: William Andrews Clark Memorial Library, University of California, 1950.

Cross, Wilbur. *The Development of the English Novel.* New York, 1889.

———. *The History of Henry Fielding.* 3 vols. New Haven: Yale University Press, 1918.

Cumberland, Richard. *Henry*. 4 vols. London, 1795.

———. "From *The Observer*, 27, 1785." In *Novel and Romance 1700–1800: A Documentary Record*, edited by Ioan Williams, 332–35. London: Routledge, 1970.

Curtis, George. "Easy Chair." *Harper's Magazine* 20 (February 1860): 413–14.

Davaux, Citoyen. Preface to *Tom Jones, ou L'Enfant Trouvé* by Henry Fielding. Paris, 1796.

De Quincey, Thomas. *Literary Reminiscences*. Boston, 1854.

Derrida, Jacques. "Différance." In *Critical Theory Since 1965*, edited by Hazard Adams and Leroy Searle, 120–36. Tallahassee: Florida State University Press, 1986.

Devonshire, Marian Gladys. *The English Novel in France, 1830–1870*. New York: Octagon Books, 1929.

Dickens, Charles. *The Letters of Charles Dickens*. London, 1893.

———. *Oliver Twist*. The World's Classics. Oxford: Oxford University Press, 1982.

Dickson, Frederick S. "Fielding and Richardson on the Continent." *Notes and Queries* 12, no. 3 (1917): 7–8.

Digeon, Aurélien. "Autour de Fielding." *Revue Germananique* 11 (1920): 209–19.

———. *The Novels of Fielding*. New York: Russell, 1925.

Disraeli, Isaac. *Quarrels of Authors; or, Some Memoirs for Our Literary History, Including Specimens of Controversy to the Reign of Elizabeth*. 3 vols. London, 1814.

Dobson, Austin. *Fielding*. New York, 1883.

———. "Richardson at Home." In *Eighteenth Century Vignettes*. 2nd ser., 2 vols., 2:50–76. London, 1892.

———. *Samuel Richardson*. New York: Macmillan, 1902.

Donaldson, Ian. "The Clockwork Novel: Three Notes on an Eighteenth-Century Analogy." *The Review of English Studies* n.s. 21, no. 81 (February 1970): 14–22.

Downs, Brian. *Richardson*. London: Routledge, 1928.

Doyle, Sir Arthur Conan. *Through the Magic Door*. London: Smith, 1907.

"Drift of London Literary Talk." *New York Times Saturday Review* 11 May 1907: 305.

Droop, Adolf. *Die Belesenheit Percy Bysshe Shelley's nach den direkten Zeugnissen und den bisherigen Forschugen*. Weimar: Wagner, 1906.

Dunlop, John Colin. *History of Prose Fiction*. Edited by Henry Wilson. New ed. 2 vols. London, 1896.

Eagleton, Terry. *Literary Theory: An Introduction*. Minneapolis: University of Minnesota Press, 1983.

———. *The Rape of Clarissa: Writing, Sexuality and Class Struggle in Samuel Richardson*. Oxford: Oxford University Press, 1982.

Eaves, T.C. Duncan. "Amelia and Clarissa." In *A Provision of Human Nature: Essays on Fielding and Others in Honor of Miriam Austin Locke*, edited by Donald Kay, 95–110. Tuscaloosa: University of Alabama Press, 1977.

———, and Ben D. Kimpel. *Samuel Richardson: a Biography*. Oxford: Oxford University Press, 1971.

Edgar, Pelham. *The Art of the Novel: from 1700 to the Present Time*. New York: Macmillan, 1933.

Edgeworth, Maria. *The Life and Letters of Maria Edgeworth*. Edited by Augustus J.C. Hare. 2 vols. Freeport, NY: Books for Libraries, 1971.

———. *Ormond*. Belfast: Appletree Press, 1992.

Eliot, George. *The George Eliot Letters*. Edited by Gordon S. Haight. 7 vols. New Haven: Yale University Press, 1955.

———. *Middlemarch*. Edited by David Carroll. Oxford: Oxford University Press, 1986.

Encyclopedia Britannica. 3rd ed. 18 vols. Edinburgh: A. Bell and C. Macfarquhar, 1797.

Encyclopedia Britannica. 9th ed. 25 vols. New York: Charles Scribner's Sons, 1878.

Fabian, Bernhard. "English Books and Their Eighteenth-Century German Readers." In *The Widening Circle: Essays on the Circulation of Literature in Eighteenth-Century Europe*, edited by Paul J. Korshin, 119–96. Philadelphia: University of Pennsylvania Press, 1966.

Fielding, Henry. "An Apology for the Life of Mrs. Shamela Andrews." In *Joseph Andrews and Shamela*, edited by Douglas Brooks–Davies. Oxford: Oxford University Press, 1980.

——— and Sarah Fielding. *The Correspondence of Henry and Sarah Fielding*. Edited by Martin C. Battestin and Clive T. Probyn. Oxford: Oxford University Press, 1993.

———. *The Covent-Garden Journal and A Plan of the Universal Register Office*. Edited by Bertrand Goldgar. Middletown, Conn.: Wesleyan University Press, 1988.

———. *The History of Tom Jones*. Edited by R.P.C. Mutter. The English Library. Harmondsworth, Middlesex: Penguin, 1966.

———. *A Journey from This World to the Next* and *The Journal of a Voyage to Lisbon*. Edited by Ian A. Bell and Andrew Varney. The World's Classics. Oxford: Oxford University Press, 1997.

Fitzgerald, Edward. *The Letters of Edward Fitzgerald*. Edited by Alfred McKinley Terhune and Annabelle Burdick Terhune. 4 vols. Princeton: Princeton University Press, 1980.

Ford, Maddox. *The English Novel*. Philadelphia: Lippencott, 1929.

Fordyce, James. *Sermons to Young Women*. 6th ed. 2 vols. London, 1766.

Forsyth, William. *The Novels and Novelists of the Eighteenth Century, in Illustration of the Manners and Morals of the Age*. Port Washington, New York: Kennikat, 1970.

Fox, Ralph. *The Novel and the People*. London: Lawrence, 1937.

Frith, W.P. *My Autobiography and Reminiscences*. New York, 1888.

Frye, Northrop. *Anatomy of Criticism*. Princeton: Princeton University Press, 1967.

Gadamer, Hans-Georg. *Truth and Method*. Translated by Garrett Barden and John Cumming. London: Sheed, 1975.

Gibbon, Edward. *The History of the Decline and Fall of the Roman Empire*. Edited by J.B. Bury. 7 vols. London: Methuen, 1897–1900.

————. *Mémoires littéraires de la Grande Bretagne, pour l'an 1767–[1768]*. Edited by G. Deyverdun and E. Gibbon. 2 vols. London, 1768–69.

Godzich, Wlad. Introduction to *Aesthetic Experience and Literary Hermeneutics*, by Hans Robert Jauss. Minneapolis: University of Minnesota Press, 1982.

Goldberg, Homer. *The Art of "Joseph Andrews."* Chicago: University of Chicago Press, 1969.

————. "Comic Prose Epic or Comic Romance: The Argument of the Preface to *Joseph Andrews*." *Philological Quarterly* 43 (1964): 193–215.

Goldsmith, Oliver. *Works*. 5 vols. Bohn's Library. London, 1885.

Gosse, Edmund. *Henry Fielding: an Essay*. Westminster, 1898.

Grant, Anne. *Letters from the Mountains*. 2nd ed. London, 1807.

Graves, Charles L. *The Life and Letters of Alexander Macmillan*. London: Macmillan, 1910.

Graves, Richard. *The Spiritual Quixote; or, The Summer's Ramble of Mr. Geoffrey Wildgoose; a Comic Romance*. 3 vols. London, 1773.

Gray, Thomas. *The Letters of Thomas Gray, Including the Correspondence of Gray and Mason*. Edited by Duncan C. Tovey. 2 vols. London: George Bell and Sons, 1904.

Green, Frederick C. *Minuet: A Critical Survey of French and English Literary Ideas in the Eighteenth Century*. New York: Dutton, 1935.

Grève, Claude de. " 'Comparative Reception': A New Approach to 'Rezeptionäs-thetik.' " In *Aesthetics and the Literature of Ideas: Essays in Honor of A. Owen Aldridge*, edited by François Jost, 233–40. Newark: University of Delaware Press, 1990.

Griffith, Elizabeth, and Richard Griffith. *A Series of Genuine Letters Between Henry and Francis*. 3rd ed. 6 vols. London, 1767–72.

"Growth of the English Novel." *The Quarterly Review* 163 (July 1886): 34–64.

Gwynn, Albinia. *The Rencontre, or, Transition of a Moment: a Novel, in a Series of Letters*. 2 vols. Dublin, 1785.

Hannaford, Richard Gordon. *Samuel Richardson: An Annotated Bibliography of Critical Studies*. New York: Garland Publishing, 1980.

Hardy, Thomas. "The Profitable Reading of Fiction." In *Life and Art by Thomas Hardy: Essays, Notes and Letters Collected for the First Time*, edited by Ernest Brennecke, Jr. New York: Greenberg, 1925.

Harpe, Jean-Francoise de la. *Lycée ou Cours de Littérature*. Dijon, 1821.

Harris, Jocelyn. " 'As If They Had Been Living Friends': *Sir Charles Grandison* into *Mansfield Park*." *Bulletin of Research in the Humanities* 83 (1980): 360–405.

————. "The Influence of Richardson on *Pride and Prejudice*." In *Approaches to Teaching Austen's "Pride and Prejudice,"* edited by Marcia McClintock Folsom, 94–99. New York: Modern Language Association, 1993.

Hawkins, Harriett. *The Devil's Party: Critical Counter-Interpretations of Shakespearean Drama*. Oxford: Clarendon, 1985.

Haydon, Benjamin Robert. *Benjamin Robert Haydon: Correspondence and Table-Talk*. 2 vols. London, 1876.

Hazlitt, William. *The Complete Works of William Hazlitt*. Edited by P.P. Howe. 21 vols. London and Toronto: Dent, 1931.

————. *Conversations of James Northcote, Esq., R.A.* London, 1830.

Henley, William. "An Essay on the Life, Genius, and Achievement of the Author." In *The Complete Works of Henry Fielding*, v–xlvi. New York: Harper, 1902.

Hill, George Birkbeck. *Writers and Readers.* New York, 1892.

The History of Charlotte Summers, the Fortunate Parish Girl. London, 1750.

Hobbes, John Oliver [Pearl Mary Teresa Richards Craigie, pseud.]. "Fielding for Girls." *New York Times*, 3 Sept. 1904, 596.

————. *Letters from a Silent Study.* London: Appleton, 1904.

Holliday, Carl. *English Fiction from the Fifth to the Twentieth Century.* New York: Century, 1912.

Holub, Robert C. "The American Reception of Reception Theory." *German Quarterly* 55, no. 1 (January 1982): 80–96.

————. *Reception Theory: A Critical Introduction.* New Accents. London: Methuen, 1984.

Honan, Park. "Richardson's Influence on Jane Austen (Some Notes on the Biographical and Critical Problems of 'Influence')." In *Samuel Richardson: Passion and Prudence,* edited by Valerie Grosvenor Myer, 165–177. London: Vision, 1986.

Horne, Charles F. *The Technique of the Novel: The Elements of the Art, their Evolution and Present Use.* New York: Harper, 1908.

Howard, Susan K. "The Intrusive Audience in Fielding's *Amelia.*" *Journal of Narrative Technique* 17, no. 3 (Fall 1987): 286–95.

Hudson, W.H. *A Quiet Corner in a Library.* Freeport, NY: Books for Libraries, 1968.

Hunt, Leigh. "A Novel Party." In *Men, Women, and Books; a Selection of Sketches, Essays, and Critical Memoirs, from His Uncollected Prose Writings,* 1:87–101. New York, 1847.

Hunt, Russell A. "Johnson on Fielding and Richardson: a Problem in Literary Moralism." *The Humanities Association Review* 27 (1976): 412–20.

Hunter, J. Paul. *Before Novels: The Cultural Contexts of Eighteenth-Century English Fiction.* New York: Norton, 1990.

Indyk, Ivor. "Interpretive Relevance and Richardson's *Pamela.*" *Southern Review: Literary and Interdisciplinary Essays* 16, no. 1 (March 1983): 31–43.

Iser, Wolfgang. *The Implied Reader: Patterns in Communication in Prose Fiction from Bunyan to Beckett.* Baltimore: Johns Hopkins University Press, 1974.

————. "The Role of the Reader in Fielding's *Joseph Andrews* and *Tom Jones.*" In *English Studies Today,* 5th ser., 289–325. Istanbul: Mataasi, 1973.

Jackson, Holbrook. *Great English Novelists: with Thirty-Two Illustrations.* Philadelphia: Jacobs, 1908.

Jauss, Hans Robert. *Aesthetic Experience and Literary Hermeneutics.* Translated by Michael Shaw. Theory and History of Literature 3. Minneapolis: University of Minnesota Press, 1982.

————. "Paradigmawechsel in der Literaturwissenschaft." Translated by J. Russell Perkin. *Linguistische Berichte* 3 (1969): 44–66.

————. *Question and Answer: Forms of Dialogic Understanding.* Translated by Michael Hayes. Theory and History of Literature 68. Minneapolis: University of Minnesota Press, 1989.

————. *Toward an Aesthetic of Reception*. Translated by Timothy Bahti. Theory and History of Literature 2. Minneapolis: University of Minnesota Press, 1982.

Jay, Elisabeth. *Mrs Oliphant: 'A Fiction to Herself': A Literary Life*. Oxford: Oxford University Press, 1995.

Jeffrey, Francis. *Contributions to the Edinburgh Review*. 4 vols. London, 1844.

Jenkins, Owen. "Richardson's *Pamela* and Fielding's 'Vile Forgeries.' " *Philological Quarterly* 44 (1965): 200–210.

Jenner, Charles. *The Placid Man: or, Memoirs of Sir Charles Beville*. 2 vols. London, 1770.

Jensen, Gerard E. "*An Apology for the Life of Mrs. Shamela Andrews*, 1741." *Modern Language Notes* 31 (1916): 310–11.

Johnson, R. Brimley. Introduction to *Shamela*, by Henry Fielding. Waltham St. Lawrence, Berkshire: Golden Cockerel Press, 1926.

Johnson, Samuel. Introduction to *Rambler* 97. In *The Rambler*, 153. Vol. 4 of *The Yale Edition of the Works of Samuel Johnson*. New Haven: Yale University Press, 1958.

————. "The New Realistic Novel." In *The Oxford Authors: Samuel Johnson*, edited by Donald Green, 175–79. Oxford: Oxford University Press, 1984.

————. "Preface to *The Plays of William Shakespeare*." In *The Oxford Authors: Samuel Johnson*, edited by Donald Green, 419–546. Oxford: Oxford University Press, 1984.

————. "Prefaces, Biographical and Critical, to the Works of the English Poets: Addison." In *The Oxford Authors: Samuel Johnson*, edited by Donald Green, 643–76. Oxford: Oxford University Press, 1984.

Jusserand, J.J. *Le Roman anglais; origine et formation des grandes écoles de romanciers du xviii siècle*. Paris, 1886.

Karl, Frederick R., *A Reader's Guide to the Development of the English Novel in the Eighteenth Century*. London: Thames and Hudson, 1974.

Kästner, Abraham Gotthelf. *Abraham Gotthelf Kästners Gesammelte Poetische und Prosaische Schönwissenschaftliche Werke*. Berlin, 1841.

Keats, John. *Poetry and Prose*. Edited by H.B. Forman. London, 1890.

Kermode, Frank. "Richardson and Fielding." *Cambridge Journal* 4 (1950): 106–14.

Kettle, Arnold. *An Introduction to the English Novel*. 2 vols. London: Hutchinson's University Library, 1951.

Keymer, Tom. *Richardson's "Clarissa" and the Eighteenth-Century Reader*. Cambridge Studies in Eighteenth-Century English Literature and Thought 13. Cambridge: Cambridge University Press, 1992.

Knight, Grant C. *The Novel in English*. New York: Smith, 1931.

Land, Myrick. *The Fine Art of Literary Mayhem: A Lively Account of Famous Writers and their Feuds*. New York: Holt, 1962.

Lang, Andrew. *Adventures Among Books*. London: Longmans, 1905.

Lanier, Sidney. *The English Novel: A Study in the Development of Personality*. 1883. Reprint, New York: Scribner's, 1914.

Lanzisera, Francesco. "I romanzi de Samuele Richardson in Italia." In *Annali del R. Istituto Orientale de Napoli (1928–29)*, 148–79. Napoli: Cimmaruta, 1929.

The Laureat: or, The Right Side of Colley Cibber, Esq. London, 1740.

Lawrence, D.H. *Pornography and Obscenity*. Criterion Miscellany 5. London: Faber, 1929.

Leavis, F.R. *The Great Tradition*. London: Chatto, 1948.

Letters Concerning the Present State of England: Particularly Respecting the Politics, Arts, Manners, and Literature of the Times. London, 1772.

Liljegren, Sten B. *The English Sources of Goethe's Gretchen-Tragedy*. Lund: C. W. Gleerup, 1937.

Lovett, Robert, and Helen Hughes. *The History of the Novel in England*. Boston: Houghton Mifflin, 1932.

Lowell, James Russell. "Fielding." In *Literary and Political Addresses*, 57–77. Boston: Houghton, 1904.

Lucas, E.V. *The Life of Charles Lamb*. 2 vols. New York: Putnam's, 1905.

Luxenborough, Lady Henrietta Knight. *Letters to Shenstone*. London, 1775.

Macaulay, T.B. "Copyright. I." In *Macaulay: Prose and Poetry*, edited by G. M. Young, 731–43. London: Hart-Davis, 1952.

Mack, Maynard. Introduction to *The History of the Adventures of Joseph Andrews and of his Friend Mr. Abraham Adams*, by Henry Fielding. New York: Holt, 1948.

Mackenzie, R.S. *Sir Walter Scott*. Boston, 1871.

Mackintosh, Sir James. *Memoirs of the Life of the Right Honourable Sir James Mackintosh*. Edited by Robert James Mackintosh. 2nd ed. 2 vols. London, 1836.

Mangin, Edward. *An Essay on Light Reading, as it May be Supposed to Influence Moral Conduct and Literary Taste*. London, 1808.

Marx, Eleanor. "Eleanor Marx on Her Father." In *The Portable Karl Marx*, edited and translated Eugene Kamenka, 48–52. New York: Viking, 1983.

Masson, David. *British Novelists and their Styles: Being a Critical Sketch of the History of British Prose Fiction*. Boston, 1859.

Mathias, Thomas James. *The Pursuits of Literature: a Satirical Poem in Dialogue*. 7th ed. London, 1798.

McCrea, Brian. *Henry Fielding and the Politics of Mid-Eighteenth-Century England*. Athens: University of Georgia Press, 1981.

McCullough, Bruce. *Representative English Novelists: Defoe to Conrad*. New York: Harper, 1946.

McKeon, Michael. *The Origins of the English Novel 1600–1740*. Baltimore: Johns Hopkins University Press, 1987.

McKillop, Alan Dugald. *The Early Masters of English Fiction*. Lawrence: University of Kansas Press, 1956.

———. *English Literature from Dryden to Burns*. New York: Appleton-Century Crofts, 1948.

———. "The Personal Relations between Fielding and Richardson." *Modern Philology* 28 (1931): 423–33.

———. *Samuel Richardson: Printer and Novelist*. Chapel Hill: University of North Carolina Press, 1936.

Meredith, George. "Essay on the Idea of Comedy and the Uses of the Comic Spirit." In *Miscellaneous Prose*. New York: Russell, 1968.

Miles, Kathleen. "A Note on Richardson's Response to Fielding's Felon." *Studies in the Novel* 1 (1969): 373–74.

Mill, John Stuart. *Autobiography*. New York, 1874.

Millar, John Hepburn. Introduction to "Samuel Richardson." In *English Prose Selections: with Critical Introductions by Various Writers and General Introductions to Each Period*, edited by Craik, 5 vols., 4:57–58. New York: Macmillan, 1903.

Montagu, Lady Mary Wortley. *Letters and Works*. Edited by Lord Wharncliffe. 3rd ed. 2 vols. London: Swan Sonnenschein, 1893.

Moore, John. "The Commencement and Progress of Romance." In *Eighteenth Century British Novelists on the Novel*, edited by George Leonard Barnett, 170–73. New York: Appleton-Century-Crofts, 1968.

Moore, Robert Etheridge. "Dr. Johnson on Fielding and Richardson." *PMLA* 66, no. 2 (March 1951): 162–81.

"The Morals of Fielding." *The Saturday Review of Politics, Literature, Science, and Art* (22 April 1893): 421.

Mudford, William. *The British Novelists: Comprising Every Work of Acknowledged Merit which is Usually Classed Under the Denomination of Novels: Accompanied with Biographical Sketches of the Authors, and a Critical Preface to Each Work*. London, 1810–17.

Nicoll, W. Robertson, and Thomas Seccombe. *A History of English Literature*. 2 vols. New York: Dodd, 1907.

North, Christopher. "Soliloquy on the Annuals." In *Critical and Miscellaneous Essays*. 3 vols. Philadelphia: Carey, 1829.

Ogilvie, John. *Philosophical and Critical Observations on the Nature, Characters, and Various Species of Composition*. 2 vols. Anglistica and Americana 27. Hildesheim: Verlagsbuchhandlung, 1968.

Oliphant, Margaret. *Autobiography and Letters of Mrs. Margaret Oliphant*. Edited by Mrs. Harry Coghill. Leicester: Leicester University Press, 1974.

———. "Historical Sketches of the Reign of George II. No. X—the Novelist." *Blackwood's Edinburgh Magazine* 641, no. 105 (1869): 253–76.

Orians, G.H. "Censure of Fiction in American Romances and Magazines 1789–1810." *PMLA* 52:207–8.

Orr, Leonard. "Reception-Aesthetics as a Tool in Literary Criticism." In *The USF Quarterly* 21 (spring-summer 1983): 35–52.

Otis, William Bradley, and Morriss H. Needleman. *A Survey History of English Literature*. New York: Barnes, 1938.

Palmer, D.J. *The Rise of English Studies*. Oxford: Oxford University Press, 1965.

Paulson, Ronald. Introduction to *Fielding: A Collection of Critical Essays*. Edited by Ronald Paulson. Englewood Cliffs, NJ: Prentice-Hall, 1962.

———, and Thomas Lockwood, eds. *Henry Fielding: The Critical Heritaǥe*. London: Routledge, 1969.

Piozzi, Hester Lynch. *Anecdotes*. London, 1786.

———, ed. *Letters to and from the Late Samuel Johnson, LL. D., to which are Added Some Poems Never Before Printed*. 2 vols. London, 1788.

Porter, Jane. *Thaddeus of Warsaw*. 4 vols. London, 1803.

Porter, Roy. *English Society in the Eighteenth Century*. The Pelican Social History of Britain. Harmondsworth: Penguin, 1982.

Pratt, Samuel. "On Novel-Writing." In *Miscellanies*, 3:116–25. London, 1785.

Praz, Mario. *The Romantic Agony*. Translated by Angus Davidson. London: Oxford University Press, 1933.

Preston, John. *The Created Self: The Reader's Role in Eighteenth-Century Fiction*. London: Heinemann, 1970.

———. "Plot as Irony: The Reader's Role in *Tom Jones*." *ELH: A Journal of English Literary History* 35 (1968): 365–80.

Price, Lawrence Marsden. "On the Reception of Richardson in Germany." *The Journal of English and Germanic Philology* 25 (1926): 7–33.

Priestley, J.B. *The English Novel*. Benn's Essex Library. London: Benn, 1927.

———. "Henry Fielding: Then and Now." *The Listener* 52 (14 October 1954): 609–10.

Pritchett, Victor Sawdon. *The Living Novel*. London: Chatto, 1946.

"The Progress of Fiction as an Art." *The Westminster Review* 60 (October 1853): 185–196.

Pye, Henry James. *Sketches on Various Subjects*. 2nd ed. London, 1797.

Ranger. "Henry Fielding." *The Bookman* 29, no. 172 (February 1906): 202–4.

Rawson, Claud. Introduction to *Henry Fielding: A Critical Anthology*. Edited by Claud Rawson. Harmondsworth: Penguin Education, 1973.

Reeve, Clara. *The Progress of Romance through Times, Countries, and Manners; with Remarks on the Good and Bad Effects of it, on them Respectively, in a Course of Evening Conversations*. 2 vols. London, 1785.

Renwick, W. L. "Comic Epic in Prose." In *Essays and Studies by Members of the English Association* 32, edited by Basil Wiley, 40–43. Oxford: Clarendon, 1947.

Review of *Ballantyne's Novelist's Library*, edited by Walter Scott. *Blackwood's Magazine* 25, no. 87 (April 1824): 406–18.

Review of *Cecilia*, by Fanny Burney. *The Monthly Review* 2, no. 67 (December 1782): 453.

Review of *The History of Amanda*. *The Monthly Review* 2, no. 18 (1758): 182.

Review of *The Italian*, by Ann Radcliffe. *The Monthly Review* 2, no. 22 (1797): 282–84.

Review of *The Newcomes*, by William Thackeray, and *The Life of Henry Fielding*, by Frederick Lawrence. *The North British Review* 19, American Ed., no. 47 (November 1855): 104–15.

Review of *The Works of Samuel Richardson*, edited by Leslie Stephen. *The Spectator* 2884 (6 October 1883): 1284–85.

Reynolds, Myra. *The Learned Lady in England, 1650–1750*. Vassar Semi-Centennial Series. Boston: Houghton, 1920.

Richardson, Samuel. *The Correspondence of Samuel Richardson*. 6 vols. London, 1804.

———. *Sir Charles Grandison*. The World's Classics. Oxford: Oxford University Press, 1986.

"The Richardson Revival." *Academy* 61 (1901): 485–86.

Richter, David H. "The Reception of the Gothic Novel in the 1790s." In *The Idea of the Novel in the Eighteenth Century*, edited by Robert W. Uphaus, 117–37. East Lansing, Mich.: Colleagues, 1988.

Roberts, William. *Memoirs of the Life and Correspondence of Mrs. Hannah More*. 2 vols. New York, 1836.

Rogers, Pat. "Richardson and the Bluestockings." In *Samuel Richardson: Passion and Prudence*, edited by Valerie Grosvenor Myer, 147–64. London: Vision, 1986.

Roscoe, Thomas. Preface to *Works*, by Henry Fielding. London, 1840.

Roscoe, William. *Poems and Essays*. London, 1860.

Rubik, Margarete. *The Novels of Mrs. Oliphant: A Subversive View of Traditional Themes*. New York: Peter Lang, 1994.

Ruskin, John. *The Works of John Ruskin*. Edited by E.T. Cook and Alexander Wedderburn. London: Allen, 1903–12.

Sabor, Peter. "*Amelia* and *Sir Charles Grandison*: The Convergence of Fielding and Richardson." *Wascana Review* 17, no.2 (Fall 1982): 3–18.

Sade, Marquis de. "Reflections on the Novel." In *The 120 Days of Sodom and Other Writings*, edited by Austryn Wainhouse and Richard Seaver, 91–116. New York: Grove, 1966.

Saintsbury, George. *The English Novel*. London: Dent, 1913.

Samson, Anne. *F.R. Leavis*. New York: Harvester Wheatsheaf, 1992.

Schlaeger, Jürgen. "Recent German Contributions to Literary Theory." In *Échanges: Actes du Congrès de Strasbourg*, Études Anglais 81, 59–71. Paris: Didier-Érudition, 1982.

Schlegel, Friedrich von. *Lectures on the History of Literature, Ancient and Modern*. Translated by J.G. Lockhart. Edinburgh, 1818.

Schlosser, F.C. *History of the Eighteenth Century*. 8 vols. Translated by D. Davison. London, 1843.

Schücking, Levin L. *The Sociology of Literary Taste*. Translated by E.W. Dickes. London: Kegan Paul, 1945.

Scott, Sir Walter. *Lives of the Novelists*. The World's Classics. London: Oxford University Press, 1906.

Segers, Rien T. "An Interview with Hans Robert Jauss." Translated by Timothy Bahti. *New Literary History* 11, no. 1 (Autumn 1979): 83–95.

Seward, Anna. *Letters of Anna Seward: Written Between the Years 1784 and 1807*. 6 vols. Edinburgh, 1811.

Shaw, George Bernard. *Plays: Pleasant and Unpleasant*. 2 vols. London, 1898.

Shaw, Thomas B. *Outlines of English Literature*. New American Ed. Philadelphia, 1854.

Shepperson, Archibald. *The Novel in Motley: A History of the Burlesque Novel in English*. Cambridge: Harvard University Press, 1936.

Sitter, John. *Literary Loneliness in Mid-Eighteenth-Century England*. Ithaca: Cornell University Press, 1982.

Slattery, William C. "Samuel Richardson in the Netherlands: Early Reception of His Work." *Papers on Language and Literature* 1 (1965): 20–30.

Smith, George Barnett. *Poets and Novelists*. New York, 1876.

Smith, Sarah W.R. *Samuel Richardson: A Reference Guide*. Boston: Hall, 1984.

Smith, Sydney. Review of *Cælebs*, by Hannah More. *Edinburgh Review* 14 (1809): 146.

Smythies, Miss. *The Stage-Coach: Containing the Character of Mr. Manly, and the History of his Fellow-Travelers*. 2 vols. London, 1753.

Southey, Robert. *Selections from the Letters of Robert Southey*. 4 vols. Edited by John Wood Warter. New York: AMS, 1977.

Spacks, Patricia Meyer. "Of Plots and Power: Richardson and Fielding." In *Desire and Truth: Functions of Plot in Eighteenth-Century English Novels*. Chicago: University of Chicago Press, 1990.

Speirs, Logan. "*Sir Charles Grandison or The Happy Man, a Comedy*." *English Studies: A Journal of English Language and Literature* 66:1 (February 1985): 25–35.

Staël-Holstein, Anne Louise Germaine, barronne de. *The Influence of Literature upon Society*. 2 vols. Boston, 1813.

Stephen, Leslie. *The History of English Thought in the Eighteenth Century*. London, 1876.

———. Preface to *The Works of Samuel Richardson*, by Samuel Richardson. London, 1883.

———. "Richardson's Novels." *Cornhill Magazine* 17 (1868): 48–69.

Stevenson, Robert Louis. *The Letters of Robert Louis Stevenson to His Family and Friends*. Edited by Sidney Colvin. 2 vols. New York, 1899.

———. *The Works of Robert Louis Stevenson*. 26 vols. London: Heinemann, 1921.

Stoler, John A., and Richard D. Fulton. *Henry Fielding: An Annotated Bibliography of Twentieth-Century Criticism, 1900–1977*. New York: Garland, 1980.

Streeter, Harold W. "The Vogue of Richardson's Novels in France." In *The Eighteenth Century English Novel in French Translation: A Bibliographical Study*, 91–105. New York: Benjamin Blom, 1976.

Stuart, Lady Louisa. *Letters of Lady Louisa Stuart to Miss Louisa Clinton*. Edited by J.A. Home. 2 vols. Edinburgh: Douglas, 1901–03.

Taine, Hippolyte. *History of English Literature*. Translated by H. Van Laun. New York, 1879.

Tennyson, Hallan. *Alfred Lord Tennyson: a Memoir by His Son*. 2 vols. London, 1898.

Thackeray, William Makepeace. *The English Humourists of the Eighteenth Century: a Series of Lectures*. New York, 1853.

———. *The Newcomes: Memoirs of a Most Respectable Family*. 4 vols. London, 1854.

Thomsom, Clara. "Old Friends." *The Westminister Review* 152 (November 1899): 579–88.

———. *Samuel Richardson: A Biographical and Critical Study*. London: Marshall, 1900.

Thornbury, Ethel M. *Henry Fielding's Theory of the Comic Prose Epic*. University of Wisconsin Studies in Language and Literature 30. Madison: University of Wisconsin Press, 1931.

Traill, Henry Duff. "Richardson and Fielding." In *The New Lucian: Being a Series of Dialogues of the Dead*, 200–215. London, 1884.

Treyssac de Bergy, Pierre Henri. *The Mistakes of the Heart, or Memoirs of Lady Carolina Pelham and Lady Victoria Nevil: in a Series of Letters*. 3 vols. London, 1769.

Tuckerman, Bayard. *A History of English Prose Fiction from Sir Thomas Malory to George Elliot*. New York, 1882.

Turner, James. "Novel Panic: Picture and Performance in the Reception of Richardson's *Pamela.*" *Representations* 48 (Fall 1994): 70–96.

Tynan, Katherine. "The Romance of a Bookseller." *The Cornhill Magazine*, n.s., 22 (1907): 678–89.

Utter, Robert Palfrey. "On the Alleged Tediousness of Defoe and Richardson." *University of California Chronicle* 25 (1923): 175–93.

Utter, Robert Palfrey and Gwendolyn Bridges Needham. *Pamela's Daughters.* New York: Macmillan, 1936.

Van Ghent, Dorothy. *The English Novel, Form and Function.* New York: Rinehart, 1953.

Vaughan, Charles Edwyn. *English Literary Criticism.* London, 1896.

Wagenknecht, Edward. *Cavalcade of the English Novel.* 1943. New York: Holt, 1954.

Warner, William Beatty. *Reading Clarissa: The Struggles of Interpretation.* New Haven: Yale University Press, 1979.

Warton, Joseph. *Essay on the Genius and Writings of Pope.* 2nd ed. London, 1762.

———. Notes on *The Works of Alexander Pope, Esq.*, by Alexander Pope. Edited by Joseph Warton. 9 vols. London, 1797.

Watson, William. *The Life of Henry Fielding, Esq., with Observations on His Character and Writings.* Edinburgh, 1807.

Watt, Ian. "The Naming of Characters in Defoe, Richardson, and Fielding." *Review of English Studies* 25, no. 100 (October 1949): 322–38.

———. *The Rise of the Novel: Studies in Defoe, Richardson and Fielding.* Harmondsworth: Penguin, 1985.

Watters, Reginald. "The Vogue and Influence of Samuel Richardson in America, A Study of Cultural Conventions, 1742–1825." University of Wisconsin Summaries of Doctoral Dissertations 6:295–97.

Wellek, René. *A History of Modern Criticism: 1750–1950.* 8 vols. New Haven: Yale University Press, 1955–81.

———. "The Theory of Literary History." *Études Dédiées au Quatriéme Congrés de Linguistes. Travaux du Circle Linguistique de Prague* 6. Prague: 1936.

West, Jane. *Letters to a Young Lady.* 4th ed. London, 1811.

White, William Hale [Mark Rutherford, psued.]. *Letters to Three Friends.* London: Milford, 1924.

Whiteford, Robert Naylor. *Motives in English Fiction.* New York: Putnam's, 1918.

Whitehead, William. *Plays and Poems.* 2 vols. London, 1774.

Whittuck, C. A. *The "Good Man" of the XVIIIth Century: A Monograph on XVIIIth Century Didactic Literature.* London: Ballantyne, Hanson and Company, 1901.

Wilberforce, William. *A Practical View of the Prevailing Religious System of Professed Christians, in the Higher and Middle Classes, Contrasted with Real Christianity.* 1st American ed. Philadelphia, 1798.

Williams, Harold Herbert. *Two Centuries of the English Novel.* London: Smith, Elder, and Company, 1911.

Williams, Ioan. Preface to *Novel and Romance 1700–1800: A Documentary Record.* Edited by Ioan Williams. London: Routledge, 1970.

Wood, Augustus. *Einfluss Fieldings auf die deutsche Literatur.* Yokohama, 1895.

Woods, Charles B. "Fielding and the Authorship of *Shamela.*" *Philological Quarterly* 25, no. 3 (July 1946): 251–53.

Woolf, Virginia. *Three Guineas*. San Diego: Harvest/Harcourt Brace Jovanovich, 1938.

Wordsworth, William. *Memoirs of William Wordsworth*. Boston, 1851.

Wünsch, Marianne. "The Status and Significance of Reception Studies in Literary History." In *Proceedings of the 12th Congress of the International Comparative Literature Association: Munich 1988*, edited by Roger Bauer and others, 5 vols., 5:324–30. Munich: Iudicium, 1990.

Zavala, Iris M. "Textual Pluralities: Readings and Readers of Eighteenth-Century Discourse." In *The Institutionalization of Literature in Spain*, edited by Wlad Godzich and Nicholas Spadaccini, 245–263. Minneapolis, Minn.: The Prisma Institute, 1987.

Index